RELIGION AND FAITH-BASED WELFARE

From wellbeing to ways of being

Rana Jawad

First published in Great Britain in 2012 by

The Policy Press
University of Bristol
Fourth Floor
Beacon House
Queen's Road
Bristol BS8 1QU
UK
Tel +44 (0)117 331 4054
Fax +44 (0)117 331 4093
e-mail tpp-info@bristol.ac.uk
www.policypress.co.uk

North American office:
The Policy Press
c/o The University of Chicago Press
1427 East 60th Street
Chicago, IL 60637, USA
t: +1 773 702 7700
f: +1 773-702-9756
e:sales@press.uchicago.edu
www.press.uchicago.edu

© The Policy Press 2012

British Library Cataloguing in Publication Data
A catalogue record for this book is available from the British Library.

Library of Congress Cataloging-in-Publication Data
A catalog record for this book has been requested.

ISBN 978 1 84742 389 4 paperback
ISBN 978 1 84742 390 0 hardcover

Cover design by The Policy Press.
Front cover: image kindly supplied by istock
Printed and bound in Great Britain by TJ International, Padstow
The Policy Press uses environmentally responsible print partners

Contents

Acknowledgements

Thank you again to The Policy Press for their support of my work. Thanks are also owed to the Universities of Warwick and Kent who awarded me the research grants that were necessary to conduct the empirical research. I hope that the organisations and individuals who met with me during the research will find some use in this book, and I thank them for sharing their time and experiences with me.

> We must continue to use to the full the spirit that made our great organizations for full Mutual Aid and that fired the philanthropists of past ... it involves making and keeping something other than the pursuit of gain as the dominant force in society.... In former days there was a great alternative to the pursuit of gain, as the guiding force in society; there was force for good inspired by religious belief and based on membership of Christian community. Now this religious force for good is less widely influential than it was in the nineteenth century. It must either be revived or be replaced by some equally good alternative, if that can be found. Perhaps it must be both part revived and part replaced. (Beveridge, 1948)

Thinking about religious welfare and rethinking social policy

My visit to the East London Mosque on Whitechapel Road (Borough of Tower Hamlets, East London) began as a run-of-the-mill interview appointment at a Muslim organisation that, I had been told by a key informant in the voluntary sector, was "doing really important work". On exiting Whitechapel underground station, I was unexpectedly greeted by the grand facade of The Royal London Hospital. A vague recollection of this name revisited me from my modest readings on Victorian philanthropy – was there not a religious connection to this place? Turning right, I walked through the street market stalls and streams of Asian people and shops. At last, I found the large mosque-cum-community centre, mundanely located in between a row of commercial businesses, as a long line of young boys in white robes and black caps were led by a male adult through a door next to the main men's entrance of the mosque – it looked like there was an Islamic school here.

During the interview, I learned that in the late 1990s, the mosque's leaders and members were joined by the local religious and secular community organisations in a campaign against the city council to obtain permission to buy a piece of land next to the mosque, where they wanted to build the community centre. With mass community support and a large protest march, photos of which are on permanent display in the mosque's reception area, the East London Mosque gained permission to buy the land and began construction of the London Muslim Centre, now a multistorey building which houses the mosque group's projects as well as various other community organisations renting out office space to offer social services. My interviewee told me that a new building is now also under construction which will be entirely focused on services for women in the local area and will include a health and fitness club. The East London Mosque was also taking part in one of the new social finance bonds currently being promoted by the Coalition government that was specifically for religious congregations (Faiths In Social Finance Bonds). It celebrated its centenary in 2011, proudly hailing its 'pluralist' ideals and non-Muslim co-founders, having grown 'from a rented hall, to a purchased house, to a purpose built mosque, to a major centre in the space of 100 years' (www.eastlondonmosque.org.uk/news/300). The East London Mosque is now a prominent member of Citizens UK (and its London wing, TELCO, The East London Communities Organisation), Britain's largest community organising network (see Chapter Eight for more on this).

Interview done, I walked back from the mosque at a more leisurely pace, with more time to take in the vicinity. Barely a few metres away, I spotted Booth House, and what I slowly recognised, looking from across the road, to be the red shield logo of The Salvation Army. This large rectangular building was indeed reminiscent of the homeless centres (or, to use their proper name, Lifehouses) that the 'Army' runs around the country. I continued back towards the station and came across a narrow entrance to a modern-looking building with 'Davenant' written on the front door and next to it, an older building, with 'The Foundation School' engraved on its front wall. Was this also some religiously inspired organisation? Next to that was an entrance to another building under the name of 'Jagonori' – perhaps another community centre of some sort?

Then I reached The Royal London Hospital again, and descended into the underground station, still not quite aware that in roughly one mile of Whitechapel Road I had walked through the best part of 500 years of religious social welfare action in this historic corner of London – symbolic home of the British working-class struggle, new home of mass immigrant populations from the South Asian continent and perennial home of innovative social welfare experiments (Bradley, 2009; Warren, 2009).

And so it is that this book stems from the recognition that the main body of students, researchers and practitioners of social policy in the UK (and England in particular) have only tacit acknowledgement of the role of religious actors, values and institutions in UK social policy, or indeed, in their more general history within the voluntary and philanthropic spheres. And furthermore, that the need to articulate this association with greater critical accuracy, let alone descriptive detail, never really seemed that relevant or pressing, until now.

Religion in contemporary UK: beyond European exceptionalism?

The heartland of secularity, Europe, is often depicted in the sociology of religion as the exception to an otherwise deeply religious world (Casanova, 1994, 2008; Davie, 1999, 2006). The UK, in particular, has held a special leading position in this regard for two key reasons (Wolffe, 2007, p 325): (1) the presence of a national established church that acted as handmaiden in the early 20th century for the transition of UK society to class-based industrialisation and urbanisation, hence ceding political and administrative power to the new modern secular welfare state; and (2) the proliferation of leading UK pioneers of liberal political thought, not to mention the 'cultural impact' of Charles Darwin on the moral credibility of the Bible. This distinguishes England from Scotland, Northern Ireland and Wales, where the respective church establishments have enjoyed much greater levels of popular commitment and support. A key reason for this is that liberal religious traditions, as found in England, have been more susceptible to decline than their more conservative counterparts in the other UK nations.

Nevertheless, the Church of England itself has continued to enjoy patriotic loyalty and a central role in English national identity (Wolffe, 2007). The religious legacy of the early modern English confessional state can still be found in the UK today. For instance, the 1701 Act of Settlement remains unchallenged, with the British monarch having to maintain the role of 'supreme governor' of the Church of England; and the Upper Chamber of the House of Lords continues to include 26 unelected senior bishops of the church (Madeley, 2003, p 3). Thus, church establishment is a fundamental part of UK national identity. In this analysis, the UK (and England in particular) represents one of three types of church–state relations in Europe, as follows: (1) the state church, where close ties are maintained (England); (2) strict separation between state and church (such as in France); and (3) church–state separation, but with discretionary privileges for the main churches (such as in Germany) (Minkenberg, 2003). This institutional perspective on church–state relations means that there is a real impact on public policy formations, since the relations between church and state are not merely seen as a reflection of other political or social factors such as class relations, but as an institutional arrangement that 'provides "opportunity structure" for religious interests in the political process' (Minkenberg, 2003, p 196).

This issue lends itself well to an apparent false separation between church and state in Europe, which Madeley (2003) calls the 'chimera of state neutrality'. Madeley (2003) cites extensive surveys that show how state control of religious groups has weakened in Europe since the 1980s, and greater state assistance has been made, such as in the form of funds to build religious temples or exemptions from state taxation. As the argument below states,

> At its simplest, a neutral state is seen as 'one that deals impartially with its citizens and which remains neutral on the issue of what sort of lives they should lead. Neutrality ... is to be regarded as the 'defining feature of liberalism: a liberal state which imposes no conception of the good upon its citizens but which allows individuals to pursue their own good in their own way. ...Arrangements based on Enlightenment liberal assumptions actually offend against the principle of governmental religious neutrality because they privilege secular beliefs over religious ones and consign religion to the margins of social life. (Madeley, 2003, pp 5, 8)

The controversies surrounding the wearing of head coverings by Muslim women (the hijab) in European societies, which is presented from a liberal secular point of view as a form of female repression, is often used by commentators on religion as a prime example of the way in which secularity imposes its moral prejudices on other worldviews (Casanova, 2008). European societies have diverse religious profiles but it is not coincidental that the most developed welfare state systems in Europe are to be found in the Protestant countries. There is a causal connection here between the high rates of secularisation and the high levels of welfare state services (Heidenheimer, 1983; Hollinger et al, 2007).

Gorski (2005: 189) sums up the main intellectual shift that has led to the increasing relevance of religion since the 1990s as follows: it is the 'decline of Whiggish modernism' and the loss of academic appetite for materialist Marxist analysis. During the 1960s and 1970s, social scientific research on the welfare state was opposed to the historicising of religion in sociological accounts (Gorski, 2005). The dominance of the 'power resources' school that emphasises class-based analysis of social welfare expenditure was central to this, and continues to animate social policy scholarship (Gorski, 2005), even among those who study religion (van Kersbergen, 1995). Thus, in the subject area of social policy, it is possible to argue that Marxist materialism has dominated the study of this applied discipline with researchers only beginning to take seriously issues of culture and identity in the last decade or so (Lewis, 2000).

Cunningham (1998) and Offer (2006) argue that this change has opened up interest in the voluntary sector and revised readings of the intellectual roots of the welfare state. As Layard (2005) notes, the socialist project worked well for a while as an alternative moral system, so it is plausible to argue that the rise of religion in public political activity has paralleled the decline of socialism and the increasing challenges to the secularisation thesis that commentators are now grappling with. This taps into a broader 'cultural turn' in social science research that in the British social policy context is becoming increasingly reflected in research on subjective wellbeing.

No doubt, the process of globalisation in the last couple of decades has also helped foster the re-entry of religion into the public sphere and the changing social trends within Western Europe (Casanova, 2008; Obadia, 2010). Globally, the closing decades of the 20th century were marked by an unexpected confirmation of the ability of religious identity to survive and indeed flourish in the late modern period (Brahm Levey, 2009). In this sense, the 1978–79 revolution in Iran is often seen as the turning point for both academic and political observers (Haynes, 2009). Moreover, religion has always been considered to be transnational in character, with adherents coming from all nationalities and a historical role for religious missionaries in conversion (Obadia, 2010).

Processes of modernisation, like globalisation, are seen to interact with religious beliefs and practices to produce new symbols, new forms of religious engagement, social organisation and meaning which social science research is only just beginning to engage with (Obadia, 2010). At a more concrete level, major events of global and regional proportions such as 9/11 and 7/7, mass inward and transnational migration into Western countries, popular debate in Western Europe about Islam versus the West along the lines of Samuel Huntington's (1996) clash of civilisations thesis, and European Union (EU) expansion have accentuated the importance of religious identity and politics in the modern world, including the UK. Indeed, the adoption by the UK of EU legislation on human rights and equality since the late 1990s has also reinforced the need to take religion seriously as a source of human identity and social welfare. Media coverage in the UK has increased on a range of issues such as the rights of public sector professionals to pray before council meetings or a Christian couple not to teach their children about homosexuality.

While these political and social factors have inevitable implications for social policy, they only partly justify the writing of this book since they can only partly account for the need to reinstate the connection between religion and social policy – indeed, they emphasise macro-social perspectives of the welfare state without making clear the deeper micro-level connections between religion and matters of personal wellbeing. This is explained below.

Aims of the book

Big questions, some perennial, some new, but which are being asked for the first time together in a contemporary social policy textbook, loom large over this book: what is the longstanding connection between religion and social policy in Britain? What is driving social policy change today towards religion, and how is this taking shape? Who are the organisations of religious character that are delivering social welfare in Britain? What services do they provide, and how are they contributing to society at large? What lies ahead for the involvement of religious groups in social policy making? How, if at all, does this affect our thinking about what constitutes human wellbeing more broadly? How can we reconcile being active members of our religious communities, and good citizens in a liberal democratic nation-state? Readers may well wish to add more questions to this list which, in the final analysis, simply reinforces a central philosophical orientation in his book, as argued in Trigg (2007) and Sutton and Vertigans (2005): that in order for religion not to fester in the 'private' sphere of life and explode sporadically in the public arena, it should undergo 'critical scrutiny', which 'dispassionate social scientific research' can offer. This can only happen when religion begins to be seen as a legitimate actor in the public sphere.

This forms the central driving force for this book: the argument that religion matters not just at the level of cultural heritage and ideas but also translates into a very real demographic variable, as argued, for instance, in Francis (2008) and Aspinall (2000), which has implications for the formulation and evaluation of social welfare policies. Thus, the book's primary objective is to give a comprehensive and critical overview of the role of religion in social policy in the specific geosocial context of the UK today.

By religion, the book focuses on the UK's nine officially recognised religions: Judaism, Christianity, Islam, Hinduism, Buddhism, Sikhism, Jainism, Zoroastrianism and Baha'i (The Multi-faith Centre, 2007). These religions form a coherent family for the purposes of empirical enquiry that, as yet, have not received direct attention as a group in social policy scholarship (the exceptions are the Abrahamic faiths, as can be found in some more recent literature such as Furness and Gilligan, 2010). Humanist and New Age faiths therefore remain out of the scope of the present discussion. The book's emphasis on the nine religions mentioned above is partly driven by a focus on minority ethnic social welfare provision that the social policy literature knows hardly anything about. Therefore, the book is biased towards a definition of religion where attachment to communal traditions of belief and ritual persist. This immediately puts the book's arguments at odds with 'individualistic' and 'humanist' definitions of spirituality (Gilliat-Ray, 2003), although it does not deny that these currents intersect (for more detail, see below on definitions of terms).

Modest references to the role of religion in British social policy scholarship have appeared in some historical and moral philosophical debates on social welfare, as can be found in Page and Silburn (1999), Deacon and Mann (1999), Offer (2006), Fitzpatrick (2008) and Bradley (2009). These authors draw attention to the important fact that religious values and ideas form part of the cultural and intellectual ether surrounding public policy making in the UK. Recent works in the fields of social work and healthcare, such as Holloway and Moss (2010), Furness and Gilligan (2010), Ashencaen Crabtree et al (2008), White (2006) and Swinton (2001), have been ground-breaking, and this book posits that social policy has much to learn from the social work and healthcare literatures in the area of religion and wellbeing research. But these are primarily practitioner-focused and do not cover all the religions that concern this book, either in relation to government policy or theoretical social policy frameworks. Hence we find that in the Western world it is mainly US and continental European historical sociologists who have given the fullest accounts of the role of religion in the development of the welfare state (for notable examples, see van Kersbergen, 1995; Skocpol, 2000; Manow, 2004; Gorski, 2005; Kahl, 2005; Orloff, 2005).

Indeed, the latter point is central to the objectives of this book: in comparison to its contemporary North American and continental European counterparts, UK social policy scholarship lags behind in terms of analysis of how religion has shaped the welfare state. Classical works on Victorian philanthropy (namely Prochaska, 1988, 2006) have paid better tribute to the way in which social services provision was the dominion of Christian charities, while Reformation historians such as Innes (1998) allow further historical insight, but still specifically in relation to charitable work. It is, however, at the historical juncture of the post-war welfare settlement (which arguably matters most for the modern UK welfare state) that UK social policy scholarship falls silent on the role of religion, missing out protagonists such as Archbishop William Temple, who coined the term 'welfare state'. More recent historical accounts of the early 20th-century 'University Settlements' in the East End of London discuss in some more depth the religious orientations of university graduate residents, as well as the religious cleavages that surrounded the two main Settlements, Toynbee Hall and

Oxford House (Bradley, 2009). Alumni of the Settlement movement included leading political and social reformers of the interwar period such as J.J. Mallon, Octavia Hill, Clement Attlee and William Beveridge, for whom involvement in the Settlement movement was a central stepping-stone in a political career (Bradley, 2009).

But is there more to religion than simply the mixed economy of the welfare framework (see Powell, 2007a; Montagné-Villette et al, 2011), or issues of diversity and social cohesion (see Dinham et al, 2009)? It is with this question in mind that the book depicts the contribution of the above-mentioned religions to the modern British social welfare landscape as both mundane/pervasive and distinctive (developed in more detail in the next section). This pervasive/distinctive continuum is an analytical heuristic device as well as an empirical description of the historically diffuse nature of Christianity in Britain, a situation which has led to a high degree of amalgamation between religious values and secular institutions (Martin, 1978; Heidenheimer, 1983). This resembles Demerath's (2003) and Norris and Inglehart's (2004) allusions to cultural and historical strands of religious identity which are inherited from previous generations, and with time, become less a matter of personal values and beliefs.

Education policy is a prime example here. Judge (2001) makes an articulate argument in this regard in his emphasis on the close connection between the Church of England and national identity in the UK, leading to a privileged, although at times ambivalent, role for the church in the education system. This is well expressed in the dual mission of the Church of England: that of a general 'public' purpose which is to educate the population at large into a shared system of common values and national culture, but also a 'domestic' mission which is to inculcate the Anglican faith in new generations (Judge, 2001, p 466).

More explicitly, prominent political figures in the UK help to maintain the presence of religion in UK society. Taylor (2003) and Weller (2009) offer useful arguments in support of this view, reminding us that Church of England and Catholic priests have a long tradition of becoming local councillors. The Archbishop of Canterbury, Dr Rowan Williams, regularly makes known the views of the Church of England on matters related to social welfare and poverty. When the Coalition government's 2010 Spending Review announced cuts to welfare spending of £17.7 billion by 2014–15 (Taylor-Gooby and Stoker, 2011), the Archbishop was among the first to criticise the impact on the poor and the bleak prospects for social equality in the UK. Gordon Brown, Iain Duncan Smith and Tony Blair have all followed suit through a string of public speeches in which they have praised the importance of faith to politics and human civilisation. For example, Blair argued in a 2008 public address for the Cardinal's Lectures at Westminster Cathedral,

> ... religious faith is a good thing in itself ... far from being a reactionary force, it has a major part to play in shaping the values which guide the modern world, and can and should be a force for progress. ... And in the West, for example, we owe an incalculable debt to the Judaeo-Christian tradition in terms of our concepts of human worth and dignity, law and democracy. (Blair, 2008, pp 11-12)

On the other hand, this book also tries to ascertain what might be distinctive about religion – is there something that sets it apart from secular state and non-state provision? Does it have some special meaning for the definition of human wellbeing? In this sense, it is also plausible to argue that the role of religion in social welfare, either as a macro-political force shaping the development of the welfare state (in Britain as in Western Europe) or as a source of motivation for non-governmental and community-based organisations to deliver social welfare services, is more than just a mundane coincidence – religion has a dynamic and intrinsic role to play in human wellbeing and social action. There is indeed a longevity factor here: Ilchman et al's (1998) extensive study of philanthropy in the major religious traditions covers a lengthy historical period extending from what the authors call the 'non-literate/aboriginal traditions' of the first century all the way up to the 20th century. There is more research in the US context on the strong links between religious affiliation and philanthropic giving or voluntary action (see Musick et al, 2000; Gronberg and Never, 2004; Lindsay and Wuthnow, 2010; Taniguchi and Thomas, 2011). But in the UK context, much less contemporary research has been done on this. However, among the most reliable available data we have are reported by the National Council for Voluntary Organisations (NCVO) (2007), the Centre for Philanthropy at the University of Kent and nfpSynergy, all of which indicate that people in the UK are more likely to be involved in volunteering and to donate money if they are religious. The Centre for Philanthropy cites this greater probability as 3 per cent. Thus, it would appear that the study of the third sector or voluntary action would be missing a vital piece of the puzzle if religious attitudes were not taken account of.

These issues of longevity and propensity for voluntary activity go hand in hand with the dynamism and energy of religiously inspired social welfare action – a further illustration of distinctiveness explored in this book. The so-called golden rule of 'Love thy neighbour' and the basic principle of compassion are common to all the major religious systems (Armstrong, 2009). This deep commitment and energy of religious actors and organisations to various social causes is perhaps driven as much by their human sense of sympathy for those less fortunate as it is by their adherence to their faith and their sense of religious obligation. A key question, therefore, is the extent to which religious social welfare is motivated by issues of social justice or religious truth. That is to say, when a religious individual or organisation help a poor person, are they steered to action by the injustice of poverty or by the duty on them to follow the religious injunctions that say that the poor should be helped?

Hence, this book offers a critical introductory overview to the role of religion in UK social policy from a firm location within the analytical perspectives of the subject of social policy – a very 'modern' academic subject distinguished by its deep connections to liberal secular ideals of egalitarianism and, in some Northern European quarters, to social democracy (Titmuss, 1970, 1976; Offer, 2006; Cohen, 2008; van Kersbergen, 2010). To this end, the book builds on firm empirical foundations in the shape of my decade-long international research on religious welfare provision culminating in four years that have focused on the UK and its four nations. Other important contemporary research referred to in the book includes the output from the Arts and Humanities Research Council (AHRC)/Economic and Social Research Council (ESRC) Religion and Society research programme.

The book fulfils two main purposes. First, it entails a mapping exercise of the role of religion in social welfare provision in the UK – religious values and norms, actors and institutions that find expression through both state and non-state bodies. This mapping exercise involves critical examination of what services religious groups provide in the typical social policy sectors, that is to say, housing, health, poverty reduction, urban regeneration and the like[1] – and their service users' perspectives. The book thus covers more breadth than depth since its aim is to take stock of what we know so far and what new directions religious welfare might be taking. A distinguishing feature that has already been alluded to is that the book covers the social welfare activities of minority faiths in the UK and how they compare and contrast to the established Church of England. More relative emphasis is given to England due to the geographical concentration of the research and the particular newness of this topic there.

The second aim of the book is to consider the conceptual ramifications of the mapping exercise mentioned above for the meaning of wellbeing as the core unit of analysis that structures the ends and means of social policy. Here, the book draws on up-to-date empirical research with the particular aim of responding to the growing appetite for discussion on the importance of ethics and moral philosophy in social policy research (Fitzpatrick, 2008; Jordan, 2008; Spicker, 2011). For instance, the meaning of social welfare from a religious perspective is explored, asking how this changes current understanding of wellbeing. Are altruism and compassion terms that are too intricately connected to religious worldviews that make religion a fundamental unit of analysis for social welfare? After all, research on voluntarism argues that religiosity increases the propensity to do voluntary work (NCVO, 2007).

To this end, the book makes a conceptual leap, as denoted in its title, by introducing the term 'way(s) of being'. This helps us think through the implications of religious welfare in its own right, but also prompts a rethinking of the meaning and purpose of social policy. The concept acts as an analytical thread that runs through the discussion of this book and helps to focus the evaluation of what religion brings to the table of social policy and social welfare. It reinforces the importance of personal identity and moral values in the work of religious welfare provision drawing on philosophical notions of 'being' and religion as a way of life that are common to the world faiths discussed. Hence, the hope is to make a contribution to the burgeoning literature on the ethics of social policy and the moral value of wellbeing, beyond their conventional utilitarian underpinnings.

Ultimately, in seeking to expand the analytical horizons of social policy, this book also marks out the boundaries of religious welfare provision in the UK. Far from making ideological claims about what religion can and cannot do, the book uses available empirical research to reflexively outline both the opportunities and limitations that face the interaction between religion and social welfare policy in the UK today. Key among these is the Kantian argument that all human experience may not be empirically testable, thus, from a religious perspective, the unit of analysis for social policy is a term much broader than human wellbeing, and encompasses a much broader array of human self-definitions and experiences that social science research may not be able to decipher. This echoes one of Jordan's (2008) key conclusions:

The value that constitutes well-being seems as difficult to capture in moral and political principles as it is within calculative individual maximisation. Disturbingly, in close personal relationship, in cultures and even in relation to the natural world, the institutions and practices through which well-being is created and sustained may not follow the pathways of justice or rationality. (Jordan, 2008, p 34)

Analytical foci of the book: from wellbeing to way(s) of being

It is for good reason that the book bears a rather intrepid title. This rests on the proposition that a qualitative shift occurs in the conceptualisation of social welfare when religion and social policy come together. The analytical unit of wellbeing is underpinned by normative understandings of the good society that have a utilitarian and liberal thrust. When this view of human nature and human wellbeing interacts with a religious perspective, the normative landscape broadens to one that includes issues of identity, culture and transcendence, denoted by the concept of *way(s) of being*. We have already alluded earlier to the ways in which religion is both a pervasive and distinctive force in society. Here we focus on two key issues: (1) how and why religion matters analytically for social policy; and (2) what this new concept of *ways of being* is about. So this section in effect sets out the analytical framework for the book.

We explore first, the rootedness of this book in the subject of social policy. Religion has not figured prominently in the teaching and research activities of social policy scholarship in the UK. Mainstream student handbooks in social policy such as Alcock (2008), Alcock et al (2008) and Baldock et al (2011), to name but a few, do not consider religion save for very minor references to its place in the contemporary voluntary sector. Admittedly, however, this situation is beginning to change, with the inclusion of a chapter on religion and various other references to religion in the 2010 edition of *The Oxford handbook of the welfare state*, and a new chapter on religion in the 4th edition of the *Student's companion to social policy* (Alcock et al, 2012). Equally, textbooks on the history of social policy in Britain, such as Fraser (2002), Lowe (2005) or Page and Silburn (1999), give no attention to the influence of prominent Christian figures or organisations in the development of the post-war welfare state save for passing reference to The Salvation Army as a charitable organisation or to the possible role of Christian Socialism. Offer's (2006) account of the influence of idealism and non-idealism on the development of social policy in Britain since the

19th century sheds some light as to why this might be the case when he cites Edward Norman (1987b), as follows:

> For decades secular historians have tended to regard the incidence of Christian belief, where they have come across it either in the lives of particular statesmen or in social groups, as a fringe cultural phenomenon, perhaps useful as a matter of social control. What they have not perceived as of importance in the modern world has not seemed to them, as noticed in the immediate past, as much more than a lingering evidence of a discarded order. (Offer, 2006, citing Norman, 1987b, pp 11-12)

The idea that human wellbeing and judgements about the outcome measures of social policies are underpinned by normative values about the good society is not new. It is odd, however, that for a subject so deeply committed to the advancement of the 'good society', more scholarship is dedicated to defining the structure of society than to the form and content of the 'good'. It seems that this has always been the case since social policy scholarship has tended to focus more on the structural, administrative and functional dimensions of the subject as opposed to its more political and philosophical ones (Plant et al, 1980). Yet the two are inextricably linked for the solution of social problems, as Fitzpatrick (2008) and Plant et al (1980) before them have argued. The focus on the 'how' is insufficient for the resolution of modern social problems if the 'why' is also not addressed (Fitzpatrick, 2008). Yet an evasion of these deeper philosophical questions is what, Fitzpatrick (2008) argues, makes social policy err on the side of empirical caution of middle range theories and second or third order principles.

Therefore, the interesting import of religion, with its unabashed proclamations to what the good is and how to achieve it, can act as a catalyst for ethical debate in the subject of social policy. The vigorous spread of neoliberal deregulation and welfare cuts in the UK affirms the demise of social democratic ideals of egalitarianism and justice – might it be possible, therefore, that an examination of religious welfare provision can reaffirm the need for ethical revival in social policy as well as address a neglected part of voluntary sector activity?

We must therefore establish some baseline or measure by which to assess the nature and scope of social welfare provision by British organisations that have a religious character, and there are two ways of thinking about this issue that the book addresses. On the one hand, the data that are discussed in this book are examined according to the three ethical ideals or principles that the subject area of social policy holds as supreme: liberty, equality and needs (Plant et al, 1980; Drake, 2001; Fitzpatrick, 2001; White, 2010). Key definitions of these concepts are provided below. Thus, the book examines the extent to which religious organisations that provide social welfare services in the UK succeed in fulfilling these key principles. On the other hand, it is evident that this book also suggests that religious organisations have something else to offer which potentially distinguishes them from secular, state and market-based provision. This is certainly a claim that many of them make, although empirical research does not always substantiate this. Consequently, new concepts and outcome measures are proposed and explored in the book that are not directly rooted in social policy analysis, ideas such as the importance of having a view of the whole human being when delivering a social service to them, the importance of embedding the provision of a service in moral values and emotional ties, and the idea that faith itself accounts for an unquantifiable dimension of wellbeing.

In sum, religious welfare is about process; it challenges the functionalist distinction between ends and means that underpins modern public policy (McGregor, 2007). Thus, the word 'service' itself is of supreme importance from a religious perspective; it is not merely an activity to satisfy a need but in its fullest sense it is a demonstration of compassion and selflessness, as encompassed in the term *seva* ('selfless service') that many Hindu and Sikh organisations in the UK use. The importance of the concept of *service* from a religious point of view thus shows that social welfare is not merely an output but a relationship of compassion and fellowship between the service provider and service user, to use modern terminology. The importance of this relationship dwells on the fact that the person who is helping undergoes a process of religious self-identification through the act of compassion and service to others. Equally, there is a process of human self-identification that the person receiving the help undergoes. In both cases, the person helping and the person being helped enact their humanity since they partake in a process of human fellowship. These ideas are not far from the arguments made by Clarke and Fink (2008), who emphasise the identity building and cultural force of social policy.

This leads us to the crux of this book's discussion, about the concept of wellbeing itself and what a religious perspective brings to our understanding of social welfare. Why does the book propose the concept of *way(s) of being*, which it is important to emphasise has been developed on the basis of empirical research and is corroborated by studies on the world religions? It is useful here to refer to Karen

Armstrong's (2009) much-cited work *The case for God* on the meaning and influence of religion in human civilisation. By way of illustrating the notion of *way(s) of being*, the following paragraph from Armstrong (2009), about the meaning of religion in the ancient world, can offer some useful insight:

> The ultimate reality was not a personalised god … but a transcendent mystery that could never plumed. The Chinese called it the Dao, the fundamental 'Way' of the cosmos.… One of the first people to make it clear that holiness was inseparable from altruism was the Chinese sage Confucius (551–429 BCE). He preferred not to speak about the divine, because it lay beyond the competence of language, and theological chatter was a distraction from the real business of religion. He used to say: 'My Way has one thread that runs right through it.' There were no abstruse metaphysics; everything always came back to the importance of treating others with absolute respect. This was epitomised in the Golden Rule, which he said, his disciples should practice 'all day and every day'. 'Never do to others what you would not like them to do to you'.… Religion was a matter of doing rather than thinking. (Armstrong, 2009, p 33)

The idea that adherence or belief in a religion is akin to a way of life is undoubtedly an idea that is familiar to many readers. Less familiar, perhaps, may be the idea that 'Being' is itself the ultimate and transcendental reality of life. Armstrong (2009) cites the German philosopher, Martin Heidegger's (1889–1976) work, on the difficulty of defining 'Being' in order to emphasise the idea of the 'religious quest' being a process, a form of practice and daily living that is meant to achieve a 'higher purpose' in human existence (a term that Iain Duncan Smith himself has employed in in discussions on the role of the voluntary sector (for example at a talk hosted in 2011 by Charities Parliament, an affiliate of the Oasis Trust).

Hence, the idea that the practice of a given religion is like a path leading to some higher status of being such as Nirvana or heaven is shared by all the religions discussed in this book. In Islam, a central tenet of the faith is for believers to follow *al-sirat al-mustakim* ('the straight path') (Ashencaen Crabtree et al, 2008); in Christianity, Jesus Christ is himself depicted as being the way to salvation (John, 14:6); in Judaism, *Mussar* ('instruction', 'conduct') is the ethical and moral way to live one's life in accordance to God's will and *Halacha* ('the way') refers to the body of Jewish law governing believers (Coleman-Brueckheimer et al, 2008). In Hinduism and Buddhism, *Dharma* is the correct way of life for believers; there are four paths or *magra* that lead to *Dharma* in Hinduism, one of which is *Karma-magra* ('the path of action'), entailing good deeds and right action (Shah and Sorajjakool, 2010, p 39). Notions of being, and the correct of way of being, are central to the study of religiously based welfare. Buddhism teaches of the 'noble eightfold way' or 'eight noble paths' which lead the human being out of worldly 'suffering' to spiritual enlightenment, which include correct conduct and earning an honest living (Sorajjakool and Naewbood, 2010, p 48). In the Zoroastrian faith, *sudreh* and *kusti* are items of white cloth and lamb wool thread that members of the faith wear underneath their normal clothing as a ritual practice. They symbolise the good deeds and pure mind of the wearer. *Sudreh* symbolises the 'advantageous path' and *kusti* symbolises the 'direction finder' towards the *sudreh*.

Box 1.1: Religious wellbeing as a way of being

Judaism: *Halacha* (the way)

Christianity: 'I am the way, the truth and the life' (John 14:6)

Islam: *Al-sirat al-mustakim* (the straight path)

Buddhism: *Eight noble paths, The middle way*

Hinduism: *Dharma,* (four) *magra* (paths)

Sikhism: *Khalsa* (purity), *Guru* (knowledge)

Zoroastrianism: (wearing of) *sudreh* (advantageous path) and *kusti* (for correct conduct)

Chinese religions: *Tao* (the way)

Baha'i: *Unity of mankind*

*****

(Compare with)

Thatcher government: *Responsible society*

New Labour: *Third Way*

Coalition government: *Big Society*

In the empirical research reported in this book, both providers and users of welfare emphasise the importance of personal self-identity and moral values to human welfare. For them, doing good or having their needs responded to cannot be disconnected from who they are and the values they live by. As one Muslim female activist expressed it, social welfare should not be about specific problems but about the identity of the person and their whole life. This holistic approach may already be familiar to some readers. It is exemplified in the way in which Christian evangelical organisations (some taking part in this research) live among the communities they are seeking to help, and this is especially the case when we recall that urban regeneration and concern for poverty in the inner cities has been a flagship initiative for the Church of England in the UK. The personal immersion of religiously motivated social welfare providers in and among the communities they work with reinforces the relationship between religion and social action, and religion and compassion.[2] It shows again the dual purpose of *service*, as a relationship and not just an output. Armstrong (2009) further illustrates this point as follows:

> Nirvana was the natural state of a life lived according to the Buddha's doctrine of *anatta* ('*no self*'), which was not simply a metaphysical principle but, like all his teachings, a programme of action. By far the best way of achieving *anatta* was compassion, the ability to feel with the other, which required that one dethrone the self from the centre of one's world and put another there. Compassion would be the central practice of the religious quest. (Armstrong, 2009, pp 32-3)

The meaning of social welfare that we have inherited in the social policy academic community undoubtedly turns the above on its head. The mainstream understanding of social welfare in social policy scholarship is as an outcome measured on an individual basis (Baldock, 2011). Assumptions about human existence and human nature – the normative underpinnings of social policy – as encapsulated in the deeply philosophical, and in Heidegger's terms, the mysterious term of 'Being' (Polt, 1999), have been neatly reduced by the addition of a prefix 'well'. The object of social policy thus turns into the pursuit of some ideal if not minimal state of wellness and happiness, generally identified in objective and money-metric terms. Yet in the last decade more subjective notions of wellbeing have become more heatedly discussed, with some authors seeking to bring in more relational elements.

Jordan (2008), for example, explores the usefulness of the concept of social capital for thinking about social wellbeing and introduces the notion of social value to argue that emotional and moral attachments matter for welfare outcomes, as he explains: a cheap gift from someone dear to us may well have a higher impact on our sense of wellbeing than an expensive gift from a stranger. Jordan's (2008) argument rests on the significance of the Easterlin paradox (Easterlin, 1974, 2001) that draws attention to new evidence on how self-reported happiness in the advanced capitalist democracies has not coincided with corresponding increases in levels of income. A recent study on the impact of income inequality by Wilkinson and Pickett (2010) also confirms these findings. These studies highlight the need to move beyond overly econometric and outcome-based definitions of social welfare. Jordan (2008) emphasises that British, and indeed Western, societies are in need of a new moral imagination that can inspire new forms of collective action to rekindle notions of solidarity and social cohesion. He argues for a 'new politics of wellbeing' (p 248), posing the real and theoretical challenge now facing social policy succinctly, as follows:

> The problem, of course, is that it has proved fairly easy to destroy the sense of commitment to common causes, to solidarity, moralities, religions and ways of life, for the sake of increased individual welfare supplied by the economic model; but it is far harder to build a new version of these forms of collective meaning. Many people remain loyal to non-welfarist communal activities, such as crafts, sports, musical styles or outdoor pursuits, but they are induced to see these as 'lifestyle choices', rather than essential aspects of well-being. So the current crises over climate change, credit and debt, and long-term fear over security, crime, health, nutrition and general well-being provide an opportunity ... it is the moment for the reconstruction of social value and collective culture to start. (Jordan, 2008, pp 249-50)

This intellectual dissatisfaction with the term 'social welfare', which also reflects deeper sociological undercurrents about the good society, in part explains the move in recent years towards the concept of wellbeing that has etymological roots in the writings and teachings of such great thinkers as Aristotle and the Buddha (Gough et al, 2007). Wellbeing emphasises subjective perceptions of personal welfare and is more deeply connected to the importance of social relationships in shaping individual perceptions of welfare. We return, therefore, to the point made above about the meaning of service in the religious sense. Bevan (2007) argues that meaning is fundamental to the notion of wellbeing and that it is not possible to separate this concept from normative discussion about the good life. To this end, the concept of wellbeing emphasises the centrality of human nature in social policy and allows the human being to step off the 'hedonic treadmill' that,

Jordan (2008, p 17) argues, obfuscates the importance of social value in definitions of wellbeing.

Definition of terms

There are two key units of analysis in this book, religion and social welfare/human wellbeing, that provide a constellation of associated terms such as spirituality, need and social justice. In many ways, as has already been alluded to above, this entire book is about meanings and definitions: the meaning of religious welfare, the meaning of social welfare from a religious perspective, the meaning of human wellbeing, the meaning of *way(s) of being*. In this section, we clarify the definitions of these terms.

First, the concept of religion: the book emphasises this concept and distinguishes it from belief, faith, ethnicity, culture or spirituality. The position taken in this book is that these are subsidiary conceptual correlates, some of which have been ascribed with a close association to religion in the UK due to contemporary intellectual and sociocultural factors. These affiliated concepts are touched on but do not constitute its main unit of analysis. The reason for this is intimately a matter of sociological definition and analytical accuracy. Beckford and Demerath (2007) argue that religion is a term that is not easily definable and indeed advise against such attempts. Contemporary authors such as Furness and Gilligan (2010) suggest that researchers should take religion to be what adherents themselves denote their religion to be. The difficulty of definition also points to the all-encompassing nature of religion and its intricate connectedness to human nature and identity. Emile Durkheim (1858–1917) and Max Weber (1864–1920), the founders of the subject of sociology who based their work on the study of religion, offer some of the following definitions:

> It can be said that both Weber and Durkheim recognised what is presupposed in this essay: that the problem of individual existence in society is a religious problem ... the relevance of sociology for contemporary man derives primarily from its search for understanding the fate of the person in the structure of the modern society. (Luckmann, 1967, p 12)

> To define 'religion', to say what it *is*, is not possible at the start of the presentation such as this. Definition can be attempted, if at all, only at the conclusion of the study. The

essence of religion is not even our concern, as we make it our task to study the conditions and effects of a particular type of behaviour. (Weber, 1993, p 1)

A religion is a unified system of beliefs and practices relative to sacred things, that is to say, things set apart and forbidden – belief and practices which unite into one single moral community called a Church, all those who to adhere them. (Durkheim, 1915, p xxi)

Among the more contemporary sociologists of religion, Robert Wuthnow (1988) offers a definition of religion which emphasises its practical qualities of social action already discussed in the work of Armstrong (2009) previously:

... religion cannot be understood very well if attention is limited only to arguments about disembodied ideas (symbols) or even abstract conceptions of organizations and actions. Religion has an organic quality, a communal and moral dimension, that binds people to one another and creates close dependencies between them and their environments.... Religions become embodied as moral communities – as networks of deeply felt obligation to one another and to collective rituals and beliefs, all of which provide a sense of belonging, even security, to the participants. The very beliefs and ideas of which any religion is comprised reflect and dramatize these moral obligations; thus, even a focus on belief requires more than abstract consideration of ideas. (Wuthnow, 1988, p 308)

What we can therefore argue is that religion is deeply public in character. The long-held Enlightenment era view that religion is a private matter and has no role to play in the development of society is thus seen to be a false one (Trigg, 2007). Casanova (2008) puts it succinctly, as follows:

The sociology of religion should be less obsessed with the decline of religion and more attuned to the new forms which religion assumes ... in all world religions: to new forms of individual mysticism, 'invisible religion' and cults of the individual; to new forms of congregational religion, from new religious movements to the global expansion of

Pentecostalism and charismatic communities in all world religions; and to the re-emergence of the world religions as transitional imagined communities, vying with if not replacing the nation-state for prominent role on the global stage. (Casanova, 2008, p 27)

It is also important to give brief attention to how the concept of spirituality enters our analysis. In many ways, the concept of spirituality has superseded religion in the re-engagement of applied social researchers. Many of the references used in this book show that authors and practitioners alike are interested in spirituality and in thinking about what it means for human health and social outcomes. The position of the book is a bit more critical and purist/orthodox in that it is interested in religion as a system of beliefs, values, institutions and practices which organises the life of a community around the concept of a superior and transcendent being. What we find, however, with the concept of spirituality, is that it can easily miss out the emphasis on organised life and coherent systems of practice and belief, as well as the existence of a transcendental superior being. In this book, this is what we focus on since it is these coherent systems of belief that exercise a moral discourse and a programme of social action on the ground in relation to social welfare interventions. As White (2006) explains:

Talk of spirituality in the past revolved around prayer or worship; now people speak rather of gardening or meditation. Spirituality has become such a broad term that almost anything with a certain warm feeling can be absorbed within it. This encourages an open approach and broad scope but can also suggest a lack of understanding and clarity ... so anything goes and who cares what other people think! In our modern pluralist society, the imposition of a specifically Christian, or even multi-faith, framework is no longer acceptable to the majority but a clear alternative framework, within which to understand spirituality has not yet emerged ... the holistic milieu is very much an emerging framework that includes a blurred and uncertain mix of mysticism and lifestyle, horoscopes and complementary therapies. This leaves a gap that makes it hard to talk with shared understanding about spirituality and even harder to develop a degree of discernment about this confusing mixture. (White, 2006, pp 14, 16)

Critiques of a generic and Eurocentric view of spirituality have been highlighted in Gilliat-Ray (2003) and Pattison (2001), who emphasise that spirituality is too narrowly defined along the lines of such terms as personal fulfilment, meaning, hope and transcendence. Gilliat-Ray (2003) argues that this signifies a 'secularisation' of the concept of spirituality into narrow 'individualistic and humanistic' terms. This is partly because the concept is being redefined by a generation of academics who are moving away from Orthodox institutional religious practices, particularly in relation to the Christian church in the UK, but also because of the need to make the concept appeal to both religious and non-religious academics and practitioners (Gilliat-Ray, 2003).

Yet, Gilliat-Ray (2003) argues forcefully that minority ethnic faiths which are an important focus of this book would not necessarily sit well with individualist and humanistic definitions of spirituality – as the research reported in this book and other contemporary research shows, adherence to scriptures or the laws of a particular religion as well as religious rituals and practices are fundamentally connected to notions of spirituality within minority religious faiths, and certainly within the Evangelical Christian tradition, which is now at the forefront of social welfare provision in the UK. Moreover, connection to family and community form the basic expression of spiritual life for many of these groups of faiths, as opposed to a solitary experience of personal meaning-making (Gilliat-Ray, 2003). So the position of this book is that spirituality is a valid, individual, transcendental experience, but it is incomplete without a connection to a creed and praxis that are based on a religious understanding of the world, its origins and purpose.

We now come to clarifying meanings of liberty, equality and need that are used as criteria for judging the work that religious welfare organisations achieve. Drake (2001), Fitzpatrick (2001) and White (2010) offer more detailed useful discussion in this regard. Suffice to note at this point that liberty is understood to be the extent to which religious welfare organisations do not constrain the free will of their members of staff and their service users. A typical example might be if religious welfare organisations impose on their staff or beneficiaries specific religious values and practices. Equality is understood as the extent to which members of staff and service users are treated in the same manner, are not discriminated against and are given the same opportunities to flourish. Finally, needs are understood as the extent to which basic and non-basic factors that are essential to human existence are satisfied. The close link between needs and rights also needs to be acknowledged, but what is of greater significance for this book is the connection between understanding of human need and theories of human nature since this underpins the normative discussion of religious welfare provision in this book.

The book takes into account the four typologies of human nature that can be detected in left and right political discourses of human nature, as proposed by Hewitt (2000, pp 21-3):

- The *atomistic model*, favoured by free marketers and proponents of residual welfare, considers human nature to be self-interested and individualistic. The atomistic model acknowledges that only subsistence level needs should be targeted by the residual welfare system; human needs are best satisfied through free market enterprise.
- The *organic model* emphasises the bonds of family, community and nation, most commonly associated with social democratic and liberal traditions. In this view, human needs are fulfilled through the individual's contribution to the common good and the promotion of the wider social good. This was a view shared by both 19th-century British Idealists and the New Liberals, and later by the Webbs, R.H. Tawney and Richard Titmuss. It was also present in the welfare philosophy of voluntary organisations that had a religious character, such as the Charity Organisation Society.
- The *basic needs model* – standing at the opposite end to the atomistic model – considers human needs to be universal in character (as opposed to subsistence-based) and to include both people who have been able to satisfy their basic needs and are able to use their capacities to help others, as well as people who have a basic needs deficiency which affects their capacities to participate fully in society. This universal and inclusive interpretation of human needs was also apparent among the New Liberals and formed the basis of the Webbs' and Beveridge's endorsement of the idea of a national minimum for living standards.
- The *mutualism model* considers human nature and the fulfilment of human needs to be closely intertwined with 'relationships of reciprocity and co-operation among individuals engaged in works of producing goods for each other' (Hewitt, 2000, p 22). There is here, therefore, a strong attachment to voluntary work that propagates the view that it is through 'cooperative ventures of labour' that qualities such as fraternity, fellowship and comradeship can be developed. Mutualism is returning to British social policy, as the next chapter argues, and is especially relevant for the religious underpinnings of social welfare. It is a concept that became especially evident in the political discourses of New Labour and Coalition leaders alike, some of whom have deep religious convictions. Again, as with the

basic needs model and the organic model, the mutualism model was especially popular among 19th-century New Liberals, the Charity Organisation Society and the British Idealists (Hewitt, 2000).

Yet these philosophical underpinnings about human nature that are crucial to the design of social policy, as Le Grand (1997) has shown, rarely rise to the surface of social welfare discussions. Social welfare forms a key part of the discussion in Chapter 2; suffice to say here that it is understood in this book to have dimensions of redistribution and recognition in line with the work of Fraser (1997). In the last decade or so, egalitarian concerns for the just redistribution of wealth have given way to newer notions of recognition of cultural values and identity, as Western Europe enters what some have termed a post-scarcity society (Atherton, 2011). Deeply connected to terms such as security, preferences and needs, the term 'social welfare' has acquired pejorative connotations in Western society due to the association between cultures of worthlessness and idleness and people who seek recourse to welfare state benefits. Here, social welfare is considered as an objective and measurable outcome. Richard Titmuss (1974) aptly highlighted the judgemental moralistic undertones surrounding the term 'social welfare' when he elaborated on the concept of the social division of welfare (Dwyer, 2007). These issues have been raised in the previous section that looked at the arguments of Jordan (2008) and his proposal that a new politics of wellbeing was needed that emphasised the notion of social value.

Before we end this section, we need to consider the term 'faith-based organisation'. Smith (2004a) alerts us to the fact that in the UK we cannot think of the group of religious people that are socially engaged in some way or another as an 'organisation'. This is merely one facet of their shape and form. Certainly, this assertion has implications for social policy and for how religious people can work with government – not all religious people are formally part of an organisation. Social welfare services are often provided on the premises of the temple where people worship and by the same people who lead them in a workshop. There is a large degree of informality and fluidity, with congregations just as likely to help their local communities as a formal organisation. This situation is confused, as Smith (2004a) points out, by the use of terminology in policy discourse such as 'faith group', 'faith community' and 'faith organisation'. All of these terms are vague, since the religious sector is diverse and fluid and cannot be bracketed neatly under the banner of the voluntary sector.

In the research conducted for this book, it was formal organisations of a religious character that were involved. The operational premises of these organisations may be directly linked to a place of worship, but they were all formal charities registered at the Charity Commission, whose mission was to serve their local communities and to offer social services. The US literature offers various typologies and definitions of faith-based organisations (see Ebaugh et al, 2003), discussed in more detail in Chapter 3 of this book. One of the most well-known of these that has been used for the identification of religious organisations in the research for this book is by Smith and Sosin (2001), who identify three main characteristics: (1) reliance on resources of a religious character; (2) affiliation with or control by a particular religious denomination or religious group; and (3) existence of a religious culture that works for the pursuit of religious values.

Organisation of the book

Since this book lays some basic groundwork for the theorisation and practices of religious welfare in the UK, it is split into two parts that deal with theory and practice respectively. The first part consists of three chapters that are conceptual in nature; they set the analytical scene for the reader by reviewing the historical and social record of the role of religion in social policy in the UK, and the key theoretical frameworks for thinking about social policy change and development under the influence of religion. Part II consists of five shorter chapters that are more applied in nature since they critically review the social welfare services that religious organisations provide in key social policy sectors, and more broadly, they consider the role of religion and spirituality in the conceptualisation and experiences of human wellbeing and social welfare. All of the chapters are concerned with the way in which religious welfare moves beyond the conceptualisation of wellbeing as a transient measure of individual happiness to the broader, more holistic values and processes of human fellowship, prayer, social order, morality, identity and belonging and service to God or will. Below is a more detailed description of each chapter.

Chapter 1 reviews the key historical currents and developments through which religious welfare in contemporary British society needs to be understood. It offers a historical account of the role of the church in caring for the poor, starting with the Middle Ages, through to the 16th-century Reformation with the establishment of a national church in Britain that had a reformed Protestant character akin to North America. The introduction of mass education in the mid-

1800s was forged by political leaders with strong religious convictions, such as William Gladstone, and the 19th-century Victorian era too was animated by the notion of 'practical Christianity'. The historical account systematically works up to the post-Second World War era, with such figures as William Beveridge and William Temple overseeing the establishment of the modern welfare state, drawing inspiration from Christian values of philanthropy and human dignity. The value of this historical overview is in showing that religion is not confined to non-state religious organisations in Britain but has been intertwined in the national political culture.

Chapter 2 begins by describing how the theorisation of social policy has developed exclusively of the role of religion in wellbeing. Even the analysis of the voluntary sector has diluted the rich import of religion to charity and voluntary activity. It looks at the main historical-institutional perspective that historical sociologists in continental Europe and North America have adopted to explain the influence of religious political parties and institutions on social spending and the shape of poverty relief in the West. It also reviews some key definitions such as the adequacy of the term 'faith-based' welfare from its North American origins and uses to the present UK context. What this chapter achieves is clarification of the common ethical and intellectual grounds which concern all political, philosophical and religious ideologies concerned with the good society, thereby laying the ground for the concept of *ways of being*. Taken together, Chapters 1 and 2 show that the impact of religion on social welfare has concerned both state and non-state action in the UK – hence, it is firmly about the social order, ethics of the good society and the basic constitution of human identity.

Chapter 3 introduces the contemporary social and policy profiles of the UK in relation to religion. It describes the changing political, social and economic climate in the UK that has engendered more religion-friendly public policy. A profile of poverty and social problems in relation to religious groups in the UK is discussed, as well as existing data on the religious welfare sector, including its size and financial base. The chapter situates pluralism and concern with social exclusion at the heart of the changing religious climate of the UK. It then describes the key policy developments that have taken place, particularly after Tony Blair won the 1997 General Election. The discussion of the UK is compared as appropriate to the situation of other countries within Europe and North America.

Part II looks at the practice of religious welfare in specific areas of provision, starting with social work, social action and health provision. Chapter 4 considers the importance of religion and spirituality in social work, arguing that social policy as a subject area has much to learn from developments in social work. It offers two key illustrations of the work that religious organisations do, in the areas of prison chaplaincy and bereavement counselling. The chapter takes a broad view of the notion of social work, and looks at the empirical findings of the research undertaken on social action and how religious organisations interpret this. For smaller or newer faith communities, such as the Zoroastrian and Baha'i communities, the concern is less about poverty alleviation and more to do with the preservation of cultural heritage and identity. Theoretically, the chapter confirms the centrality of human nature in the understanding of religious welfare. This will help illustrate how the theoretical conceptualisation of wellbeing is not confined to income and social security, but moves into more cultural and psychological understandings.

Chapter 5 looks at health: based on the contemporary analytical shift away from the biomedical model of health to a psychosocial one, the chapter not only examines how religious organisations provide health support services, but also the challenges and opportunities surrounding the mainstreaming of religion into healthcare provision within the NHS. This includes chaplaincy services, health counselling and general education about lifestyle choices, as well as other services such as visiting patients in hospital and help with transportation. The more holistic view of health which faith groups purport to offer, as well as the engagement of some NHS trusts with issues of religion and spirituality, help to illustrate the shift from transient and individual wellbeing in the mainstream social policy literature.

Chapter 6 complements the focus on health by reviewing the work which religious welfare organisations carry out in the area of social care, broadly defined. In many ways, religious organisations represent 'caring communities' (Wuthnow, 2004) and are the embodiment of the 'ethic of care'. Personal social services are a niche for religious groups precisely because of their personalised character that appeals in particular to older people. The chapter also highlights the challenge facing some ethnic communities in the UK where dependent family members no longer have the support of able members of their families to care for them within the traditional family setting. The future of social care provision in the UK is a hot topic of debate, and in many ways the growth of religious social care organisations in the UK is led by the demand of service users, particularly those from minority ethnic groups in the UK who want to be cared for in an environment which is in harmony with their religious beliefs and identity.

Chapter 7 considers the variety of ways in which religious groups deal with poverty, particularly in relation to low income. It describes how some organisations have set up credit unions, while others collect religious almsgiving such as the Islamic welfare tax *zakat* to distribute to socially disadvantaged families or individuals. The chapter also considers a variety of in-kind services such as re-employment, job advice, food banks and clothing distribution that alleviate poverty, purchasing goods locally to help local economic development or setting up 'fair trade' stalls. Thus, this chapter emphasises the moral mission that religious groups seek to accomplish which is underpinned by a particular understanding of human nature, social morality and order. The international dimension of this chapter highlights how faith groups are particularly active in international poverty campaigning and humanitarian relief work.

Chapter 8 takes the discussion of the book full circle by looking at housing, homelessness services and urban regeneration – hence building on key themes in the book related to social action and social transformation. Like education policy, urban regeneration is a sector in which government policy engagement with religious groups is fairly advanced, with the Local Government White Paper (CTBI, 2006) giving special importance to the role of faith groups. The chapter highlights the housing services which religious welfare organisations offer in terms of advice, homeless shelters, housing for young people, support for independent living for people with disabilities and neighbourhood regeneration. It also shows how neighbourhood regeneration relates to the more intrinsic and long-term role that many faith groups play in their local communities. This is one way of moving beyond the instrumental use of the concept of social capital which is increasingly informing social policy in the UK to a more normative dimension which emphasises the holistic approach faith groups have towards the communities they work in.

The concluding chapter considers the theoretical and practical implications of the book's discussion for social policy. It synthesises all the preceding chapters in order to home in on the debate surrounding the legitimate role of religion in liberal societies, and ultimately, the concept of *ways of being*. The argument focuses on social relationships, personal identity, self-worth and cultural values that matter for human wellbeing and social policy. In this sense, religious values can sensitise service providers to the perennial concerns of egalitarian social policy by breathing new life into concepts such as compassion and service. This in turn shows the way in which the utilitarian approach to social welfare is flawed. By positing individual happiness as the ultimate good, it allows the possibility that welfare will not be shared by all. But as the research in the book shows, personal welfare cannot be separated from the wider condition of society. In this sense, religious perspectives on welfare share a similar approach with cultural understandings of social policy analysis and idealist thinking of the 19th century. Thus, in thinking about religious welfare, there is a need to rethink the moral philosophical premises that underpin social policy.

By way of conclusion, it is apt to return to the beginning of this book and to explain to readers who may not be familiar with the history of social action in Whitechapel that much religious social welfare enterprise did indeed begin in this area. The Salvation Army was born in Whitechapel in the 1860s and the University Settlement movement, a sociopolitical breeding ground (not devoid of religious sentiment and inspiration) for the architects of the post-war welfare state, was also located in this area. 'Davenant' refers to Reverend Ralph Davenant who set up The Foundation School, a 17th-century Christian educational establishment, now turned academy; and The Royal London Hospital was one of the first voluntary-based health providers in England, originally known as the London Infirmary in the 1700s. The young boys referred to at the very beginning of this introduction were entering their school, the East London Academy for boys.

Notes

[1] The research for this book covered both the role of religion generally and the services provided by contemporary religious welfare organisations, particularly in the field of education (such as faith schools or academies). However, due to considerations of space, a chapter on education has been omitted from this book. For further references on education, readers are advised to see the work of John Flint, Clare Tinker and the volume by Marie Parker-Jenkins and colleagues (listed in the References). Religious organisations in the UK such as Oasis and the East London Mosque run a number of city academies which future research would do well to focus on. This follows in a long tradition of religious involvement in education provision as the engine for personal salvation and societal change. This latter point is explored in some depth in Chapter 2, which charts the historical background of religion in British social policy developments.

[2] The salience of these ideas was raised at the time of writing. A commission of experts on care for the elderly recommended to the government that compassion should be as important a job trait of nurses and care professionals as technical competence (Tiggle, 2012).

Part I

Religion, social welfare and social policy
in the UK

Conceptualising the relationship between religion and social policy I: historical perspectives

Summary

- The earliest historical records show that between the 11th and 16th centuries, churches played the primary role in collecting money to spend on the poor and for caring for the poor. As of the 17th century, and with the introduction of the Poor Law of 1601, more organised institutional control at local government level began to take shape as poverty began to be seen as a social problem in need of organisation and redress. In the early 20th century, religious philanthropy reached its apogee with the proliferation of Christian social activism and social care work. But as the demands of industrialisation and pauperisation increased, the church found itself shrinking in resources and membership. By the end of the Second World War, Archbishop William Temple led the way in arguing that the British state was a Christian state and responsibility for social welfare was handed over to a secular administration that would be better able to respond to the needs of the British population.
- Some of the most significant political leaders and social reformers of Britain, from William Gladstone to William Beveridge to Tony Blair, have been driven or in part inspired by their religious faith. Key milestones in British social policy history such as mass education and ragged schools (which were specifically for children from poor backgrounds), the University Settlement movement and the Charity Organisation Society have grappled with the place of religion in public life. Christianity has thus played a central role in the shaping of British national identity. Today, it may be said that church and state have come full circle in Britain, and once again the church is being called on to fill the gaps in welfare provision.
- The changing religious and ethnic profile of the UK since the 1950s has increased the diversity of religious welfare provision, with a growing number of non-Christian faith groups engaging with government in public service provision, although the Jewish population has had a much older history in Britain.

Introduction

In order for us to understand the relationship between religion and social policy in the British context, it is useful to adopt two complementary approaches, one historical and one theoretical. The first of these is the subject of this chapter; the second is taken up in the next. These two perspectives fulfil two important purposes: on the one hand, our view of the welfare state is stretched to the period before the Second World War which is often missing in contemporary social policy scholarship since it is post 1945, which is generally depicted as the watershed moment of the classic Beveridgean welfare state (Page and Silburn, 1999; Fraser, 2009). This allows us to see that social welfare is a much broader and older endeavour than the modern welfare state, with religious values, identities and political mobilisation supplying much of the moral and material resources shaping its pathway.

Most importantly, the historical overview presented in this chapter shows that religious welfare in Britain has much wider connotations than charity or volunteerism; instead, it is firmly concerned with the societal, nation-building and civilisational enterprises that have preoccupied leaders of the British nation-state since early medieval times, including and up to Beveridge in the 1940s. These manifest themselves in issues of social order, ethics of the good life and the basic constitution of human identity. This historical overview also equips us with useful conceptual baggage for studying the relationship between religion and social policy. Thus, concepts such as the mixed economy of welfare, the role of social and political institutions and the influence of moral philosophical thinking in shaping the welfare state become evident. As a result, the historical and theoretical discussions that cut across this chapter and the next are closely intertwined, and this is due in part to the poor development of the theoretical literature on religion in social policy scholarship, and its more advanced status in other subjects such as the history of the welfare state and historical sociology.

We come therefore to the contribution of this chapter. The aim is to provide a basic scene-setting discussion that brings out the key historical phases and currents that have shaped the development of the British welfare state. It begins with an account of the role of the church in caring for the poor in the Middle Ages (Midwinter, 1994), and how this role progressed through to the 16th-century Reformation with the establishment of two national churches (the Church of England and Presbyterian Church of Scotland) (and the persistence of smaller church denominations) in Britain, which had a reformed Protestant character akin to North America, but different from the largely Catholic and Lutheran traditions which took hold in the rest of Europe (Kahl, 2005).

As the role of the church in British social welfare intertwined with growing state involvement from the reign of Henry VIII in the 16th century through to the 19th century, this chapter shows how Christian understandings of welfare have helped form the foundations of social policy in Britain. However, questions remain, as Pacione (1990) notes, over the extent to which, as an established church, the Church of England has been too close to the monarchy, the government and the middle classes to be able to mobilise the working classes sufficiently. These are more fundamental questions about the nature of church–state relations in the UK that the chapter explores since they have direct implications for understanding the British welfare regime structure. The chapter thus develops the historical account systematically up to the end of the Second World War, when the Church of England effectively gave up its right to administer social welfare provision by actively endorsing the establishment of a secular state apparatus to meet the social needs of the time. Simultaneously, new minority religions would soon begin to grow, etching out a new religious profile for the UK.

The chapter is divided into three sections that look at the historical profile of religious welfare from early Christian provision in the 11th century (the shortest of the three sections due to the lack of sufficient historical records), through to the 16th-century Reformation and 19th-century Victorian philanthropy to the final emergence of the modern welfare state after the Second World War (1945).

Historical overview of religion and social welfare provision in Britain

This historical overview is broken down into two large historical periods: the first spanning medieval England until the period of the Reformation, roughly the 11th to 15th centuries, when religiously based social welfare provision was the norm; the second period looks at the 16th century, a watershed moment that began with the Reformation, leading to the 18th-century Enlightenment up until the first half of the 20th century, as changes began to take root in the fusion of religious welfare provision with state and secular voluntary action leading to the near-total marginalisation of the church after the Second World War. The focus of the historical overview is Britain, and England in particular. It is clear from the outset that most of this historical overview will have a Christian focus since non-Christian religions have only come to the fore in the social welfare landscape of Britain in the last 20 years, and in some respects, the reporting of the empirical research in this book constitutes a continuation of the historiography of welfare provision by minority ethnic religions in the UK.

Medieval period (11th to 15th centuries): church dominance in welfare

The medieval period is characterised by the parallel predominance of two systems of social organisations, that of feudalism, where a landed warrior class offered work opportunities and patronage to the peasant population and the church, which in the English case had the archbishops of Canterbury at its apex and a network of bishoprics, monastic orders and village-based parishes (Midwinter, 1994). Issues such as the alleviation of poverty and sickness were not formally recognised or treated in the administrative structures of feudal life, notwithstanding the existence of contracts between feudal landlords and their peasant labourers, whereby shelter and work were offered to the latter in exchange for their labour and service to the former. Thus, peasant families first and foremost had to fend for themselves by living off the land that they worked on. The rule of self-help was supplemented by the supportive role of the church in matters of assistance to the poor and vulnerable.

During this period, the church was a well-resourced institution, owning land and estates and collecting dues from the laity. Churches often acted as conduits for gifts and endowments aimed at the poor with much of this activity taking place at parish level, although in some cases revenues were kept by the church leaders. The church thus acted as both the source of inspiration for social welfare and the mechanism for the actual delivery of assistance (Midwinter, 1994). Christian notions of being 'God's debtor' through good works done to help the disadvantaged animated social welfare provision at the time (Midwinter, 1994, p 14). So the idea that by helping those less fortunate, one would gain God's favour in the afterlife is deeply associated with religious welfare practice, and this has survived down the ages to give expression to various forms of religious social welfare practice today. This idea of an 'afterlife insurance' (Midwinter, 1994, p 15) also meant that the impact of the social assistance offered was perhaps not thought to be of great importance. This is an issue that would also need to be looked at in contemporary studies of religious welfare.

At the height of the medieval period, the church monasteries played the lead role in helping the poor by distributing food, money, clothes and alms at the monastery gates or even delivering these to poor people's homes (Whelan, 1996). Eventually, these services became institutionalised in the shape of the establishment of almshouses which were the first such examples of non-cash or kind domiciliary service to the poor. Although widespread, almsgiving was not a very well organised activity and arguably increased the plight of the poor and their dependency as opposed to bringing about more long-term improvements to their lot – anyone who presented themselves as poor at the monastery gates would receive poor relief as no independent inspection of their circumstances was made (Whelan, 1996). It certainly did not overturn the feudal system. With time, the development of merchant and craft guilds saw the emergence of more secular forms of welfare provision aimed at helping the widows and orphans of guild members (Midwinter, 1994).

Midwinter (1994) further explains that in terms of illness and the treatment of the sick, the church took two contradictory stances: on the one hand, it saw disease as a form of 'divine retribution' (Midwinter, 1994, p 17) and was inclined not to intervene; and in other instances, the church was actively involved in charitable service whereby the almshouses sometimes specialised in helping lepers, the blind or people with disabilities. Nursing and hospital orders were a commonplace church activity, as were the travelling Franciscan or 'grey' friars who offered help to the infirm. Almshouses formed the precursors to the workhouses and hospitals, the two earliest of which were St Bartholomew's and St Thomas', established in London in 1123 and 1200 (Midwinter, 1994). Significantly, these institutions were located in towns and offered care to the poor, sick, aged, disabled and orphans.

In matters of education, dealing with lawlessness and crime, the role of the churches was also important. It began to make large-scale contributions by the 14th century when over 300 schools were in operation under the control of monasteries, cathedrals, hospitals or charities. Modern-day institutions such as Winchester School (1382) and Eton (1440) were established in this way, although even then, their primary purpose was to serve the children of the nobility. The Universities of Oxford and Cambridge later followed with firm identities as ecclesiastical colleges. The role of the church as 'opinion former' and social authority continued to prevail even when new forms of secular apprenticeship, urban trades and the law training Inns of Court evolved (Midwinter, 1994, p 19). In terms of keeping the social order, since church establishments were also large landholders, they had jurisdiction over the rural communities, thereby instilling very firmly in them a culture of crime as sin. Eventually, this gave way to the more secular role of the local constable (predecessor to the modern–day policeman/woman) and legal structures of local government.

The 16th-century Reformation to 19th-century Victorian era: merging of state and church in welfare

Under Henry VIII, England was transformed into a Protestant country and church property was confiscated by the state. This period, from the 1500s onwards, became known as the Reformation. It saw the spread of Calvinism and Lutheranism across Northern Europe as more secular forms of political rule began to take root, thus requiring new forms of public social welfare to replace the old system of poor relief that was under the charge of the medieval Catholic Church. In England, this brought about the passage of the Act for the relief of the Poor of 1597, to be known posthumously as the Poor Law 1601 (Whelan, 1996).

The overseers of the Poor Law remained the local churchwardens, although no clerical responsibility or involvement in dealing with the poor was written into the Act itself. Christian motivation for social action continued to flourish in voluntary form as well, especially in the area of education. The principle of the joint stock company took root during the 17th century and was the basis of the establishment of the Society for Promoting Christian Knowledge (SPCK) in 1699 by Reverend Thomas Bray. SPCK fostered the establishment of charity schools for poor people (Whelan, 1996). By 1729, 1,419 schools had been established in England, teaching 22,503 children. This initiative formally established the idea of education within Christian social thinking in England and was the precursor to the Sunday schools and ragged school movement (Whelan, 1996).

Cunningham (1998) and Innes (1996) note that, by the mid–18th century, there was no real distinction between state and non–state action in the social welfare realm. The terms 'charity', 'philanthropy' and 'welfare' denoted areas of social intervention as opposed to specific ways of addressing social problems. Cunningham (1998) discredits 'historiographical' attempts to assign charity to religious roots and philanthropy to secular ones, arguing that the English Poor Law was itself sometimes referred to as 'legal charity' (Cunningham, 1998, p 2), and in the Catholic countries of Europe, voluntary funding also provided the main resources for poverty relief. Innes (1998) also notes that community volunteers supported state action as a matter of extending public relief. Thus,

> What bound together state and voluntary bodies was that they were both concerned with formulating and implementing policies towards the poor ... across Europe, we can discern a 'mixed economy' of welfare in which state, church and voluntary organization were often inextricably mixed. The English Poor Law, the most obvious example of state regulation and tax funding, depended on volunteers for its operation. (Cunningham, 1998, p 2)

According to Innes (1998), therefore, the Reformation was crucial in setting European countries on specific social policy trajectories. It produced a geosocial demarcation of European welfare provision into a largely Protestant North and a Catholic South. The main characteristics of the emerging Protestant/Catholic divide in welfare provision were that in the former case, welfare was mainly coordinated by the state, through local, municipal or parochial bodies, whereas in the latter case, especially after the counter-Reformation, the church continued to dominate welfare provision through religious orders and confraternities (Innes, 1998, p 21). These differences remained a matter of degree; indeed, the same types of services were such as 'lodging houses ... residential and non-residential workhouses ... home nursing-care ... regular or occasional pension or dole schemes ... and grants for special needs such as marriage' (Innes, 1998, p 23). According to Innes (1998), the practice of institutional care for the 'impotent' poor (the young, old, sick, homeless and vulnerable) was also begun by the church and later developed into poorhouses or 'hospitals' in the 18th and 19th centuries.

Christian understandings of morality and social order underpinned many of the key changes taking place at this time in relation to social welfare in Britain. An emphasis on individualisation and moralisation of the relationship between donor and recipients saw more religious groups taking to the fore of social welfare such as the nuns in early 19th-century Ireland. Many leading 18th-century philanthropic organisations, such as the Philanthropic Organisation of England, were led by progressive social reformers who, even though Christian, did not necessarily attribute to their organisations a Christian mission. Rather, their aim was the benevolent service of humanity. Many philanthropists were Christian and the popularity of belief at the time in the rehabilitation of the poor was a central tenet of the Christian faith (Cunningham, 1998).

Cunningham (1998) goes further in arguing that it was the Christian strands of philanthropic activity that were the more progressive, dynamic and long-lasting, able to survive the upheaval of revolution in Europe and seeking new approaches to deal with poverty in the shape of reforming or rehabilitating the poor. Stand-alone secular forms of charity inspired by Enlightenment thinking collapsed quickly; indeed there was fusion between Enlightenment and Christian ideals and methods in the treatment of the poor. Concern for child welfare was an important development in late 18th-century England led by such evangelicals as Lord Ashley.

Indeed, the 19th century was a period of vibrant intellectual and social activity among Christian groups. As the era of the birth of British and in particular English liberalism, it is a time of transformation, both in church–state relations (the repeal of the Test and Corporation Acts of 1828 and the passing of Catholic Emancipation in 1829) and great Christian evangelical revival, when many of the ideas that were to form the basis of the post-war welfare state were to be formed. Indeed, there were very close links between the Liberal Party and the non-conformist movement (1870–1920), with adherents of the latter later forming the Labour Party (Pelling, 1965; Heidenheimer, 1983; Parry, 1986; Martin, 1999). Thus, even though Brent (1987) argues that England is in the unique position of not allowing religion to play a formative role in its national politics (in contrast to countries such as Northern Ireland or the 'moral majority' in North America), he nevertheless states that:

> ... no history of nineteenth-century English liberalism can be complete if it fails to take account of the role which Anglicanism played in the development of Whiggery in this period ... the Whigs were no more immune from the contagion of nineteenth-century Christian renewal than were their Tory opponents, and that this affected their outlook on policy and politics every bit as much as it did their Conservative rivals. Whig governments had a distinctive religious outlook in the 1830s ... this is best termed 'liberal Anglicanism', and ... in politics this was revealed most clearly on questions involving the Church of England. (Brent, 1987, pp 1-2)

In particular, Brent (1987) sees the contribution of the liberal Anglican politicians of the 1830s in terms of setting the British political landscape that led to the university and school education reforms under William Gladstone in the 1870s which allowed non-Anglicans to study at Oxford and Cambridge, established a national system of elementary education for the poor in England and helped dampen sectarian cleavages between Protestants and Catholics, by disestablishing the Irish

Church, for instance. A project of nation-building was in the making here – liberal Whig parties were keen to expand their political support base and some leaders, such as John Russell, managed to gain allies from a diverse array of social and political figures who were not part of the mainstream Anglican fold such as the evangelical William Wilberforce, the Quaker Elizabeth Fry and the radical Jeremy Bentham (Brent, 1987).

The education system was especially important in this regard. The new ethos aimed at fostering social cohesion and a 'common morality' (Brent, 1987, p 220) among children from all sectarian backgrounds, as opposed to class backgrounds, since religion formed the main sociopolitical fault line of the time. So as well as teaching working-class children about their duties in society and equipping them with skills that would benefit the growing industry of the time (Brent, 1987), the education system was underpinned by a liberal Anglican social vision propagating Christian virtue that was presented as universal to all sects and would support the establishment of the liberal Anglican state (Brent, 1987).

This was not far away from the thinking of Alexis de Toqueville who saw religion as the cornerstone of freedom and admired the religious voluntary associations of the US in the wake of democratic development (Prochaska, 2006). Nineteenth-century liberal Anglicans were also keen to forge alliances between the sacred and the secular. Inspired by the image of the enlightened aristocrat, their view of Christianity was inclusive and non-dogmatic. These politicians were instrumental in establishing the modern notion of a national religion as a 'constitutional necessity' that would serve as the moral foundation of government (Brent, 1987). Thus, the church would care for spiritual matters while the state cared for secular and temporal matters.

The importance accorded to education, as opposed to political action, was a central feature of Christian idealist thinking in the 19th century. The emergence of the Victorian Christian Socialist movement in the 1840s/50s, under the leadership of well-to-do Anglican academics such as Frederick Denison Maurice and Stewart Headlam (Norman, 1987a, 1987b), also needs to be addressed. This group were clerical contemporaries of the liberal Anglican politicians and in many respects their paths were intertwined. Prochaska (2006) explains that the attachment of 19th-century liberalism to individual freedom came from conceptions of the human personality in Christianity. Maurice, for example, was an inspirational religious leader although not formally a politician. The ideas of the Christian Socialists were more closely concerned with issues of social justice and poverty, as proponents sought to overturn the key intellectual trends of the time, namely their opposition to political economy and Benthamite utilitarianism (Norman, 1987a).

The 1800s were thus a period of immense intellectual revival and activism among a new generation of socially conscious Christians who included William Booth (1890), founder of The Salvation Army, whose book, *In darkest England and the way out*, was one of the most significant studies of working-class deprivation in London. A similar detailed survey of poverty in London, Charles Booth's *Life and labour of the people in London* (1892), appeared around the same period, where the connection between poverty and moral degradation was made clear by Booth, who described parts of East London as 'a moral cesspool towards which vice and poverty flow' (1892, p 273). This connection between poverty and immorality is also evident in Booth (1890), who wrote of the poor people The Salvation Army worked with that: 'Their vicious habits and destitute circumstances make it certain that, without some kind of extraordinary help, they must hunger and sin, and sin and hunger' (p 273).

This connection between sin and hunger is not only a matter of moral judgement that the poor are immoral people but that their situation of destitution drives them to engage in criminal activity in order to satisfy their most basic needs. It is as a result of this that in the 19th century, social activists such as William Booth would argue for the rehabilitation of the human being as the key to curing their social problems – this was 'social regeneration' through 'regeneration of the human heart', hence:

> To get a man soundly saved it is not enough to put on him a pair of new breeches, to give him regular work, or even to give him a University education. These things are all outside a man, and if the insider remains unchanged you have wasted your labour. You must in some way or other graft upon the man's nature a new nature, which has in it the clement of the Divine. (Booth, 1890, p 45)

Employing a language to later form the bedrock of the post-war modern welfare state, General Booth spoke of the gigantic evils and twin devils of destitution and despair consuming three million poor people in England – the 'submerged tenth' as he called them in *In darkest England and the way out*. Likening his plan to resolve the social problems of the day to be as revolutionary in the philanthropic sphere as the invention of the railway was to the age of industrialisation, Booth proposed a scheme which consisted of transferring poor people through three stages of social regeneration which, for lack of space, we cannot explore here. The process of social regeneration entailed:

> ... the formation of these people (poor people) into self-helping and self-sustaining communities, each being a kind of co-operative society, or patriarchal family, governed and disciplined on the principles which have already proved so effective in The Salvation Army. (Booth, 1890, p 91)

Indeed, evangelicals came to dominate the philanthropic landscape of 19th-century England, many of them working among the destitute in the East End of London (Whelan, 1996). Rejecting the Calvinist doctrine of predestination and original sin, leading English figures such as William Wilberforce and John Wesley emphasised the need to treat social ills such as poverty and unemployment since these were seen as resulting from immoral action and could detract from the road to salvation. Lord Shaftesbury became the leading evangelical Christian of the time and was seen as the successor to William Wilberforce, the conscience of the nation (Whelan, 1996, p 19). His association with over 200 philanthropic organisations during his lifetime, as well as his pioneering legislation for industrial work, especially against the exploitation of women and children factory and mine workers, bore testimony to the centrality of the Christian faith in social welfare action of the 19th century (Whelan, 1996).

Strongly opposed to the principle of competition, 19th-century Christian Socialists sought to 'Christianise socialism' not through political action but through the moral revival of society and educational enterprises – particularly among working-class men (Norman, 1987a). They also developed small-scale cooperative enterprises as a way of cultivating self-help attributes and moral responsibility, and fostered a sense of human dignity among the downtrodden working class that the existing competitive society of the time ignored. The basis of this was a system of mass education, particularly among the adult working class, and not social engineering or political legislation (Norman, 1987a). The leading thinker of the time was Frederick Denison Maurice, who was inspired by Samuel Taylor Coleridge (1772–1834) and idealist thinking (Norman, 1987b). Thus, the first wave of Victorian Christian Socialism in the 1840s owed little to socialism – it was strongly anti-collectivist and anti-centralisation (Norman, 1987a).

The second generation that was active in the 1880s became much more strongly allied to collectivism as a sacramental form of socialism developed within the Church of England (1987a). This combination of religious and humanist tendencies is a longstanding trait of the Church of England that has long allied it to secular political enterprise. Although they continued to act within the social mores of their privileged class status, the late 19th-century Christian Socialists were among the first public figures of the Victorian era to critique and act against human exploitation for selfish economic gains, and helped to change social attitudes about the social ills of 19th-century laissez faire economics (Norman, 1987b). Key figures of the time, such as Stewart Headlam, saw the importance of secular political reforms. Headlam was a contemporary associate of the Fabians and actively supported developments such as collective bargaining trade union rights, wealth redistribution by the state as well as state-provided education and welfare (Norman, 1987b).

In sum, the key feature of 19th-century Christian social action is its emphasis on the moral quality of the human being. This attachment to individual virtue, self-help and the work ethic (Himmelfarb, 1995) can be seen in the personal drive of Christian philanthropists in social welfare action (as opposed to corporatist action which is more common in our modern times, as exemplified in the idea of the welfare state) (Whelan, 1996). Thus, gradual expansion of social legislation from the mid-19th century onwards in the areas of schooling, nursing and welfare charities undermined the idea of a social purpose and relevance of the Church of England inherent in the local parish charities and the local associational attachments to denominational and congregational bodies of the Victorian era. The Education Act of 1870 brought an end to the tradition of voluntary and self-governing schools funded by local collections and subscriptions. It formalised a system of mass state education funded by taxation which, liberal politicians reasoned, had to be universal and could not be seen to support any particular Christian denomination (Prochaska, 2006). Churchmen of all the different denominations saw this as the death blow to the Christian faith.

Early 20th century to post-Second World War (1945): the church hands over responsibility for social welfare to the (Christian) state

The centrality of Christian virtue and social service, no matter how great a matter of national pride and standing for Britain of the late 19th century, could not withstand the mounting pressure of mass poverty and urban deprivation (Prochaska, 2006). A combination of factors in the form of a steady decline in religious observance in Britain, a global economic recession in the 1930s, a growing population with mass social needs for education, health and public services and two world wars that were to follow in the early 20th century, meant that the state eventually replaced the church as protector of needs and guarantor of social order (Davis et al, 2008). Prochaska (2006) describes this transition effectively in terms that show the intricate connection between Christianity, democracy and social policy, as follows:

> In a representative democracy, social policy had shifted from the local to the national, from the religious to the secular, and the parish and the congregation bowed to the constituency ... the ministerial, civil-service state had dislodged civic pluralism, whose foundations lay in Christian notions of individual responsibility. The shift from voluntary to state social provision was significant not only for social policy but also for religion. Christian institutions were conducive to the growth of grass-roots democracy, but democracy in its representative form proved less conducive to Christianity. (Prochaska, 2006, p 150)

The Second World War imposed the most damaging impact on associational life and the basic infrastructure of the church and British families. Hence, there was a turn towards a centralised state apparatus to fulfil the role previously performed by the local voluntary charities (Prochaska, 2006). Eager to support state expansion, the church presented a report called *The church and the modern world* which, for Prochaska (2011), was a key complementary document to Beveridge's Plan, at the 1948 Lambeth Conference. At this event, Archbishop William Temple, a contemporary of Beveridge who led the way in endorsing the post-war welfare state, together with the bishops of the Church of England, stated that:

> We believe that the State is under the moral Law of God, and is intended by Him to be an instrument for human welfare. We therefore welcome the growing concern and care of the modern state for its citizens, and call upon the Church of England to accept their own political responsibility and to cooperate with the state and its officers in their work. (William Temple, cited in Prochaska, 2011, p 44)

The couching of Christian faith within the wider national interest proved to be a double-edged sword. It instantly put an end to pastoral visitation practices, a central plank of the church welfare edifice, as the church bowed to the pressure of resource constraints and the promise of a centralised administration to tackle the social problems caused by war. Collective provision of benefits and a growing culture of materialism went counter to the localised Christian associational culture of the late 19th and early 20th centuries which linked families to their churches and congregations through bonds of piety and social service in the community (Prochaska, 2006).

But there was also another very important and much more basic reason for the decline of church-led social services: this was the huge drain that the war effort exerted on church personnel and members (Prochaska, 2006, 2011). Thousands of priests became war chaplains and ordinary members of the population were either sent off to war or had to fill the place of family members who were absent. This greatly affected the day-to-day activities of church life at a time when state provision was taking over existing forms of provision. For instance, women became more involved in the Women's Voluntary Services (WVS) which was set up by the government in 1938, taking them away from their traditional church parish groups (such as schooling, nursing and various forms of social care such as district visiting, neighbourly care and mothers' meeting groups). Also, large numbers of Sunday schools and city missions that had long been bastions of 19th-century social work were destroyed by the bombing. This shift was also apparent in the changing nomenclature as charity became social work and major organisations such as the Charity Organisation Society became the Family Welfare Association. Very few organisations, such as the City Missions and The Salvation Army, were able to maintain the traditional religious welfare practices, albeit in modified form due to the new climate of social work.

The important argument made by Prochaska (2011, p 38) is that it was the physical destruction of the religious infrastructure that had supported the day-to-day running of 'practical Christianity' which was the more important reason for the decline of religious charities than any revived sense of post-war 'egalitarianism' or decline in actual religious belief. Indeed, during the 1948 Lambeth Conference, the church delegates present did not hide their fear of a totalitarian state, arguing that even though the state was fulfilling a moral duty by providing social welfare services, it was important to preserve the local voluntary associations as a safeguard of democracy. Their concern for social conscience was shared by Beveridge (1948) in *Voluntary action*, suggesting possible regret on the part of the latter at the establishment of an impersonal and standardised welfare state machine (Prochaska, 2011). Indeed Harris (2011), Beveridge's biographer, states that Beveridge envisaged a relationship of equal partnership between the voluntary sector and the state. This is underpinned by a deeper philosophical tension in Beveridge's thinking about the need to develop civic identity and moral character as a support for effective social welfare services that addressed the political–economic conditions of poverty: the welfare state lacked the former, while religious charities lacked the latter (Harris, 2011).

In spite of Beveridge's clear support both for standardised state provision and personalised voluntary care and mutualism (Harris, 2011), the academic social policy literature falls silent on the role of religion in the inter-war period and especially after the Second World War. Davis et al (2008) argue that the Church of England played a very real role in the political momentum for a universal secular welfare state, through such events as the Malvern Conference of 1941, the Archbishop's conference of industrial and economic experts, and most importantly, the book by Archbishop of York, and later of Canterbury, William Temple's (1942) *Christianity and social order*. Temple played a key role in helping to merge church schools into the public education system in the early 20th century. He became a member of the Labour Party and also President of the Workers' Education Association from 1908 to 1924 (Heidenheimer, 1983, p 23). Heidenheimer (1983) argues that by attributing to the secular state a distinctly religious purpose, Temple helped further the rapid growth of a universal and comprehensive welfare state in the post-war era, one in which the National Health Service (NHS) would achieve such symbolic resonance of nationhood that no subsequent British government has been able to dismantle its hegemony over health service provision.[1]

In *Christianity and social order*, Temple (1942) consciously asserted the characteristic need for the church to move with the times – as alluded to previously. Thus, he outlined the three Christian social principles that should guide the good society (post-war Britain). These, he noted, were based not on 'ancient authorities' but on 'first principles', thus they broadly concurred with universal values. They were 'freedom' and 'fellowship', which he saw as intricately connected because human beings were part of one family created by God; the spirit of social 'service', which, he argued, was a strength of the Christian church, but should underpin all professions and interactions within. These three principles were based on the Christian postulate that '... Man is a child of God and is destined for a life of eternal fellowship with Him' (Temple, 1942, p 74). This elevates the human personality, endowing the human being with the responsibility of stewardship of the natural world that should be used in a way that pleases God and does not undermine the survival of future generations.[2] On the basis of these principles, Temple (1942, pp 100-1) laid down six key social objectives of the post-war government:

- Every child should live decently and with dignity within a family.
- All children should receive an education that develops their aptitudes and is centred around Christian worship.
- Every citizen should have a secure income that enables them to maintain a family and a home.
- Every citizen should have a say in the conduct of the trade or business that relies on their labour, and that this is directed at the welfare of the community.
- Every citizen should have sufficient daily leisure time.
- Every citizen should enjoy freedom of worship, speech, assembly and association.

Temple was the first to use the term 'welfare state' in contrast to the 'power state' of the Nazi regime in Germany (Davis et al, 2008; Pierson and Leimgruber, 2010). He recognised and supported a neutral and social democratic Keynesian approach to government and public provision (Davis et al, 2008, p 32). Thus, Temple advocated for a taxation system and the nationalisation of the banking sector by means of supporting the state's duty to guarantee the basic social and economic needs of the British population by war (Davis et al, 2008). Pierson and Leimgruber (2010) have reasserted this new reading of the history of the welfare state through their examination of its intellectual roots which, they argue, owe as much if not more to liberal and conservative currents than to social democratic ones. Taking a broader European view, Pierson and Leimgruber (2010) give substantial attention to the role of 'practical Christianity' in forging alliances with a new class of secular social formers and, thereby, influencing the climate of ideas that shaped the post-war welfare state.

In the case of Britain, Temple (1942, p 50) aptly recalled that many Labour leaders began their career as local preachers, by way of seeking a middle ground between Christian truth and secular government. Thus, he asserted that the role of the Christian church was to set the moral principles by which society should be ordered and to act as a sort of moral guardian and power broker of public order and civility. His book presents an argument for the involvement of the church in public affairs in its capacity to appeal to universal moral principles, a longstanding practice of the Anglican Church, as evidenced above. These moral principles were a non-sectarian interpretation of Christianity. In this way, Temple was able to couch the spirit of Christian faith within the broader national interests of Britain and he saw no contradiction in British citizens acting out their civic duties with Christian spirit. For Temple (1942, p 31), every citizen had to do what was 'best' for their country, and this 'best' was to be based on Christian principles. In a passage highlighting the perennial problem of church interference in state affairs, Temple (1942) said:[3]

> The political problem is concerned with men as they are, not as they ought to be. Part of the task is to order life as to lead them nearer to what they ought to be.... The Church should tell the politician what ends the social order should promote, but it must leave to the politician the devising of the precise means to those ends.... I cannot tell what is the remedy; but I can tell you that a society of which unemployment (in peace time) is a chronic feature, is a diseased society....The Church is likely to be attacked from both sides. It is likely to be told it has become 'political' when in fact it has been careful only to state principles and point to breaches of them; and it will be told by advocates of particular policies that it is futile because it does not support them. (Temple, 1942, pp 51, 53)

Thus, the church's approach in the inter-war and post-war period was increasingly characterised by compromise and adaptation due to dwindling funds, membership and personnel (Prochaska, 2011). Historically speaking, this tendency towards compromise has been a longstanding feature of the relationship between the Christian churches and wider forces of secularisation (Heidenheimer, 1983). Thus, as charities and friendly societies slipped into what Prochaska terms the 'constructive anonymity' of the 1950s and 1960s, the post-Second World War welfare state set forth in providing 'political solutions' to social problems under the new mantra of redistributive justice and egalitarianism (Prochaska, 2006, pp 152, 160). This new politics was one of 'dutiless rights' and had replaced the old liberal ideal of balancing duties with rights (Prochaska, 2006, p 154). This leads Prochaska (2006) to the following conclusion:

> It was not a coincidence that the expansion of government and the contraction of religion happened over the same period, for the modern British state was constructed against religious interests and customs of associational citizenship. The reform of the suffrage that prompted welfare legislation

may be seen as an underlying cause of Christian decline. Indeed, the expansion of the state into education and social services was both cause and effect of a Christian decline. It is notable that high levels of welfare and low levels of religious adherence go together across much of Europe. (Prochaska, 2006, p 150)

Hence, the impersonal and centralised post-Second World War welfare state would become the hallmark of British civic identity and national pride in the 1940s to 1960s, as Christian charity had been for them in the Victorian period a century before. By the 1940s, British society had become so much less attached to religion that the legislative enactment in the Education Act of 1944 of daily non-denominational worship in state schools rang hollow (Prochaska, 2006).

Yet, some of the last vestiges of the religious voluntary social order of the 19th century were to be seen in the social work and community action of the University Settlement movement, whose alumni included some of the most distinguished figures of the modern British welfare state, that finally came into being in the aftermath of the Second World War (Sherr and Straughan, 2005; Bradley, 2009). William Beveridge and Clement Attlee were two such figures. Bradley (2009) notes that we should not 'overstate the end of Christianity' in the Settlement movement of the early 20th century since the idea of giving service remained a calling for many of the settlers: Oxford House had a deeply religious orientation, and there was also a Jewish settlement at Oxford St George's Club in Stepney.

Although Beveridge played a key role in entrenching the idea that poverty was the result of industrial activity and not personal character (Prochaska, 2006), he retained recognition of the legitimate place of religious belief as part of the fabric of a socially active and progressive society, as evident in *Voluntary action*:

> The making of a good society depends not on the State but on the citizens, acting individually or in free association with one another, acting on motives of various kinds – some selfish, others unselfish, some narrow and material, others inspired by man and love of God.... That there has been loss of religious influence is certain. That this means a weakening of one of the springs of voluntary action for social advance is equally certain. The lives of the pioneers ... show how much of their inspiration for service to society most of them owed to their religious belief. Diminished

influence of the Churches must be taken as one of the
changes in the environment of voluntary action. Now
this religious force for good is less widely influential than
it was in the nineteenth century. It must be revived or be
replaced by some equally good alternative, if that can be
found. Perhaps it must be both in part revived and in part
replaced.... When and how shall we replace the lost power
of widespread religious belief, the material resources which
must support the Philanthropic Motive as the body clothes
the soul, and the sense of brotherhood in the human race?
(Beveridge, 1948, pp 225, 322, 323)

Was Beveridge merely paying lip-service to the waning church
establishment of the time, or should we read more into his homage
to religious values and philanthropy? This depends in some part on
how posterity has interpreted the significance of Beveridge's welfare
programme. For Milward (1992, p 43), the latter was 'no more than
the administrative completion of the moral programme of the British
nineteenth century nonconformism', and in many ways this can
indeed be discerned in the inspiration Beveridge seemed to draw
from Victorian England's social values. More than half a century later,
Beveridge's attachment to the values of mutualism were also voiced by
the Archbishop of Canterbury, Dr Rowan Williams, in his controversial
New Statesman entry in June 2011 where he warns that due to 'cultural
fragmentation', many areas in Britain have lost the tradition of
syndicalism and cooperatives. Mutualism also figures centrally in the
Coalition government's 'Big Society' agenda.

In a seminal work by Oppenheimer and Deakin (2011), *Beveridge and
voluntary action in Britain and the wider British world*, in which a select
group of historians reviews Beveridge's thinking on philanthropy and
the role of voluntary action, Oppenheimer and Deakin attest to the
persisting vitality of religion in the British voluntary sphere. They note
that although Beveridge was not himself religious, he fully appreciated
the positive social contribution of faith groups to society and was
concerned to find an alternative social force, were religious belief and
practice to continue to decline (as highlighted above). In the same
edited volume, Prochaska (2011, p 37) refers to the transcendental
symbolism that the welfare state had for Beveridge and his generation
when Beveridge referred to the 'divine vocation' of self-less service
and social solidarity that would underpin the post-war social welfare
enterprise. Prochaska (2011) concludes that the war helped to create
an appetite for large-scale state planning, relegating voluntarism to

piecemeal and rudimentary provision, no matter how sincerely heartfelt it was. Nevertheless, the continued dynamism and indeed growth of Christian evangelicalism across the world, and indeed in the UK, has meant, according to Martin (1999), that this movement has been at the forefront of Christian voluntary social welfare provision, a phenomenon explored further by the empirical research reported in this book (see for instance examples of the work of the Manchester-based youth organisation The Mission or the London-based Oasis Trust).

This brings us aptly to the second phase of discussion and an appropriate conceptual framework for analysing the relationship between religion and social policy: the current state of theoretical enquiry, which is the subject of the next chapter. This will review the prevailing analytical perspectives in light of the near-total silence of contemporary British scholarship on this subject until the very late 2000s, despite important policy developments in the UK and changing demographic profiles, partly due to the growth of minority religions.

Conclusion

This chapter has given an overview of the role of religion in social welfare and the development of the welfare state in Britain. From early medieval times, the churches were the main body in charge of collecting money to spend on the poor and caring for them. This role progressed through to the 16th-century Reformation, with the emergence of diverging Protestant and Catholic models of welfare in Europe, whereby the former favoured state action and the latter favoured philanthropic action. Thus, the significance of this historical overview has been to demonstrate the deep connections between the national state religion adopted by European countries, including the UK, of course, and processes of nation-building and political action. Religion has been about much more than just charity and philanthropic action.

Indeed, as early as the 17th century, and with the introduction of the Poor Law of 1601, more organised institutional control at local government level had begun to take shape as poverty began to be seen as a social problem in need of organisation and redress. Welfare provision intertwined both church action and the early modern state that was itself of a confessional character at this time, thus the church would administer welfare provision at local level. Prominent religious figures who were also part of the political establishment influenced the developing liberal political ideas of the day and Christian Socialists led the social reform agenda of the 18th and 19th centuries. In England, the church preserved the civilising core of the nation and fostered its prosperity by taking a non-orthodox view which: (1) admitted dissenters into the education system; (2) withdrew institutionalised religion from the state; and (3) established a system of non-dogmatic religious education (Brent, 1987, p 183).

Religious welfare as a state-based force began to dwindle in the early 20th century. At this point religious philanthropy reached its apogee with the proliferation of Christian social activism and social care work. By the end of the Second World War, the church would hand over responsibility for social welfare to the new secular administration, which it justified as being a Christian state. Thus, we see that some of the most significant political leaders and social reformers of Britain, from William Gladstone to William Beveridge to Tony Blair, have been driven or were in part inspired by their religious faith. Key milestones in British social policy history such as the establishment of the University Settlement movement and the Charity Organisation Society have grappled with the place of religion in public life.

Questions for discussion

1. How has religious welfare action changed from the medieval period up to our present times?
2. How and why was the Victorian era distinctive in the role that religion played in social welfare?
3. Who were the Christian Socialists and how did they influence liberal politics of the early 20th century?
4. What can modern Britain learn from the history of the role of religion in social welfare?
5. Has the Church of England undermined itself by advocating the establishment of a universal secular welfare state?

Notes

[1] It should be recalled that both the Thatcher and Coalition governments tried to implement major reforms to the NHS in the 1980s and 2011 respectively and in both cases, wide public disapproval forced them to detract.

[2] Temple (1942) tempered his description of private property as sin by alluding to the new interpretations of the Bible which emerged during the Reformation that lay new emphasis on individual responsibility as spiritually good, making private property necessary because man was imperfect in his capacities for justice and love. Also, reference to theft as a sin in the Bible provided further argument in favour of the freedom to acquire and dispose of property. This endorsement of private property and profit making

was expressed in the terms of 'exclusive rights and moral responsibilities'. Simultaneously, the duty to give charity to the poor also became part of the equation. In this tradition of thought, Temple cited John Wesley who said: 'Gain all you can; save all you can; and give all you can' (Temple, 1942, p 43). Temple then eloquently explained the irony that Methodist individualism paved the way for 18th-century industrial activity and wealth accumulation, which turned into a new form of economic materialism that outlived the decline of faith in God in the centuries that followed.

[3] This aptly echoes the predicament of Reverend Dr Rowan Williams following his critique of the Coalition government's political practice and policies in the 9 June 2011 issue of the *New Statesman*.

TWO

Conceptualising the relationship between religion and social policy II: theoretical perspectives

Summary

- Thinking theoretically about the role of religion in social policy takes two forms: on the one hand, it involves looking at how religion can shape the *content* of social policy and social welfare, for instance, what values and definitions should constitute social welfare, the common good and correct moral action. This draws heavily from theology and scriptural teachings such as helping the needy, paying alms or not practising usury. On the other hand, it involves the *form* of social policy, meaning the way in which religious *actors* and *institutions* have shaped the actual development of the welfare state and/ or non-state social welfare action. Typically, Western countries have been divided along Protestant and Catholic lines, with the former favouring state welfare provision and the latter charity and voluntary action.
- Historical sociologists and sociologists of religion in the US and continental Europe as well as social work academics in the UK have been at the forefront of theoretical engagement with the role of religion, and indeed spirituality, in their subject areas. Social policy scholarship in the UK offers only cursory mention of the Christian Socialist movement or 19th-century religious voluntary activity.
- Religion in social policy is more than just about the mixed economy of welfare or faith-based organisations; it can provide a radical starting point for rethinking the nature of social welfare and, to a certain extent, the economic system. However, some authors argue that a religious perspective on social welfare favours an emphasis on moral obligations and social order over universal rights and emancipation.
- Religious perspectives on welfare challenge reductionist utilitarian notions of wellbeing by advocating an holistic understanding of human beings based on their innate agency and dignity, and the broader moral dimensions of the social relationships which determine their wellbeing. These resonate with secular arguments about the need to maintain the moral purpose of contemporary social policy and the 'social value'[1] with human interactions. The term *ways of*

being is proposed as a way of moving beyond narrow material conceptions of wellbeing or welfare.

Introduction

Following on from the historical focus of the previous chapter, here we examine how religion has been studied within social policy scholarship. This immediately contrasts the British (and English) context with continental Europe and North America in the sense that the role of religion has been more or less lost in the obscurity of the voluntary sector in the UK, whereas in Europe and North America it has figured much more centrally in the analysis of social welfare provision, for example, through the role of Catholic political parties and the Catholic Church or through faith-based social welfare provision funded by federal states in the US. There are two broad axes along which the theoretical perspectives discussed in this chapter will be organised. These are the *form* which the relationship between religion and social policy has taken and the *content* of this relationship, explained further below.

The first axis is about form: it is a macro-level politico–institutional perspective. This dimension of theorising is much more international in origin and scope, stemming from research in the 1970s on the role of Catholicism in the welfare state formation of continental European countries (Flora and Heidenheimer, 1981). To this end, it is perhaps the more developed dimension of research on religion and welfare state formation and has been led by the work of historical sociologists, social work scholars and sociologists of religion in the European Continent and North America (see Flora and Heidenheimer, 1981; Wilensky, 1981; Heidenheimer, 1983; van Kersbergen, 1995; Skocpol, 2003; Cnaan, 2004; Manow, 2004; Wuthnow, 2004; Kahl, 2005; Orloff, 2005). This macro perspective looks at the institutional configuration and political cleavages that have occurred in Western Europe and North America, and the role of religious parties and welfare organisations in forging or hampering public spending and the development of welfare states. Of interest here are broad state–church relations, processes of industrial modernisation and the sociopolitical cleavages resulting from political mobilisation. Within the UK, contemporary scholars mostly discuss the institutional role of religion in social welfare within the context of the voluntary sector (Page and Silburn, 1999; Powell, 2007a) and the heritage of mutuals and friendly societies or community development and local governance (Chapman, 2009; Lowndes and Dinham, 2009). Taken from the long-term historical perspective presented in the previous chapter, it will become immediately clear that religion has been an institutional driver, both in the private and public spheres, and advocating social welfare action, but at state and non-state levels.

The second axis is about content and has greater claim to British academic focus: it is the micro-level normative perspective which is relatively less well developed in the literature and explores the substantive influence of religious values and perspectives on social welfare. Of interest here are how values, attitudes and behaviours linked to processes of modernisation and secularisation intertwine with conceptual frameworks in social policy and shape definitions of social welfare. For example, Manow and van Kersbergen (2009), Jawad (2009) and van Kersbergen and Manow (2011) show that whereas modern professionalised and secular social welfare systems are founded on the logic of 'rights', 'emancipation', 'entitlements' and social insurance from material risk, religiously motivated or inspired social welfare action may be more concerned with maintaining 'obligations' and 'social order', and more closely founded on the principles of salvation or redemption, faith, personal ties and affective relationships. British scholarship on the topic has been led so far by scholars who, strictly speaking, are situated outside the traditional disciplinary boundaries of social policy, and have primarily framed their research in terms of the political place of religion in the public sphere and its role in social cohesion (such as Farnell et al, 2003; Ashencaen-Crabtree et al, 2008; Davis et al, 2008; Dinham et al, 2009; Furness and Gilligan, 2010; Atherton, 2011); the landscape is fast changing and new publications more closely located in social policy are beginning to emerge, although none, as yet, has engaged with how religion relates to the meaning of social welfare at a theoretical level.

In focusing on the two dimensions of: (1) macro-level institutional process and political relations, and (2) micro-level normative values and patterns of identity, this book diverges from Opielka's (2008) four-tier classification of micro-meso-macro-meta analyses in the theorisation of the relationship between religion and social welfare. This chapter simplifies this debate by highlighting, on the one hand, how the interplay of institutional forces has shaped the role of religion in social policy (form); and how religious identity provided the moral basis for conceptualising social welfare (content). This broadly echoes van Kersbergen and Manow's (2010) classification of 'political' and 'ideational' perspectives on the relationships between religion and social policy.

The chapter is divided into four sections: the first sets the theoretical discussion in motion by considering the debates on the public role of religion and its right to provide social welfare services in modern-day liberal democratic societies. The second explores the macro-institutional perspective highlighted earlier, which roughly divides Europe and the US along the lines of church–state relations and the dominant Christian denominations of their various territories. The third focuses on the term 'faith-based organisation' and how it has been critiqued in the literature. It hones in on the role of faith-based organisations in the Anglo-Saxon countries. The fourth explores some of the normative dimensions of the religion and social welfare debate and how some scholars have sought to conceptualise the substantive contribution of religious perspectives to social policy. This has largely taken the form of debate around the role of culture and social capital. The social work literature stands out in particular here with some authors looking at the health-related impact of spirituality and others exploring the values and ideational elements that a religious perspective brings to social work practice.

A right to provide? Utilitarian, moral and religious claims to social welfare

Before we can embark on a more detailed consideration of the place of religion in contemporary social policy scholarship, it is important to briefly address the more fundamental question regarding the claim of social policy to the moral high ground of social welfare provision, and the claim of religion to public social welfare provision at all. Put another way, is modern society justified in allowing the secular (egalitarian) strain of social policy to dominate the moral argument surrounding human wellbeing and relegating religion to the sphere of personal and private activity with little implications for the moral principles on which society is based? Surely religion has some moral claim over human life too, and indeed does not differ from modern secular social policy in the types of moral concerns that it is grappling with – for example, poverty or crime are social concerns to all worldviews. The two main themes that concern us, in this section are, therefore: (1) the deeply moral nature of human welfare questions; and (2) the distinctions between the private and public spheres. This has implications for definitions of human nature, as explained in the introduction to this book, and ultimately for human identity.

One of the most enduring legacies of the 18th-century European Enlightenment was to seal the fate of religion to the inconsequential private sphere of life as a backlash against centuries of prolonged conflict and war inspired by religious and sectarian differences (Casanova, 1994). Yet, in our times, the question of the private/public division of social life has been challenged by the emergence of new social groups seeking to claim political power, most notably the feminist movement and feminist scholarship (Hewitt, 2000). Here, the personal sphere of life has been shown to be intricately connected to issues of public power. In the same vein, the question of religious welfare also has implications for the remit of religious values, actors and institutions in the public sphere (Dinham and Lowndes, 2009).

A key contribution of the feminist critique is that it has helped to highlight dissatisfaction with the classic post-war welfare state which was predicated on standardised and universal provision through public taxation (Deacon and Mann, 1999). Citing various communitarian and religious thinkers such as Amitai Etzioni, Philip Selznick and Chief Rabbi Jonathan Sacks, who lament the loss of moral direction in social welfare policy, Deacon and Mann (1999) offer the following succinct predicament for social policy:

> Welfare policy is either about enabling people to make responsible choices or it is a form of social engineering. If it is the former, then it must engage with behaviours and the moral decisions that people make. If it is the latter, then the debate is about what sort of society it wants to engineer and which set of moral codes it wishes to impose. The tension between these options can not be resolved: policy will either treat the poor as moral defectives or as moral agents. (Deacon and Mann, 1999, p 433)

These arguments about the effects of institutionalised social welfare may help to explain why there have been very few theoretically oriented publications on the normative aspects of social policy since the 1940s. One publication, *Moral philosophy and social welfare* (Plant et al, 1980), has not been followed by similar titles and indeed, at the heart of Plant et al's (1980) book is a concern with advancing theoretical analysis of the concept of human need. Fulfilling human need does indeed constitute *a*, if not, *the*, central organising principle in social policy studies. White (2010, p 20) sees this fundamentally as a matter of the 'ethical ideals' which the welfare state represents. Together with upholding the values of liberty and equality, social policy has important political import: T.H. Marshall described the advancement of 'social rights' as the hallmark of the modern welfare state and the provision itself of welfare benefits in society represents, at least in some quarters, a concern for social justice and equal opportunities.

Moreover, the challenges facing welfare states in the affluent capitalist countries over the last two decades, together with the rise of neoconservative political parties, have brought back debates about the moral and economic strain caused by the welfare state, both on the public purse and on the personal responsibility of poor people to fend for themselves. Indeed, it has long been a tradition within social policy scholarship to separate the latter 'morally judgemental' approach to social welfare from the non-judgemental one (Deacon and Mann, 1999). It is the non-judgemental interpretation which has dominated since the end of the Second World War, prompting commentators to note the gap in moral leadership. Yet, Deacon and Mann (1999) highlight the uncanny similarities between New Labour's discourse of welfare recipients' duties and responsibility and Christian Socialist and communitarian perspectives. Indeed, Pierson and Leimgruber (2010) also note this strong 'remoralising' tendency in the politics of welfare since the late 1970s, with the return of neoliberal intellectual forces to the fore. Tony Blair's Third Way and David Cameron's Big Society are part of this process.

Spicker (2000) offers further insight on the moral debates underpinning social policy. Locating the moral implications of and for social policy requires concern with what is the right course of action, as opposed to merely advocating what policies have a good effect. This is the classic juxtaposition of focusing on outcomes as opposed to process, and it highlights the central influence that utilitarianism (as defined by Jeremy Bentham and John Stuart Mill in the 19th century) has played on social policy. As Spicker (2000) notes, Esping-Andersen's welfare regime approach has played a key role in showing how institutional level dynamics, such as policy processes, ideological underpinnings, rules of benefit and administrative structures for benefit distribution, can have a direct impact on welfare outcomes – in short, to use Spicker's (2000, p 173) term, social policy is not a 'black box' whereby inputs and outputs can be measured in a technical manner. Hence, Spicker (2000) states:

> It is possible to examine policies in a neutral fashion, seeing whether they achieve their stated ends, but the study of social policy has to consider whether the ends are appropriate as well as whether they are achieved.... The provision of welfare is a moral activity and the values it enshrines are the values of the society it operates in.... In the field of welfare provision, there are no neutral outcomes. (Spicker, 2000, pp 4, 107, 110)

Part of the impetus behind Spicker's (2000) emphasis on moral values in his theoretical approach to welfare provision is that his analysis begins with social relationships and society as opposed to the more conventional mode of thinking which emphasises the role of the state and broad political-economic processes such as industrialisation as the main driving forces behind social policy. This emphasis on social relationships is important for the empirical research and analytical discussion that are the subjects of this book; they are also important for the new social policy climate of the UK which, ever since the New Labour era, has become increasingly concerned with social issues such as social cohesion, community, partnership and now the Big Society. As Spicker (2000) notes, the social and the moral are closely intertwined; this is where notions of the individual's obligations towards society and vice versa emanate from. This close connection between the social and the moral has formed an important line of argument for scholars within the broader field of the social and political sciences and is one which the subject of social policy is likely to have to face up to more closely in the near future as it battles to preserve its standing in the fierce climate of welfare retrenchment.

Thus, Jordan (2008) succinctly articulates the moral challenge facing social policy scholarship and policy making as follows:

> The problem of course is that it has proved fairly easy to destroy the sense of commitment to common causes, to solidarities, moralities, religions and ways of life, for the sake of increased individual welfare supplied by the economic model, but it is far harder to build a new version of these forms of collective meaning. Many people remain loyal to non-welfarist communal activities such as crafts, sports, musical styles or outdoor pursuits, but they are induced to see these as lifestyle choices rather than essential aspects of wellbeing. (Jordan, 2008, pp 249-50)

These ideas point to a more fundamental argument about the welfare state itself as having transcendental symbolism and forming an expression of ultimate values and ideals for human life in advanced capitalist democracies (Tinder, 1987; Hollinger et al, 2007). It is not a coincidence that some Christian commentators and political reformers have seen a spiritual Christian duty in the establishment of a welfare state (Temple, 1942; Tinder, 1987). If, then, social policy is fundamentally tied to the moral values upheld by a society (Spicker, 2000; Rowlingson and Connor, 2011), and if religious values and institutions play a key role in shaping the histories and cultures of human civilisation (Wilber and Jameson, 1980; Trigg, 2007), then it is important to allow religious reasoning space in the public sphere as a faculty of human reasoning (Trigg, 2007). For, as Trigg (2007) argues, if religion is to promote the values of equality and freedom in society, it needs to play a formative public part in the definitions of these same terms. The implication here is that religious reasoning can be allowed expression and scrutiny on the same par as scientific reasoning. After all, the right to express and act on one's faith publicly is enshrined in Article 18 of the United Nations (UN) Universal Declaration of Human Rights and Article 9 of the European Convention on Human Rights (Trigg, 2007, p 32). Hence, echoing Madeley (2003), Trigg (2007, p 149) argues that democracies require open public space for all voices to be heard and that far from state neutrality towards religion, it has been the state's religious commitment in many countries, including the European countries with a Christian heritage, that has fostered the modern liberal ideals of freedom and equality. The previous chapter demonstrated this argument.

Trigg (2007) effectively outlines the dangers and weaknesses of keeping religious concerns and views out of public life as follows:

> Religion is a private matter, in that it is a free personal choice, not dictated by the State. Political voices themselves, however, should be in that category, and that does not mean they cannot be publicly discussed. The demands of freedom and those of rationality are intertwined.... Religion is prevented from making any public truth claims, or from being able to share in any overarching rationality. Thus a relativist view of truth in religion comes to prevail, coupled with a touching faith in science as the sole arbiter of objective truth.... A restriction on the idea of public reason, confining it to what is generally acceptable, prejudges democratic debate before it has begun. We cannot be told what cannot be discussed.... The enemy of a rational discussion is a misplaced certainty.... (Trigg, 2007, pp 206-7)

For Trigg (2007), therefore, a truly democratic state cannot be self-sufficient but must, as in the US way, fall under the will of God. The state's power must be superseded by a higher authority which can provide moral restraints to secular government. Using the example of the Church of England, Trigg (2007) argues that this religious establishment opens the space of public debate and for the voice of minority faiths to be heard. Trigg's (2007) argument ends with the important proposition that religious views should be publicly debated since, if their truth claims are then proved, they can then lay the basis for universal human principles and social ethics.

But what we find is that the normative underpinnings of modern social policy are from the above. Utilitarianism has provided the backdrop to political philosophical thinking in social policy since the 18th century, infiltrating the way happiness, wellbeing and human nature are conceptualised in British social policy. The key thinkers in this tradition were David Hume, Jeremy Bentham and John Stuart Mill (Kenny and Kenny, 2006; West, 2006). Utilitarianism posits that human nature is fundamentally geared towards the pursuit of happiness and the avoidance of pain. Happiness is understood in a very inclusive way to encompass all notions of physical, emotional and intellectual 'pleasure' which all have equal weighting, so, in Bentham's famous remark, 'Quantity of pleasure being equal, push-pin is as good as poetry', because the key thrust of utilitarianism is quantifiable measurement (Kenny and Kenny, 2006, p 27; Jordan, 2008). To this end, according to utilitarian theory, social action is to be judged by its utility, which 'is the degree to which it produces better consequences than alternatives' (West, 2006, p 1). Moreover, the maximisation of utility or happiness is sought in terms of the greatest number of people; this is the utilitarian principle of the greatest happiness of the greatest number (Kenny and Kenny, 2006).[2]

In this view, welfare is understood in *hedonistic* and *consequentialist* terms as outcomes that are characterised by a happy feeling (West, 2006, p 1). This understanding of human wellbeing may be seen as promoting the technical social administration view of social policy which separates ends from means. Morality is thus understood primarily in terms of happiness, and not duty, as discussed above. For Jordan (2008), this perspective has helped to foster the influence of economist, individualistic and consumerist interpretations of social welfare, to the detriment of social solidarity and social value. Utilitarianism has also helped to foster aggregate analysis of social welfare and the public good as opposed to the process of distribution and differentiation (Kenny and Kenny, 2006). Indeed, a key problem is that utilitarianism accepts the misery of an individual or a minority for the happiness of the majority, and in this sense, its compatibility with neoliberal capitalist thinking is evident (Kenny and Kenny, 2006). Modern advocates of utilitarian thinking, such as Layard (2005), defend it in that they argue that social justice can be a primary end of utilitarian thinking. For John Stuart Mill in the 19th century, the golden rule of 'Do unto others as you

---

would have them do unto you' was equally shared in utilitarianism, and there was thus an 'ethic of utility' in the teachings of 'Jesus of Nazareth' himself, according to Mill (West, 2006, p 75).

The extent to which the religious perspective advocates a critique of utilitarian thinking is part of the overall objective of this book and will be explored in the course of it. Certainly, an emphasis on character and virtue as having a higher moral value than happiness will be a major fault line underpinning the discussion. A central theme here is the extent to which a religious perspective prioritises morality over happiness. In this sense, religious welfare organisations help the poor, not just because this is just and because the poor need helping, but because it is a religious duty to help them. Likewise, for many religious organisations, as in the tradition of William Booth, the poor do not just need material help but also spiritual help.

In sum, we can add more flesh to these arguments by going back to the all-encompassing notion of *service* which emphasises the importance of human fellowship and compassion over and above the transfer of material forms of help. The concept of *ways of being* is a way of expressing the narrow utilitarian notion of wellbeing or happiness in that it, first, identifies human relationships, identity and moral values as central to the human condition but second, that it abates unrealistic expectations about the possibility of uninterrupted happiness. Misfortune and suffering happen to all people and perhaps, therefore, the challenge for social policy is more in relation to what attitudes people have to their lives as opposed to how much utility they are able to extract or maximise. It is their *way of being* rather than their wellbeing that matters.

We now turn to how religion has been studied in social policy scholarship to further develop this argument.

Thinking theoretically about religion and social policy: macro-institutional processes

In order to consider the status of the academic study of religion in social policy and the development of welfare states more generally, this section contextualises religion within two broad frameworks: (1) a political-institutional framework that has come to characterise the welfare regime tradition (Titmuss, 1967; Esping-Andersen, 1990); and (2) a less well-known cultural-geographical framework which emanates from the 'families of nations' school of thought in welfare state analysis (Castles, 2010). These perspectives place the study of religious forces in welfare provision with wider processes of political mobilisation, particularly in relation to party politics and class coalitions in the formative years of European welfare states at the end of the 19th century and the beginning of the 20th.

The political-institutional approach, most closely associated in recent years with the work of Esping-Andersen (1990), seeks to explain divergence in social welfare provision in the rich Western democracies (Castles, 2010). Its three-legged typology of liberal, social democratic and conservative-corporatist regimes is criticised by commentators for hiding unexpected differences or anomalies within the regime clusters such as the 'women friendliness' of corporatist countries such as France and Belgium, the liberal character of the Swiss welfare state and the delayed but subsequently rapid development of Dutch welfare (Manow and van Kersbergen, 2009, p 33).

A parallel although less well-known framework in comparative social policy research is the 'families of nations' framework propagated, for example, by Castles (1993, 2010) and Therborn (1993), which differs from the political-institutional regime approach in that it explores the influence of common genealogical factors (language, culture, history and geography) on policy outcomes. This approach argues that policy divergences may occur among countries with similar characteristics but that these will revert to type due to their 'common ancestry' (Castles, 2010, p 634). To a certain extent, the 'families of nations' approach is in some ways implicit within the Esping-Andersen typology, specifically in relation to the liberal welfare regime model which Esping-Andersen (1990) himself links closely to the Anglo-Saxon countries.

The 'families of nations' approach has been particularly corroborated by empirical research that supports a specific welfare grouping generally referred to in the literature as 'England and its settler colonies' (America, Canada, New Zealand and Australia), all of which belong to the reformed Protestant faith initiated by John Calvin (1509–64), which, as seen in the previous chapter, in welfare state terms, combines strong anti-state tendencies with self-help and mutualism (Gorski, 2005; Kahl, 2005; van Kersbergen and Manow, 2010). This tendency differs from orthodox Protestantism or Lutheranism (Martin Luther, 1483–1546) which characterises Germany and the Nordic Scandinavian countries where the national church merged more smoothly into the emerging secular welfare state enterprise of the late 19th century. This point helps to respond to the specific absence of consideration of Protestantism in social policy analysis (Manow, 2004).

As argued in Manow (2004), a cultural-institutional framework is especially relevant for the analysis of welfare regimes from the perspective of religion because it highlights the significance of state–church configurations in the development of welfare, as well as the moral values that motivated political activism in European welfare state development. These were especially evident in church–state conflict over education legislation, the influence of Catholic and Protestant parties and conflict over control of the provision of social protection services (Manow, 2004). In Manow's account, these are the institutional variables that emphasise the role of social Protestantism in particular in explaining the contradictions in Esping-Andersen's welfare regime typology.

Accordingly, this section argues that the two key variables that distinguish the Western countries for our purposes are the levels of religious pluralism and diversity and the strength of liberal political traditions in them. The stance that religious groups and representatives took in relation to liberal politics in Europe is fundamental for understanding the different pathways of development that the welfare state underwent. The understanding of liberal here is first in the moral terms of self-help, work ethic and individual responsibility which has a great affinity with reformed Protestant traditions, and not just in the economic terms of free market enterprise (Manow, 2004; van Kersbergen and Manow, 2010). Typically therefore, Catholicism and Protestantism fell on opposite sides, with Protestantism finding affinities with liberal politics and Catholicism the inverse (Manow, 2004). For example, the latter case is well exemplified in Catholic countries such as France, Spain and Italy, where social legislation, especially in the late 19th and early 20th centuries, was advocated by liberal parties that were deeply anti-clerical in nature. This contrasts with Sweden, New Zealand, Australia and Britain, which had liberal Protestant traditions that went with the grain of a secular welfare state.

These two factors of religious pluralism and liberal political mobilisation therefore help to determine not only the extent to which non-state religious welfare organisations are active in the provision of social welfare services but also how comprehensive and universal state-based social welfare provision has been in Western Europe. Manow (2004) further argues that the religious character of European countries shaped labour relations, patterns and degrees of economic development and the strength of non-majoritarian institutions, all of which had an impact on welfare state development. Van Kersbergen (1995) puts the distinction between Catholic and Protestant influence on the welfare state succinctly, as follows:

> Christianity is related to welfare capitalism only so far as Protestantism involved a first step in the process of secularisation and individualisation.... Protestantism

> qualitatively changed church–state relationships which, in turn facilitated the construction of the welfare state....This contrast between the Protestant and the Catholic nations explains the qualitative differences between the welfare states. These differences concern the degree of "stateness" (the level of centralisation; the level of state-church integration; the degree of state intervention in the economy) and the degree of institutional coherence (universalism versus fragmentation). (Van Kersbergen, 1995, pp 194-5)

In the existing literature, these various patterns of relationships between religion and the welfare state in the rich Western democracies have been mapped out onto three types of church–state relations that began to shape welfare policies from the 19th century onwards. For Morgan (2009, p 57), who omits Britain from her typology, these patterns of church–state relations are as follows:

- The Nordic European model characterised by religious homogeneity, church–state fusion and no significant sociopolitical conflict based on religious lines where liberal forces were in close alliance with the social Protestant (Lutheran) tradition (for example, Sweden, Norway, Finland and Denmark).
- The Catholic European model where strong church–state conflict dominated the political and electoral scene and liberal forces became closely associated with the anti-clerical movement (for example, Belgium, France and Italy).
- Countries where religious forces gained political prominence and their policies and interests were therefore accommodated in society (for example, Germany, Austria and the Netherlands).

Morgan's (2009) typology focuses on party political cleavages, especially between the left wing and religious/Catholic parties of Europe, and can be broadly superimposed onto the more standard church–state classification offered by Casanova (2008, p 111), which describes more clearly the liberal nature of religious practice in some countries and now others as follows:

- Formal church establishment with relative 'free exercise' of religion in society (England, Scotland and the Nordic countries).
- Formal disestablishment of the church and strict regulation of religious practice (France and the former Communist countries).

- A half-way house between formal separation of church and state but with the existence of informal single or multi-church establishments (Germany, Southern European countries).
- Disestablishment with a very high degree of religious pluralism (US).

Based on the patterns of church–state separation mentioned above, this section examines the academic literature on the role of religion in social policy in the advanced capitalist Western world through a cultural-geographical lens. This responds to the patterns of influence of religion on social welfare, a matter of cultural values and religious traditions which saw a so-called 'westward' direction in the birth of welfare states (Heidenheimer, 1983). Thus, the three main groupings that are proposed in this chapter are as follows:

- The Catholic Southern European countries such as Spain, Italy, Greece, Cyprus and to some extent France, where moderate to high levels of religiosity prevail (with the exception of France) and low levels of religious pluralism exist.
- The Protestant Northern European countries with low levels of religiosity and high levels of welfare state provision which may also be subdivided into reform Protestant and Lutheran traditions, thus distinguishing between Germany and Sweden on the one hand, and Switzerland, the Netherlands and Britain on the other. Notably, strong Catholic presence exists in some of these countries such as Germany and the Netherlands.
- The English-speaking world which notably includes the US, Britain, Australia and New Zealand, all of which experienced a late onset of the welfare state (Heidenheimer, 1983; Manow, 2004) (even though quick and comprehensive once finally implemented, as in the case of the Britain in 1906 and then 1945), where strong liberal political traditions now operate in a context of religious pluralism.

Clearly, we see here the amorphous position of Britain. This geographical sub-classification will help to categorise Britain among the various theoretical currents that can feed into a fuller picture of the study of religion in social policy. It will be shown that as the birthplace of the classic universal welfare state, British social policy has had a residual relationship with religious values, actors and institutions making academic study and contemporary empirical enquiry in this area still in its infancy – certainly in relation to the US and continental Europe. The dividing line between countries of a Catholic or Protestant confessional background is important since research has shown that the welfare state developed along different lines depending on the relative importance of Catholic social teachings or social Protestantism (Manow, 2004; Kahl, 2005; Casanova, 2008). Indeed, as Gorski (2005) further notes:

> ... corporate-conservative welfare states were most likely to emerge in predominantly Catholic societies, such as France and Italy ... liberal welfare states emerged only in areas heavily influenced by Reformed Protestantism (that is England and its settler colonies) ... social democratic states emerged only in the homogenously Lutheran countries of Scandinavia. (Gorski, 2005, p 163)

Like van Kersbergen and Manow (2010), Gorski (2005) emphasises the links between values and institutional formations in the welfare regimes of Western Europe, making the study of religion ever more pertinent. Based on this, historians of the welfare state are increasingly emphasising that in many respects, the welfare state is not the culmination of activities and aspirations of either labour movements or of social democratic parties (Offer, 2006; van Kersbergen and Manow (2010)). Nor was welfare state development in Europe necessarily delayed by religion. Rather, religious political mobilisation, particularly of the Catholic political parties such as in Italy and Germany, played a fundamental role in pioneering social legislation in the formative periods of the welfare state from the 19th century up until the Second World War. What follows is a brief consideration of the three main pathways that welfare states in Europe have followed based on the classification offered above.

Catholic corporatism: 'subsidiarity' and church–state conflict

The role of Catholicism in the development of the welfare states of the European countries where it has been the dominant religion has been most documented in the literature. It has taken two forms: (1) the role of Catholic social doctrine in informing state and non-state social welfare action, as can be found in Esping-Andersen's welfare regime typologies (1990); and (2) the role of the Catholic Christian Democratic parties which became especially prominent and successful in the inter-war period, exercising at times a much more important influence on welfare spending and the shaping of social security and family policies than their secular Social Democratic counterparts (Wilensky, 1981; Heidenheimer, 1983; van Kersbergen, 1995; Hornsby-Smith, 1999).

Catholicism in Western Europe has been the dominant religion of the Southern European countries (Italy, France, Spain and Portugal) and it also has a significant presence in Germany, the Netherlands, Ireland, Austria and the UK. As the dominant religion of the ruling monarchic dynasties of Europe, Catholicism has tended towards an uneasy relationship with the modern Republican nation-state (Manow, 2004). Thus, it aspires towards 'supra-national' forms of identity in that it defines human allegiance as being to God first and then to nation (Hornsby-Smith, 1999). This is one reason why, according to Hornsby-Smith (1999), the project of European integration has been most deeply supported and promoted by Catholic politicians such as Jacques Delors. The unwillingness of the Catholic Church to be submerged into the emerging secular political institutions of the early modern era, coupled with a view of poverty as a chance for the believer to please God by helping a person in need who was not responsible for their plight, can be seen as the defining features of Catholic social doctrine (Kahl, 2005). This has meant that acts of charitable compassion and voluntary social welfare are the norm in Catholic countries (Kahl, 2005).

Moreover, the family unit has primary responsibility for social welfare, to the extent that the role of the church in conflict over family and education policy was more indicative of welfare state development, according to Manow and van Kersbergen (2009), than the mobilisation of the working class in Catholic countries. The Catholic principle of 'subsidiary' stipulates that the state is only the welfare provider of last resort, since the greater concern is on how best to preserve the social order and moral obligations (as opposed to citizens' rights and duties toward the state) (Manow and van Kersbergen, 2009). This helps to explain why there is a strong corporatist tendency in Catholic-influenced welfare states which fosters collaboration and consensus as opposed to class conflict based on industrial relations (Hornsby-Smith, 1999). In Esping-Andersen's (1990, p 131) terms, Catholic social doctrine is more in favour of subsidising family wellbeing than in guaranteeing employment. In effect, countries such as Italy, Spain, Portugal and also Greece have hardly any coverage for particular client groups such as the young, or particular social risks such as unemployment (Kahl, 2009).

Van Kersbergen and Manow (2010) argue that Christian Democratic parties in, for example, Italy and the Netherlands, were able to mobilise workers on the basis of their Catholic identities, since Catholicism was able to develop a successful critique of capitalism through the notions of the fair wage and the prohibition of usury (van Kersbergen, 1995). Van Kersbergen denotes this as a particular welfare regime strand, which he calls 'social capitalism'. His argument is based on the fact that political parties of Catholic orientation in the inter-war period often had to enter into cross-class coalitions between the Catholic middle classes and the working classes, particularly within the electoral system of proportional representation that dominates continental Europe. Thus, they needed to seek both the support of the Catholic Unions and the working classes if they were to win elections, which obliged them to enter into political compromises that eventually shaped the institutional configurations of the modern-day welfare states (van Kersbergen and Manow (2010). The 'social capitalism' or Christian Democratic regime may be distinguished by several features favouring the following forms of social provision: (1) preponderance of in-cash rather than in-kind services; (2) income replacement and job protection as opposed to employment creation; (3) family wellbeing as opposed to individual wellbeing predicated on the male breadwinner–female carer model; (4) a fragmented, decentralised administrative system; and (5) a tax-benefit system tending towards the preservation of social status (based on income level and social standing), usually of the male breadwinner with female labour participation being restricted by the joint taxation of income.

Hence, Manow and van Kersbergen (2009) argue that the traditional distinction between Catholic and Protestant welfare as one of timing and qualitative variation in provision, which was the main argument of commentators in the 1970s and 1980 such as Flora et al (1981), is insufficient. By looking at the role of social cleavages and political parties, as well as the various political coalitions and compromises which Catholic-leaning parties entered, it is possible to explain the distinguishing features of welfare regimes such as: the women friendliness of the French and Belgian states; the liberal character of the Swiss welfare state; the belated welfare generosity of the Dutch welfare state; and the strong role of the voluntary sector in the US (Manow and van Kersbergen, 2009, p 33). These variations, Manow and van Kersbergen (2009) argue, are missed in Esping-Andersen's (1990) welfare regime types. Indeed, Kahl (2005, 2009) adds to this that poor relief and social assistance programmes are also missing from Esping-Andersen's welfare regime analysis and yet, the subsequent social insurance systems that developed in Europe were built on such social assistance programmes. Thus, the countries that introduced the earliest forms of social insurance in the 19th century were those that already had in place a tax-financed, centralised system of poor relief, meaning that they were Lutheran countries, or orthodox Protestant, as exemplified by the Nordic Scandinavian countries, discussed next.

Lutheranism: social Protestantism in the welfare state

In the critiques of Esping-Andersen's conservative-corporatist regime typology and the lack of attention to religion in Europe, Manow (2004) refers in particular to the near absence of discussion of the Protestant religion and in particular, the anti-state stance of countries with a strong reformed Protestant strand (Calvinist/Puritan), as typified by the US and the UK. Indeed, scholars note the paradoxical situation whereby the impact of Protestantism on the welfare state is that it allowed the church to enter into an alliance with secularisation and modernisation processes, thereby surrendering its role in social welfare to the state. Hence, the paradoxical impact of Protestantism is that it had no impact on the development of the welfare state (Manow, 2004; Manow and van Kersbergen, 2009). As the citation from van Kersbergen (1995) above suggests, the key effect which Protestantism unleashed after the 16th century was to ease the way for rational, autonomous and individual interpretations of social life, eventually forming the building blocks of secularisation.

In contrast to the international and communitarian tendencies of Catholicism, Protestantism has a very clear preference for individualism, and individual responsibility (Hornsby-Smith, 1999). Among Martin Luther's key innovations during the Reformation were to change the medieval views of charity and indulgences as an act that purified sins and brought the donor closer to God, work as an attribute of the poor, and poverty as a blameless condition (Kahl, 2009). Thus, in his writings, Luther elevated the status of work as a daily duty that was pleasing to God which we have come to know in contemporary times as the 'work ethic', and separated it from the status of being poor. Instead, he argued, faith alone (*sola fide*) was the route to God's love;[3] work was a way out of poverty, and all people, both rich and poor, had a share in God's grace, therefore they could not be excused from work. In this sense, poverty became equated with non-work or laziness, and the idea of individual responsibility for one's fortunes was thus slowly introduced (Kahl, 2009, p 271). Luther was author of the first Protestant Poor Law which was eventually introduced into all of the Lutheran countries. These countries were primarily the Nordic Scandinavian countries (Sweden, Norway, Finland and Denmark). This law instituted practices of the poor tax, secular and localised administration of poor relief. From here also developed the notion of deserving and undeserving poor, with the latter being channelled to the workhouses to be punished to earn an honest living and the former benefiting from outdoor relief. At the same time as Luther condemned begging, he called for state and church authorities to provide for the poor – and here the Scandinavian countries have the roots of their universal welfare systems in place – to enact this new Lutheran religious ethic, the church became swiftly incorporated into the emerging nation-state, since the state rulers would set the laws and the parish priests would ensure that they were implemented (Kahl, 2009).

Thus, the distinguishing features of the Scandinavian countries and Germany is the near-homogeneous adherence of their populations to the orthodox strand of Protestantism, as promulgated by Martin Luther, and thus, the near-total absence of a church–state conflict when secular political institutions began to take over social welfare provision and lead the way in social legislation (Kahl, 2005, 2009). This was the model par excellence of a sub-national church religion. Its hallmarks were universalism, but that work was a duty of all able-bodied citizens. Thus, we see the principles of state responsibility for the citizen's welfare in the 19th-century Bismarckian social insurance laws in Germany or the generous state welfare provisions in Denmark that marked the early formative phases of universal welfare state provision up until the Second World War.

Calvinism: welfare liberalism and religious pluralism

Calvin took the teachings of Martin Luther further, and developed new strands of Protestantism that acquired particularly deep roots in England, Scotland, the Netherlands and the US. For Calvin, work was an absolute duty of spiritual significance. Poverty was a sign of damnation, and wealth a sign of God's grace. This sealed the notion of poverty as a source of social stigma and the primacy of the work ethic and personal responsibility – God only helps those who help themselves (Kahl, 2009). Social enterprise and wealth accumulation thus became defining characteristics of Calvinism, hence opening it up to the emerging forms of capitalism (Kahl, 2009).

It was Calvinist reformers in England, inspired by Dutch reformed Protestant communities, who established the first workhouse, Bridewell, in London in 1555 (Kahl, 2009). British and Calvinist/reformed Protestants (Puritan, Dutch reformed, Presbyterian and Anglican) were the main settlers of the New World, and workhouses were also established there. In this sense, the US, the Netherlands and England share similar features in terms of the liberal and residual aspects of social provision. Calvinism was also similar to Catholicism in its anti-statist stance, favouring church-based funding of poor relief – hence we can explain why voluntary and religious social welfare charity is popular today in the US.

For Manow (2004), consideration of the impact of reformed Protestantism in the Western European countries where it has been most dominant can help explain the peculiarities of some of the countries which do not find an easy fit in Esping-Andersen's welfare regime typology, namely, the UK, the Netherlands and Switzerland – in particular due to the dualism of publicly funded minimum social protection programmes and private, group-specific insurance schemes in these countries. Manow (2004) argues that the influence of reformed Protestantism in these countries, which share the same ancestral roots as North America, is the reason why they were 'late' welfare state developers and also institutionally different. The UK, for instance, only introduced the social legislation that had been sweeping Europe since the late 1800s between 1906 and 1911 but very quickly, thereby introducing the four main types of publicly funded social insurance schemes in one raft (Heidenheimer, 1983; Manow, 2004). Thus, Protestantism allied itself with liberal currents, as in Switzerland against centralised state control, but equally, it developed radical forms of liberalism which opposed right-wing politics, so the idea that the state should provide basic human necessities was a fundamentally Protestant religious idea, which a more liberal Protestant country like the UK shares with an orthodox Protestant country like Sweden (Manow, 2004).

The UK has tended to follow a liberal capitalist economic model of welfare, but with a mix of universalism/state provision, such as in the NHS and the national pension insurance system (Hornsby-Smith, 1999; Manow, 2004). The Dutch employment benefit system appears to follow the continental 'welfare without work' regime and yet, this is a country that Esping-Andersen has included in the Social Democratic mould. Like van Kersbergen's (1995) and Manow and van Kersbergen's (2009) arguments for the Catholic countries, Manow (2004) also argues that anomalies in the welfare regime approach may be better explained by looking at the two different types of Protestantism: orthodox and reformed. Thus, Manow (2004) refutes the claim that Protestantism did not influence welfare state development, but rather, that its influence was indirect or 'negative' in the sense that is was strongly anti-statist and promoted self-help, strict state–church separation and the independence of local congregations. So how apt is the term 'faith-based welfare organisations' as a signifier of the non-state religious bodies that do social welfare action work?

'Faith-based' welfare organisations in the Anglo-Saxon countries: a rethinking of definitions and functions?

Today, contemporary British scholarship situates religious welfare in the voluntary sphere and generally does not distinguish between secular and religious organisations. Chapman (2009) focuses on this issue by exploring the ways in which secular and voluntary organisations are similar, arguing that it is the faith dimension itself which is the most distinguishing feature. Chapman (2009) draws attention to the work of US researchers, Sider and Unruh (2004), who discuss the concept of 'faith-based' in detail and provide their own typology of faith-based organisations based on US congregations, as follows:

- *Faith-permeated organisations:* faith is fundamental to all services, staffing and mission.
- *Faith-centred organisations:* faith is evident in all aspects of the services and staffing and mission of the organisation but there is an opt-out from religion for some participants.
- *Faith-affiliated organisations:* mainly the leadership is religious but staff and services are not.
- *Faith-background organisations:* faith is part of the historical inception of the organisation, and while some members of staff may be motivated by their religion, the organisation no longer has any religious aspect.
- *Faith-secular partnerships:* secular organisations that work in partnership with religious organisations relying on their volunteers and resource base.

Also borrowing from the US literature, Bretherton (2010) notes that religious welfare organisations in the UK exhibit a combination of religious and secular characteristics, and we should not assume that 'faith' is their defining feature. Although primarily concerned with the engagement of Christianity with politics in contemporary liberal democratic societies, Bretherton (2010) argues that the term 'faith' is too general and derived from a Protestant Christian understanding of religion. To this end, the term risks homogenising different religious identities and phenomena, and indeed hiding the often mutual coexistence of secular and religious dimensions in any particular religious grouping. Bretherton (2010, p 38) thus employs the term *faith-designated group*, which even eschews the term 'community' as a way of getting round the risks of essentialising and homogenising diverse religious identities, social groupings and practices. Borrowing from the US literature like Chapman, Bretherton (2010, p 39) outlines seven key dimensions for ascertaining the degree of religiosity in an organisation:

- the organisation's self-identity
- the religious convictions of the organisation's members
- how religion affects access to resources
- how far religion shapes the goals, products and services of the organisation
- how far religion influences decision making
- how much authority religious figures have over the organisation
- how far religion determines inter-organisational relations.

Bretherton (2010) also makes the apt observation that the term 'faith' emphasises a private or personal dimension of spiritual experience, leaving the much less used term of religion with connotations of the public sphere and matters relating to social order, rules and codes of behaviour. This dichotomy is misleading and indeed potentially stigmatising, according to Bretherton (2010), and part of the emphasis in this book falls in line with this critique, since its aim is to show that matters of personal belief and lifestyle cannot be separated from social and political action. Similarly, the outcome notions of social welfare, wellbeing or happiness cannot be separated from structural and process issues related to identity.

In the North American context, Farnsley (2007) argues that the term 'faith-based' became commonly used to refer to the broad range of organisations that had some religious feature. The term has also come to refer to religious welfare provision in all other countries and is the main signifier of religious welfare provision in the social science academic literature, but is not without its critics, as highlighted below (see Melville and McDonald, 2006; Bretherton, 2010). In the US context, some commentators such as Tangenberg (2004), have argued that the term *faith-related* may be more appropriate as a general reference to organisations that have a religious character since not all services are based on faith and many have a totally secular character regardless of the orientation of the organisation. This is certainly the case of some of the larger professional agencies, as can also be found in the UK.

The emphasis in British scholarship on the voluntary sector and urban governance has also seen the development of research about the role of religious organisations in community development (Bretherton, 2010; Dinham and Shaw, 2012), drawing particularly from the work of radical political activists of the 1940s–60s such as Saul Alinsky and Paulo Freire. Here, religious organisations are seen as agents of social change and initiators of local democratic politics, ready to get their hands dirty, to live among the most deprived communities and to help them bring about their own social transformation, guided by key principles such as empowerment and participation (Dinham and Shaw, 2012). Lowndes and Chapman (2007) and Weller (2009) also examine the engagement of faith groups in local governance and via multi-faith forums and how they offer opportunities and challenges for civil renewal. These governance issues are discussed in more detail in the next chapter, but what is useful here is to briefly review the academic research on faith-based organisations in the US context in order to assess comparisons and likely lessons for the UK.

The deeply religious character and widespread provision of religiously based social services in North America are well discussed in the academic literature (Heidenheimer, 1983; Skocpol, 2000; Wineburg, 2001; Farnsley, 2007; Quadango and Rohlinger, 2009; Lindsay and Wuthnow, 2010; Taniguchi and Thomas, 2011). For Skocpol (2000), the key historical contribution of the religious and secular voluntary associations in North America was that they acted as a link between central and local government since they stressed the ethos of mutual aid. Mutuality is considered to strengthen social solidarity since it takes a view of human need as being intrinsically connected to community interests (Hewitt, 2000).

Today, the US has around 340,000 congregations, outnumbering all other types of community organisations, and in 2006, 36 per cent of all charitable donations went to religious organisations, with new research on changing tax policy legislation leading to an enhanced role for private foundations in fostering and channelling religiously based donations (Lindsay and Wuthnow, 2010, pp 108-9). Factors such as regular church attendance, private prayer and other religious activities are all strongly linked with volunteering (in both secular and religious organisations) in the US. Liberal Protestant denominations in particular have a strong ethos of participation in the local community and civic engagement, in contrast to their Catholic and evangelical cousins who tend to be more inward looking and isolationist (Taniguchi and Thomas, 2011).

Church-based welfare agencies have been at the forefront of administrative developments in social welfare provision in the US and have enjoyed a long tradition of receiving state funding for this work. Religiously inspired social action has thus had a strong national thrust, seeking to promote participatory citizenship as much as to alleviate individual suffering and deprivation (Skocpol, 2000). For instance, public schools were established by travelling reformers who were often members of regional or national associations and closely connected to leading local citizens, churches and voluntary groups (Skocpol, 2000, p 28). This type of 'translocal' activism was epitomised by the 'federation' which themselves had local, state and national tiers. This allowed a harmonisation between forms of representative government and biblical moral values. Crucially, it was the involvement of non-clerical individuals and ordinary Americans that helped to keep the balance between religious morality and civic association. This helped to foster a national egalitarian culture of cross-class solidarity and inclusion which has come under increasing pressure due to the more short-term character of modern-day volunteering and the growing social divisions in US society.

The contemporary partnership between government, private and charitable organisations in the provision of social services in the US is discussed in more detail by Farnsley (2007) than can be allowed for here. In brief, this is 'web-shaped', with overlapping provision by federal, state, local as well as secular and religious organisations. Added to this are the political tensions surrounding proper implementation of the US Constitution's First Amendment relating to religious disestablishment: 'Congress shall make no law respecting an establishment of religion, or prohibiting the free exercise thereof'. What is changing in the US, according to Farnsley (2007), are the incremental government initiatives since the 1980s (under Ronald Reagan) to strengthen the working links between government and faith groups and to allow the latter the right to keep their religious identity while benefiting from public funds to deliver social welfare services. Such moves were given a further push by the Clinton administration with the introduction of the 'charitable choice' initiative in 1996 as part of wider legislation known as the Personal Responsibility and Work Opportunities Reconciliation Act (PRWORA). In 2001, the Bush administration gave further impetus to the positive promotion of faith groups in social welfare provision with the creation of the White House Office of Faith-based and Community Initiatives.

Farnsley (2007) notes that religious organisations receiving government funds and subject to strict rules on secular service provision are only a fraction of the larger landscape of religious welfare provision in the US which is independent of government grants and able to fund welfare services that are sectarian or evangelical in character from its own private funds.

But in the new climate of the 'faith-based initiative' legislation, the government is now much more worried about discrimination against faith-based organisations, and consciously seeks to add clauses which stipulate that religious groups are offered opportunities to provide welfare services. This resonates more loudly with the current UK and especially English context since the 1990s. In the US, state funding now considers that welfare services which have a distinctly religious character can and should be legitimate recipients of public funds since they are 'effective and legally secure' (Farnsley, 2007, p 347). In the US context, local congregations have become the new focus of devolution and are lauded as having three key advantages over state-provided welfare: they know the needs of the local environment better than the state bureaucracy; being small, they are more flexible and responsive to these needs; and they transfer not just services but positive social values to rehabilitate the character of the poor (Farnsley, 2007). So here, not only do we have further confirmation of the arguments put forth in this book about the nature of religious welfare being more focused on social relationships and moral principles but also, the emphasis on social values is reminiscent of secular arguments around the need to find a moral purpose for social policy, as voiced by Jordan (2008) and others.

Academic research in the US has offered a mixed verdict on the success of religious groups in offering social services and their partnership with federal government. Campbell (2009) draws attention to the large discrepancies between rhetoric and reality and the lack of sufficient reliable data on the true impact on client groups of faith-based services. Leading commentators such as Wineburg (2001) and Wuthnow (2004) note that faith-based groups can often be limited in their resources and in their willingness to work with government, much like in the British case. Cnaan (2004), on the other hand, gives a largely positive account of congregations, arguing that their work should be further supported. But again, the issue of resources remains.

Other challenges remain in terms of general organisation and programme effectiveness and the effects of public state funding on the identity of religious groups (Fitzgerald, 2009). There are parallel streams in the US academic research on the extent to which faith groups can act as radical community-based organisations that can empower and transform their communities or are trapped in short-term, isolated project work that hinder more enduring community partnership work (Campbell, 2009; Fitzgerald, 2009). For Wineburg (2001, pp 140-6), in spite of these constraints, faith-based charities have seven 'assets': a mission to serve; a large volunteer base; use of sacred space for social welfare provision; ability to apply for grants; political strength; moral authority; and they are able to be creative and to experiment. But much like the current UK climate, Wineburg (2001) and Wuthnow (2004) warn against high expectations of what faith-based organisations can actually deliver. In the final analysis, experiences vary (Wuthnow, 2004) as in the case of Campbell's (2009) case study of the Community and Faith-based Initiative in the state of California, where large amounts of resources were invested and continued efforts made to build the capacities of faith-based organisations, but with little impact due to the top-down approach of the partnership's effort. For Campbell (2009), the key lesson is the need for government policy to seriously develop local community networks, instead of satisfying short-term political objectives. The intensifying debate of faith-based welfare provision in the US is located squarely within the broader debate about the growing political presence of conservative Christian evangelicals, and the continuing renegotiation of boundaries in the state–church relations of the US.

To a certain degree, the situation in the US is also mirrored in Australia and New Zealand with religious welfare organisations, particularly of the various Christian Protestant denominations, increasingly gaining the attention of policy makers and academic research. For Conradson (2008), the progressive drift in government policy toward neoliberalism since the 1990s in New Zealand has presented a challenge for faith-based organisations in balancing their aim of providing relief assistance and lobbying government on issues of social justice. Conradson (2008) sees a steady move since the 1990s among faith-based organisations in New Zealand, from charity and social service to social development as a result. In this, he focuses his assessment of the achievements of the major faith groups in terms of having a moral vision that seeks social/structural transformation such as lobbying for the rights of deprived communities, or merely acting as professional service providers, particularly in the context of government contracts. These arguments about the need for the church to bring about social transformation through its moral vision are also made in the British context by Pacione (1990). Like Bretherton (2010) in the British context, Australian authors, Melville and McDonald (2006), note that the religious welfare sector has been the dominant type of voluntary sector organisation in Australia and highly mainstream, to the extent that there is a need to rethink the term faith-based and to assess the impact of these organisations on wider society.

Micro-normative perspectives

The discussion now comes to the way in which commentators have conceptualised the relationship between religion and social policy from what has been called at the beginning of this chapter micro-normative perspectives. By this we mean how religious values have shaped modern definitions of social policy. This dimension of the literature is much less well-developed since social policy has tended to steer clear from normative and cultural considerations, remaining faithful to perennial utilitarian precepts. As Fitzpatrick (2008) bemoans, social policy is a deeply applied field that scholars and practitioners are more likely to argue against the need to philosophise about social problems when we know that they exist and need to get on with the job of solving them. But the main task of this book is to emphasise the importance of these normative considerations by examining the substantive contribution of religion to the meaning and experience of wellbeing.

There has been some debate in the literature outside of the social policy disciplinary boundaries on the substantive contribution of religion to human society. I deliberately use this larger concept of human society since much of the British scholarly debate has been led by scholars outside of social policy whose analytical terms of reference are not rooted in the conceptual constellation attached to the welfare state. The debate has been led mostly by scholars in the sociology of religion, where there has been an increasing interest in spirituality (such as Heelas and Woodhead, 2004; Spalek and Imtoual, 2008; Holloway and Moss, 2010); in practical theology, where there has been an attempt to chart the broader engagement of religioun and religious groups within British society (such as Baker, 2009; Dinham et al, 2009; Atherton, 2011); moral philosophy (such as Bayley, 1989; Kenny and Kenny, 2006), where the focus is on concepts such as happiness, morality or social justice; in governance and public policy (such as Harris et al, 2003; Powell, 2007b; Chapman, 2009), which focus on the mechanics and dynamics of local government partnerships with faith groups; community development (such as Farnell et al, 2003; Dinham and Shaw, 2012), where the interest is in urban regeneration and social cohesion; and most recently, in social work (such as Ashencaen Crabtree et al, 2008; Furness and Gilligan, 2010), where the concern is to take an holistic approach to human needs or respond to ethnically determined social needs. Thus, the analytical frameworks from which these authors draw vary from post-secularity to local governance frameworks and local strategic partnerships, to holistic approaches, to dealing with social needs in minority ethnic communities.

This is a fast-changing landscape, however, and the social work publications mentioned above herald that religion has started knocking on the doors of social policy. New publications continue to emerge, for example, the European-based comparative project on church welfare by Bäckström et al (2010, 2011) and the new research publications coming out of the Arts and Humanities Research Council (AHRC)/ Economic and Social Research Council (ESRC) Religion and Society programme. It might seem that this section, and this book, are exaggerating the contribution of religion to the experience and definition of wellbeing. Other forces may be playing an equally if not more important role, such as climate change or the international financial crisis. The issue is not to credit religion with more than its fair share, so the task at hand is to ascertain as accurately as possible what this fair share is – and to give religious organisations credit according to the size of that share.

How, then, has British scholarship conceptualised the substantive contribution of religion to human wellbeing and flourishing broadly defined? It is possible to categorise this answer in terms of the following themes that emerge from the literature, which in turn can be grouped into themes measuring social welfare outcomes and themes that motivate or structure social welfare provision. Hence (1) happiness, (2) spirituality and holism, (3) cultural identity and (4) social capital are areas of research where a religious perspective has been applied with the aim of advancing, modifying or adding meaning to the contemporary understanding of human flourishing.

Happiness has long been a theoretical correlate of social welfare (Fitzpatrick, 2001) and a central plank of philosophy (Kenny and Kenny, 2006). In more recent years, it has regained the focus of social science researchers, particularly in the field of economics, most notably in the work of the utilitarian economist Richard Layard (2005), through greater interchange with the discipline of psychology. Kenny and Kenny (2006) suggest that happiness is one of the pillars that constitute human well-being: contentment (which is an attitude or mental state of happiness akin to the utilitarian notion of happiness), dignity (which is a form of psychological welfare related to one's freedom and sense of self-worth in relation to others) and welfare (which is about the satisfaction of our material 'animal' needs, that is, food, clothing and shelter). Kenny and Kenny (2006) argue that these components of wellbeing may not all be present or achievable simultaneously, and indeed that trade-offs in any one of them may occur when the other components are pursued. But they see these as fundamental human rights enshrined in the US Declaration of Independence: life, liberty and the pursuit of happiness (Kenny and Kenny, 2006, p 43). Crucially, by separating wellbeing into these three components, and conducting an extensive review of research on subjective wellbeing and the weak connections between income and welfare, Kenny and Kenny's (2006) policy recommendations come out in support of minimal public interventions that can have an impact on welfare and dignity but not contentment – which, they argue, is determined more by issues of individual character and actions.

Thus, they accord to morality a higher value than happiness, arguing that individual happiness can be found through and is often tied to the happiness of others. Altruism for them is inherent in the biblical injunction and golden rule, shared by all religions, which is to 'love one's neighbour as one would love one's self'. Significantly, the parable of the Good Samaritan reinforces the importance of helping others on the basis of their need (the Samaritan stopped to help a stranger on the road), as opposed to their ethnic origin (a family member or compatriot, for instance) (Kenny and Kenny, 2006, p 185). Altruism is a trait of individual personality, and not necessarily cultivated through the state apparatus.

What authors reviewing the meaning of happiness draw attention to is that there are other values over and beyond the pursuit of pleasure and personal satisfaction. In particular, the emphasis on morality and duty as the basis for protecting social justice and our social obligations towards others advances a notion of wellbeing which is much more deeply related to the human character, human nature and human identity. This expanded view of what constitutes the human character can also be found in the literature on spirituality and holism, which is another way in which researchers are commenting on the way in which religion shapes social welfare.

The burgeoning literature on spirituality and holism has engendered a rethinking of the role of religion in contemporary understandings of wellbeing. Empirical research on spirituality in the UK has been reported in the terms of a revolutionary paradigm, with key works by Heelas and Woodhead (2004), Spalek and Imtoual (2008), Holloway and Moss (2010) and Furness and Gilligan (2010), to name some of the most notable. These researchers highlight more subjective and relational understandings of wellbeing which take into account the individual's moral values, their ethnic identity and concerns, and how their relationship with God or another transcendental force shape their attitudes, self-perceptions and coping strategies. Whether these individuals are New Age therapists, unemployed young people or older people of a minority ethnic background, a new wave of research in the sociology of religion and in social work in the UK is now beginning to take serious account of spiritual values and needs. For some this is part of a broader engagement with the notions of quality of life (see, for instance, Holloway and Moss, 2010); for others, it is a more effective way of meeting the cultural needs of an increasingly demographically diverse British population. These researchers echo the recurring results of public surveys where people report that their religion is very significant to them in their daily lives (Furness and Gilligan, 2010).

Two interrelated issues which are the inverse of each other become apparent here: (1) social problems cannot be treated in an isolated manner but require contextualisation in the identity of the individual; and (2) the individual's identity is formed not in isolation but in relation to other members of society who may be within their close vicinity of family and friends, or in relation to a transcendental force or ultimate meaning which guides their life. Taking into account the spiritual dimension of wellbeing emphasises the role of emotions and social relations and responds to the growing discontent with the impact of individualism on contemporary society (Hay, 2006; Kenny and Kenny, 2006). Particularly in the fields of mental health and palliative care, and in relation to older people, the search for meaning in one's life becomes ever more pertinent (Holloway and Moss, 2010). Spirituality is understood not only in terms of belief in a superior 'Being' or God – research by Lynch (2008) and Heelas and Woodhead (2004) shows that the search for meaning also engages atheists or people who do not follow the conventional Abrahamic and Dharmic faiths. This search for meaning is appreciated by the social work profession in particular, and highlights the need to rethink the basic constitution of the human condition – the basis of which is a sense of personal dignity which is rooted in religious thinking, as highlighted in Kenny and Kenny's discussion of happiness above (2006).

The importance of dignity in social welfare provision has not gone amiss. Kwan Chan and Bowpitt's (2005) study highlights the centrality of this concept to the effectiveness of services provided both in the UK and in China. These concerns raise the broader issue about the impact of the impersonal and bureaucratic welfare state, far removed from the daily lives of benefit recipients, and indeed potentially an important reason why the latter are being urged to demonstrate a sense of personal responsibility for ties of social solidarity and social cohesion are increasingly loosening. Again, this brings us back to definitions of the human condition and human identity, and the increasingly important role that culture is playing, both in social science research and in the study of the welfare state.

A small number of contemporary scholars have studied both directly and indirectly the implications of religion for social policy from the point of view of culture – indeed, cultural analyses of social policy and the welfare state have been few and far between in the British context (Clarke and Fink, 2008). The eminent sociologist of religion, Jim Beckford, in his contribution with Demerath (see Beckford and Demerath, 2007), has long argued that religion is a 'cultural resource' in Britain; churches, choir singing, religious rites such as marriages, births and funerals are symbols that uphold national identity in Britain, for example. Moreover, there has been much debate and research in the UK since the 1980s about the growing multicultural profile of Britain and the challenge for social policy to respond to diverse minority ethnic needs. The urban riots of Brixton and Bradford brought home fears about cultural segregation in Britain, which has become particularly centred around the cultural integration of British Muslims (Modood, 2009). This is intricately related to the broader policy concerns with social cohesion, to be discussed later.

Cultural considerations in social policy reflect two important and interrelated lines of analysis: on the one hand is the relative importance of *recognition* (respecting difference based on cultural identity, values and needs, such as the feminist or gay movements) as the key principle of social justice, which is a matter of identity politics over the importance of *redistribution* (fair access to natural resources and low levels of wealth inequality), which is a matter of class conflict (Fraser, 1997). Concern with redistribution is the perennial fault line in production-based industrialising societies, while concern with recognition is seen to be more a phenomenon of post-industrial consumer societies that have become increasingly multicultural. Related to this is the argument which posits that moral values and emotional/social relations matter for the experience of social welfare, as opposed to the focus on how much government spends on welfare benefits or how much income citizens earn (Pfau-Effinger, 2009). This, in turn, relates to the second line of analysis as propagated by Clarke and Fink (2008), which is that social welfare is a 'political–cultural project' intrinsically intertwined with the structuring of national identity, political power and social control. These arguments serve to reinforce the importance of religion in cultural debates about social policy: it is a system of moral values, symbols and meanings; it is a source of personal and national identity; it is a driver of ideological values underpinning the provision of social welfare.

Writing in the continental European context, Opielka (2008, p 103) offers a functional typology of religion in relation to social policy which encompasses all the major religious and political ideologies present in the Western world. Thus, he categorises Marxism and Nietzschean philosophy as forms of scientific or subjective religion based on science as the source of knowledge and meaning and advocating strong and weak welfare states respectively. The spiritual religions, in Opielka's (2008) functional typology, are the main world religions (Daoism, Islam, Judaism, Christianity, Buddhism and Hinduism), none of which has actively inspired the development of the welfare state except for Christianity, which, Opielka (2008) argues, has been the most successful in this regard. Islam and Judaism come second in promoting self-help and paternalism, with the other religions stopping at the doors of spiritual worship. Jawad (2009), on the other hand, has provided a broader analysis of non-Christian faiths which shows their very direct links to social welfare provision, whether in private or public form.

Closely linked to the debate around culture is the extent to which religion can be a source of social division or cohesion, and scholars have linked this to social policy. Primarily, it is the issue of social capital and the ability of religious groups to work at community level and to respond to/solve local problems more effectively than government which has gained the attention of government policy and scholars alike. Since the seminal publication of *Bowling alone* by Robert Putnam (2000), the concept of social capital as the relations and networks of trust between groups of people which help them enjoy better life outcomes has gripped the imagination of politicians and academics alike. In Britain, concern with such issues became especially prominent under Tony Blair's leadership and have received a new lease of life under the Big Society concept and the invocations of volunteering and localism as better forms of social welfare provision than state bureaucracy. Research on religion as a source of social capital has been quite prominent in the work of urban geographers and sociologists with an eye on religion such as Furbey et al (2006) and Baker (2009), who explore the contribution of religious groups to their wider communities on the basis of Putnam's bonding, bridging and linking typology of social capital. Powell (2007b), on the other hand, takes a much more sceptical view of Britain's faith-friendly politics, and sees religious social welfare as a divisive threat to the humanist ideals of social citizenship.

In view of what has been discussed in this chapter, our view of the modern secular state is undeniably altered. In a sense, the welfare state symbolises the 20th century's utopian dream of the modernist, secularist political project. Norris and Inglehart (2004) note that for a time, this was able to replace a social purpose in the advanced capitalist democracies based on religious values, but it appears that, in the 21st century, the pendulum is beginning to swing the other way as we enter what some are terming a post-secular society (Bäckström et al, 2011; Beaumont and Baker, 2011). Thus, we end this chapter with Bäckström et al's (2010, 2011) seminal two-volume research on the contemporary face of majority church (that is, the national churches such as the Church of England or Church of Sweden) welfare in Europe. These authors assess the renewed vigour of church welfare provision in Europe which they situate within the broader sociopolitical cleavages underpinning European secularisation.

To this end, Pettersson (2010) notes that the social phenomenon under study is better denoted as 'religious change', rather than secularisation, since there are competing trends in Europe: church membership is declining but the churches have become more active in the social welfare sphere. In this new landscape, the main European church bodies preserve their positions as the main religious social welfare institutions; typically, prison chaplains in the UK have a responsibility to ensure that prisoners of all faiths can access chaplains from their faith (Beckford, 2001). For Pettersson (2010), these church groups symbolise the new wave of voluntary social action of our times and are thus central players in the emerging 'social economy'. In this new 'social economy', European societies have the modern facility of choice to exercise a faith and to belong to a church group (Pettersson, 2010). At the same time, social welfare activists of a religious leaning are concerned to enact their religious obligation towards their fellow humans in need (van Kersbergen and Manow, 2010).

Bäckström et al (2011) thus highlight the inherent tension in religious involvement in social welfare in the European context, echoing the macro-institutional and micro-normative lines of analysis pursued in this chapter: religious groups have been a useful and perhaps inevitable institutional resource for the welfare state in Britain but they are more problematic as sources of moral values in society. It is indeed a fine line that religious organisations walk between being neutral channels of social welfare services and morally driven people seeking to enact their faith.

Conclusion

This chapter has offered a thorough review of the theoretical perspectives informing the study of the role of religion in social policy, based on two broad lines of argument:

- The micro-institutional processes whereby key church teachings both within the Catholic and Protestant faiths, as well as the role of political cleavages particularly around the inter-war period, are noted as having played a key role in either expanding public spending or integrating the social work function of the church into the emerging secular state. These two roles of the state have been in part determined by the dominant national religion, with Catholicism and reformed Protestantism/Calvinism being the most anti-state, as can be found in the proliferation of voluntary groups or the Catholic Church in the Southern European countries, the US, the UK and the Netherlands; and orthodox Protestantism/ Lutheranism favouring universal state provision, as can be found in the Scandinavian countries. This chapter has then reviewed the term 'faith-based organisations', arguing that it fails to capture the diversity of ways in which organised religious activity takes place and that the term 'faith' itself has an Anglo-Saxon Protestant bias.
- The micro-normative perspective, which has looked at how religious welfare and social action has been conceptualised in contemporary British scholarship. A variety of concepts have been explored from the way in which religion is seen as a source of social capital, to how it reinforces the relevance and importance of spirituality to human wellbeing, to how it makes us think differently about the deeper societal assumptions we carry within us about being modern and secular.

What emerges from these perspectives is that modern, secular social policy is as concerned with the human condition as religious welfare, in spite of the dominance of utilitarian thinking of social policy and the focus of the latter on problem solving as opposed to philosophising about social problems. However, concepts such as social value, compassion, service and ethics, which appear to elude secular forms of state social welfare, find expression in religious welfare. Hence what has been emphasised in this chapter is the role of social relationships, human agency and moral values in giving meaning to welfare and wellbeing. This chapter makes clear therefore that the concept of *ways of being* is one way of moving our thinking forward and laying the emphasis more clearly on the quality of social relationships and the ethical dimensions of our society.

Questions for discussion

1. How have Catholicism and Protestantism shaped welfare states in North America and Europe?
2. How does the historical–institutional literature help shape the debate on the role of religion in social policy?
3. What are the relative advantages of focusing on human needs and human identity in solving social problems?
4. What have been some of the key entry points for the study of religion in social policy, sociology and social work?
5. Why is it useful to consider the moral dimensions of social welfare?

Notes

[1] Jordan's (2008) argument, which is also corroborated by other authors writing on the religious welfare sector.

[2] John Stuart Mill later added to the theory by differentiating between moral and material pleasures (most notably liberty), the former being superior and more worthwhile, but he retained the same basic parameters in his definition of utilitarianism as Bentham.

[3] It is not a coincidence that today we speak of faith-based welfare, the term having particular Protestant European/North American origin.

THREE

The contemporary British context: social and policy profiles in relation to religion

Summary

- Britain has become a post-Christian and a post-secular society where interest in spirituality is gaining ground, and minority religious communities are finding a new public voice. Nevertheless, Christianity remains a cornerstone of national identity and the Church of England has a special role in terms of access to Parliament and policy debate.

- Very little data and research exist in the UK on how social and economic disparities map out onto religious identity (as opposed to ethnic identity). The 2001 Census provides the most reliable data that affirms that the highest levels of social and economic deprivation in the UK exist among the Muslim population.

- Since the early 1990s, government policy has articulated a discernible interest in engaging with religious groups as well as opening up opportunities for them to provide welfare services and be involved in local governance. But this positive interest has not necessarily been matched by the level of understanding at policy level of the positive contributions, challenges and drawbacks of engaging religious communities in social policy in the UK.

- The Coalition government has not been as active in the generation of policy statements and guidelines on engaging religious communities as the previous New Labour government; indeed public spending cuts have led to the dismantling of some local government units specialising in religious communities as well as the government funds that some religious charities have received. However, the push towards philanthropy, volunteerism and local community-based provision of social welfare may work in favour of religious communities, with key members of the Coalition political establishment themselves being people of faith.

Introduction

What role does religion play in social life in Britain today? Is there a religious profile of social inequality and deprivation? What do we know about the 30,000[1] or so religious welfare charities that are currently operating? What is the contemporary policy context in Britain with regard to the role of religion in social policy?

These are four guiding questions for this chapter, which sets out the contemporary situation of social problems and social policy in relation to the religious welfare sector. Government policy since 1997 (under Tony Blair's leadership) has been etching out an agenda to engage religious groups in social welfare provision and social policy making. However, there is little empirical information on the structure of the religious welfare sector and on the way in which religion intersects with social problems. This chapter uses what information we do have, for example, grey literature from the Charity Commission or from various regional development agency publications. It also uses available socioeconomic indicators from the 2001 Census data on the religious profile of social deprivation in Britain that shows the Muslim population to be the worst off in terms of educational achievement, self-reported health status and labour market participation. These issues are in addition to broader policy concerns about national security and social cohesion, making the Muslim population a matter of concern not just in terms of poverty, but also in terms of political and cultural integration.

The chapter is made up of four sections: the first gives an overview of the status of religious affiliation in Britain today which testifies to the original thesis of this book about the pervasive and distinctive nature of religion in contemporary life; the second looks at the available 2001 Census data on how religious affiliation intersects with poverty and social deprivation; the third considers what available information we have on the profile of the religious welfare sector, giving general information about the structure of the sector and its financial worth, as cited in the Charity Commission and the National Council for Voluntary Sector Organisations (NCVO, 2007); finally, the fourth section looks at the current policy context – what is the government's current policy stance on the role of religion and religious groups in social policy, and how is the collaboration between religious groups and government (both at national and local levels) taking shape?

Religious profile of contemporary Britain

The most accurate view of contemporary religiosity in the UK is one of potential ambiguity and contradiction, as also reflected in its type of welfare regime discussed previously. Certainly, religion has a diffuse nature in the British context that is partly the result of the universalist approach of the Church of England and semi-established character (Heidenheimer, 1983). According to Weller (2009), British society is now made up of three pillars: Christian, secular and religiously plural.

The issue of ambiguity is also reflected by discrepancies in the various methodological approaches used to define and research religiosity in national surveys and what statistical sources researchers rely on. Typically, researchers juxtapose data on religiosity from the 2001 UK Census by the Office for National Statistics (ONS) with that of the British Social Attitudes survey which collected data on religion in 2008, and also with the European Values Survey (Beckford et al, 2006; McAndrew, 2010; Voas and Ling, 2010). Hence, the 2001 Census estimates that almost 71.8 per cent of the population in the UK identified themselves as Christian (split between 72 per cent in England and Wales and 65 per cent in Scotland), with 15.1 per cent as having 'no religion', whereas in the British Social Attitudes data, the figure was 50 per cent for Christians and 43 per cent for 'no religion' (Voas, 2010, p 67). Differences also occurred with respect to the non-Christian populations of the UK that were estimated at 10 per cent in the 2001 Census and 7 per cent in the British Social Attitudes survey.

Table 3.1 below gives the breakdown of the entire UK population by religion, according to the 2001 Census.[2] Muslims formed the second largest faith group, at 2.8 per cent of the total population, followed by Hindus (1 per cent) and Sikhs (0.6 per cent). The group 'Any other religion' includes smaller faiths such as Spiritualists, Jain, Baha'i, Zoroastrian, Rastafarian and Wicca. It is important to note that the religion question was the only voluntary question in the 2001 Census yet only 7.8 per cent of respondents chose not to answer it (ONS, 2004).

Table 3.1: British population by religion (2001)

	Total population		Non-Christian religious population
	Numbers	%	%
Christian	41,014,811	71.8	
Muslim	1,588,890	2.8	51.9
Hindu	558,342	1.0	18.3
Sikh	336,179	0.6	11/0
Jewish	267,373	0.5	8.7
Buddhist	149,157	0.3	4.9
Any other religion	159,167	0.3	5.2
All non-Christian religious population	3,059.108	5.4	100.0
No religion	8,596,488	15.1	
Religion not stated	4,433,520	7.8	
All population	57,103,927	100.0	

Source: 2001 Census, Office for National Statistics, www.statistics.gov.uk/cci/nuggett. asp?id=979, accessed 10 May 2001

In terms of geographical distribution, most people from non–Christian religious backgrounds live in England (as opposed to Scotland or Wales). In 2001 they constituted 6 per cent of the English population, compared to 2 per cent in Wales and 1 per cent in Scotland. Figure 3.1 below shows that around half of the minority religious groups in England were also mostly concentrated in London, with Jews and Hindus being the largest and Muslims, Buddhists and Sikhs having a greater presence in the East and West Midlands, Yorkshire and Humber and the North West. London had the least number of Christians (around 58 per cent), whereas between 78 and 80 per cent of the North East and North West described themselves as 'Christian' (ONS, 2004).

Comparing England to the other nations of the UK, Pacione (2005, pp 238-9) presents disaggregated data for Scotland from the 2001 Census. He notes that 94.5 per cent of the Scottish population responded to the question on religious affiliation. Sixty-seven per cent stated they had a religion while 28 per cent said they did not. In terms of religious affiliation in Scotland, 42.4 per cent were Church of Scotland, 15.9 per cent were Catholic and 6.8 per cent were from other Christian denominations. A total of 1.9 per cent of the Scottish population belonged to another main non-Christian religion. But it is Northern Ireland that has the largest religious population, at 86 per cent (Purdam et al, 2007). What is also noteworthy is that across the UK, significant pockets of poverty and social deprivation exist among the Catholic working class of Irish descent (Pacione, 2005).

Figure 3.1: Percentage of each religious group living in London (2001)

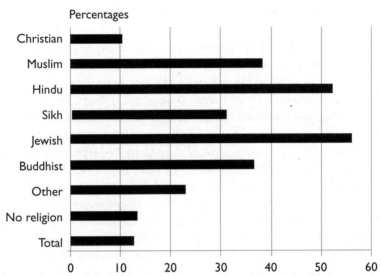

Percentages

Source: 2001 Census, Office for National Statistics, www.statistics.gov.uk/cci/nuggett. asp?id=979, accessed 10 May 2001

Nevertheless, as Purdam et al (2007) argue, the religion question is asked in different forms for these countries so comparisons need to be made with caution. Much of the conflict around how to measure the exact number of religious people in the UK inevitably centres round the phrasing of the religion question itself in the national census ('What is your religion?'), which critics say is misleading and traps respondents into choosing a religion, when in reality, they may not practise that faith (see Aspinall, 2000, for a fuller discussion). This was the argument made by the British Humanist Association around the time of the 2011 Census. In the British Social Attitudes survey, the question is phrased as 'Do you regard yourself as belonging to any particular religion?' Wolffe (2007) aptly surmises this issue of conflicting interpretations of religiosity in the UK that has existed since the Second World War along the following lines:

> ... almost any other activity that attracted the committed involvement of up to a tenth of the population, the passive sympathy of two-thirds or four-fifths of a sample, and was totally rejected by only one-twentieth of respondents, would be regarded as a successful and influential historical force. Thus we confront immediately the place of religion in the life of the people of Britain during the decades after 1939:

should we dwell on how far the tide of faith had gone out, or concentrate our attention rather on how much water remained in the sea? (Wolffe, 2007, p 323)

Two leading British sociologists of religion represent these two opposing camps of sociological observation on religiosity in the UK. The secularist view of the definite and ultimate decline of religion in the UK is presented by its ardent spokesperson, Steve Bruce (2003). Examining 'the facts' behind his thesis of the 'demise of Christianity in Britain', Bruce (2003, pp 54-7) argues the following: church attendance has seen a consistent decline, from 40-60 per cent in 1851, to 12 per cent in 1978 to under 8 per cent since 1999. Indeed, there is a pattern of generational decline of religious observance in the UK (McAndrew, 2010; Voas and Ling, 2010), with committed churchgoers being increasingly elderly and accounting for around 40 per cent of total churchgoers. According to Bruce (2003), the aggregate figure for church attendance would be even lower were people not living longer in the UK. With regards to church membership, Bruce argues that even to speak of such a term is indicative of the increasing precariousness of religiosity in the UK since in medieval times members of the population were automatically subjected to the will of God and it was not possible to even think of opting out of church membership. Bruce discussed similar patterns of decline in relation to clergy numbers, Sunday schools and religious significance in key aspects of the life course such as birth and marriage. In political life, Bruce significantly downplays the importance of religion in relation to voting patterns, immigration and the European Union (EU).

Most importantly, Bruce (2003) argues that religious beliefs and faith have also followed the institutional patterns cited above, with around 26 per cent of the population believing in a personal god or that Jesus was the son of God. This contrasts with 48 per cent, the figure cited in the British Social Attitudes survey's 26th report in 2008 (McAndrew, 2010). But the crux of Bruce's (2003) reasoning for the disappearance of Christianity as an important force in British sociopolitical life is, ironically, the same reason why it has been argued by other authors, such as Wolffe (2007), that religiosity in Britain is best characterised by its ambiguity and contradiction. For Bruce, British culture is distinguished by its 'indifference' to religion as opposed to the more active kind of anti-clericalism that can be found in the Catholic European mainland, for, although they may not profess to committed adherence to the church, British people (barring, perhaps, vociferous intellectuals such as Richard Dawkins and Christopher Hitchens) have not sought to dismantle the Church of England, they continue to offer religious services in their state education system and their church leaders continue to express public opinion on issues of national concern.

In a seminal work on the role of religion in Britain since the post-war period, Grace Davie (1994) coined the term 'believing without belonging' in order to depict the decline of formal institutional religion and church attendance in the UK and the subsistence of personal interpretations of faith and new forms of religious self-identification. Davie (1999) presents an altogether different take on the religious identity of both Britain and Europe when she refers to the 'vicarious' religiosity of Europe:

> ... enough of the religiously inactive of Europe have retained a nominal attachment to the churches that the churches' representative role is still possible. Indeed, in many respects that role is encouraged whether in terms of worship, the life-cycle, ethical issues or political debate.... Might it not be the case that Europeans are not so much *less* religious than citizens of other parts of the world as *differently* religious? If so, the implications for public policy may well be considerable. (Davie, 1999, p 65)

In this sense, the argument goes that while traditional religious practice in Europe has dwindled steadily since the 1960s, vast majorities of Western European populations still ascribe a Christian identity to themselves, no matter how tokenistic. Casanova (2008) explains this as being primarily due to the internalisation of secularism as a knowledge system in Europe, and not due to the processes of urbanisation, education and rationalisation that are normally associated with modernisation. Casanova (2008, pp 144-5) describes the Christian character of Europe as 'unspoken' and 'rarely verbalised' – a conundrum of European identity which makes the Christian identity of Europe at once implicit and explicit, pervasive and distinctive, to use the analytical language proposed in this book. It is this implicitness that makes the integration of Turkey problematic for Europe – which, after all, claims to be secular, liberal and multicultural.

In the British context, what we find are diverse levels in both degree of religiosity and type of religion. The British Social Attitudes survey aptly accounts for the ambiguity of the British case by using three types of religious groups: religious, fuzzy religious and unreligious, the largest being the second group which accounts for 36 per cent of the 2008 survey. The religious profile of the population is thus characterised by people who do not identify themselves with a religion even though they were brought up in one. This is especially the case among the Church of England group. Seventy-five per cent of the 2008 survey also expressed the view that religious leaders should not influence voting behaviour, and 67 per cent answered that they should also not have a say in government policy (Voas and Ling, 2010, p 74). But there is also contradictory evidence in this regard. It has been a long-held view that religious influence on voting behaviour no longer matters in Britain ever since the demise of the Liberal Party in the inter-war period, except perhaps in Northern Ireland (McAndrew, 2010).[3] Class and socioeconomic background were thought to matter more for voting preferences. Yet, McAndrew (2010) draws attention to research on the 1992 General Election showing a higher proportion of Labour voters among middle-class Catholics, high proportions of the secular middle class voting Conservative and more middle-class non-Anglican Protestants and Methodists voting Liberal Democrat. In a further study on voting behaviour in 2005, McAndrew (2010) found that having a religion was more likely to mean that voters identified with one of the three British parties than not having a religion, although McAndrew states that this finding was not so clear cut as this might be due more to the influence of family socialisation.

But what is also significant in the British case and potentially points against the secularisation thesis is that there has been a 10 per cent increase in people who consider themselves to be religious despite growing up in a non-religious background (Voas and Ling, 2010). This new trend in religious identity in the UK is also highlighted by Hay (2006, pp 8-9), who notes a 60 per cent increase in the number of people reporting religious or spiritual experiences in a survey he had first conducted in 1987 and was repeating in 2000 for the BBC *Soul of Britain* review on spirituality in Britain. Hay (2006) argues that this is indicative of a wider split between religion and spirituality in the UK. Indeed, this would seem to confirm the argument that contemporary religion is much more individualistic and personalised in character, with people finding spiritual meaning a matter of growing relevance to their lives and not one for which traditional institutional religion necessarily has the answer. Although for Farias and Hense (2009), the empirical difference between religion and spirituality is hard to define for research purposes.

Nevertheless, one final issue remains, that of the importance of religion in British people's lives. Survey data, such as from the fourth Policy Studies Institute (PSI) Survey for Ethnic Minorities (cited in Beckford et al, 2006), shows that 95 per cent of Muslims, 89 per cent of Hindus and 86 per cent of Sikhs in Britain consider that their religion is 'very' or 'fairly' important in their lives. This is significantly higher than the rates reported in the same survey for White members of the Church of England (46 per cent) and Roman Catholic Church (69 per cent). These findings are also broadly corroborated by the 2001 and 2003 Home Office Citizenship Surveys and by the European Social Values Survey (Beckford et al, 2006; Purdam et al, 2007). Thus, what we find is that religion matters a great deal to the minority ethnic populations of the UK, which potentially makes the case for its more central role in social policy making. Moreover, religious affiliation in Britain is more likely to be connected to volunteering. The Home Office (2004, p 199) *2003 Citizenship Survey* found that 57 per cent of respondents who had a religious faith participated in some form of voluntary work, in comparison to 37 per cent of people with no religious faith who took part in voluntary work.

Religious profile of social problems and deprivation in contemporary Britain

So what do we know about social problems and deprivation among religious groups in the UK? At present, there is limited empirical data on the religious distribution of social problems and deprivation in the UK, as confirmed by Beckford et al (2006) and Purdam et al (2007). However, some research has been conducted on religious discrimination in the UK, for example, the right to celebrate religious holidays or to follow specific dietary and dress requirements (Purdam et al, 2007). The more usual variable is ethnicity but this is not an adequate proxy for religion expect perhaps in some policy sectors such as housing (for a fuller debate, see Beckford et al, 2006). Indeed, while this is not the place to debate the connections between ethnicity and religion in the UK, it is useful to note that intellectual and public debates about minority ethnic groups in Britain have a shifting nomenclature from 'colour' in the 1950s and 1960s, to 'race' in the 1960s–80s, to 'religion' since the 1990s (Beckford et al, 2006, p 11). The reasons for the latter are explored throughout this chapter.

For our present purpose, two secondary data sources are cited here. The first source is 2001 Census data from the ONS and the second is a 2006 government report, *Review of the evidence base on faith communities* (see Beckford et al, 2006) for the Office of the Deputy Prime Minister (ODPM, now the Department for Communities and Local Government, CLG), which also relies heavily on ONS data. Some useful data is also reported in Purdam et al (2007) from the Labour Force Survey of 2003–04 on unemployment and education, which corroborate the data from the 2001 Census. Purdam et al (2007) advocate the inclusion of a question on religious identity in the ONS' Integrated Household Surveys in order to fill the significant gap in data between religion and social inequality.

Nevertheless, thanks to the 2001 Census, it is now possible to correlate indicators on social deprivation with religious identity, although these remain limited in scope. To this end, the Muslim population fares the worst in terms of unemployment levels, educational achievement and self-reported health. As Figure 3.2 shows, 13 per cent of Muslim men were unemployed at the time of the 2001 Census in comparison to 4 per cent among their Christian counterparts and between 3 and 8 per cent in the other religious groups. Rates of unemployment are highest in the under-25 age group among Muslim men, at 28 per cent in comparison to 11 per cent among Christian men (ONS, 2004). Similar high rates of economic inactivity among people of working age are also reported among the Muslim population (ONS, 2004). According to the ONS (2004), the young age profile of the Muslim community and the presence of large proportions of students within it are two of the main reasons that can explain these high levels of unemployment or economic inactivity. Rates of unemployment or economic inactivity are significantly high among Muslim women, at

Figure 3.2: Unemployment rates: by religion and gender (2001)

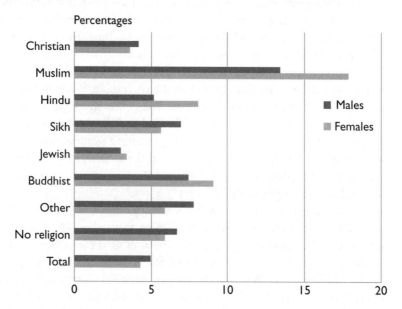

Source: 2001 Census, Office for National Statistics, www.statistics.gov.uk/cci/nuggett. asp?id=979, accessed 10 May 2001

18 and 65 per cent respectively (ONS, 2004). In the former case, this is four times more than their female co-religionists. Family and domestic responsibilities are cited as the most common reasons for these high rates, with Christian women being the least likely to be economically inactive, at 25 per cent (ONS, 2004).

Difficulties related to the labour market are also reflected in housing patterns in the census data. In terms of housing tenure, according to the 2001 Census, the Muslim population occupied the largest proportion of social housing among their co-religionists, as can be seen in Figure 3.3. According to the ONS (2004), the situation was especially grave among households that had never worked and those experiencing long-term unemployment. Overcrowding, lack of central heating or sole access to a bathroom were other aspects of housing deprivation by which Muslims were more affected. As Figure 3.3 shows, Muslim households showed the highest proportion living in social housing (around 28%), followed by members of other religions (which in the ONS data could include Rastafarians, Wicca and Pagans). Christians and Buddhist were the next two largest groups after that. Conversely, just over 50 per cent of Muslims and Buddhists owned their own homes,

Figure 3.3: Religion of households by type of tenure (2001)

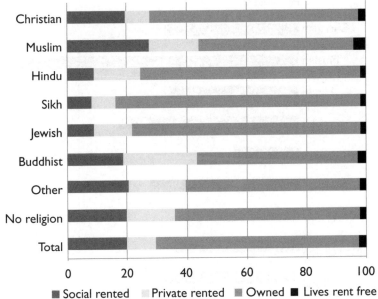

Source: 2001 Census, Office for National Statistics, www.statistics.gov.uk/cci/nuggett. asp?id=979, accessed 10 May 2001

making them the least likely private owners among the other religions. Sikh, Hindu and Jewish households were more likely to own their own homes at well over 70 per cent for each religious community. People who answered 'no religion' in the 2001 Census also figured highly as living in social housing, at 20 per cent, as in Figure 3.3.

Muslims also fare the worst in terms of educational achievement. As Figure 3.4 shows, over 33 per cent of Muslims of working age in Britain had no qualifications at the time of the 2001 Census and around 12 per cent did not have a university degree or equivalent. The second largest group not to have any qualifications were from the Sikh community. Members of the Jewish community fared the best in this regard, with only around 7 per cent of them not having any qualifications.

According to the 2001 Census data, 44 per cent of Jewish people had a university degree, followed by Buddhists (30 per cent) and Hindus (29 per cent), with 16 per cent of the Christian community holding a degree. The ONS data also notes that across all the religions, women were more likely to have no qualifications than men, but also that Muslims and Sikhs born in the UK were twice as likely to have a degree or equivalent than those born outside of the UK. This is not

Figure 3.4: Religion of people of working age with no qualifications (2004)

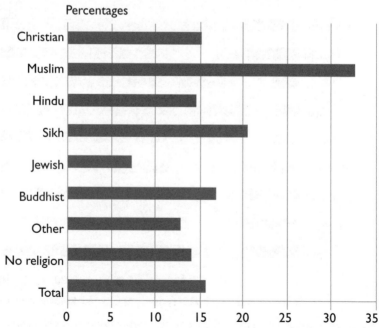

Source: 2001 Census, Office for National Statistics, www.statistics.gov.uk/cci/nuggett. asp?id=979, accessed 10 May 2001

the case for Hindus where place of birth did not seem to be connected to acquisition of a degree.

The final segment of data relates to how many people of specific religious backgrounds reported that their health was 'not good' in the 2001 Census. Again, both male and female Muslims came out as the worst, closely followed by members of the 'other' religions and Sikhs. Figure 3.5 shows these figures to be 16 per cent (Muslim women), 13 per cent (Muslim men), 10 per cent (Sikh men) and 14 per cent (Sikh women).

Figure 3.5: Religion of people reporting 'not good' health rates (by sex, age standardised) (2001)

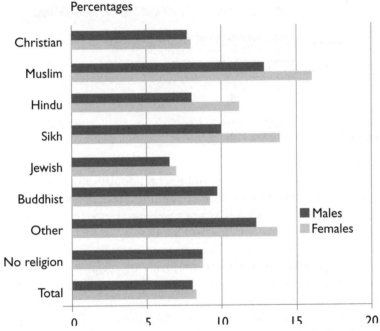

Source: 2001 Census, Office for National Statistics, www.statistics.gov.uk/cci/nuggett. asp?id=979, accessed 10 May 2001

For almost all religious categories rates were 3 to 4 percentage points higher than their respective male counterparts. The exception was the Buddhists, where the rate for males was higher than for females; and in the cases of 'no religion', Christians and Jews, there were no gender differences in reported health. In terms of long-term illness and disability rates, the 2001 Census data also show that Muslims were most affected, followed closely by 'other religion' and Sikhs, as shown in Figure 3.6. Once older age groups are accounted for (more

Figure 3.6: Religion of people with long-term illness or disability (by sex) (2001)

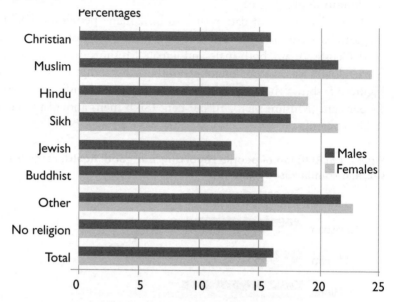

Source: 2001 Census, Office for National Statistics, www.statistics.gov.uk/cci/nuggett. asp?id=979, accessed 10 May 2001

predominant in the Christian and Jewish populations), it is the other minority ethnic faiths that reported limiting health conditions on their everyday lives. Most notably, women were more affected by than men, especially among the Muslims and Sikhs.

The low levels of female economic participation among the Muslim populations reinforce problems of social integration and economic marginalisation for this particular community (Beckford et al, 2006). This situation is now changing, however, with second or third generation Muslim women becoming better educated. The Muslim population is the fastest growing in the UK, with a third of the population under the age of 15 compared to 20 per cent, which is the English national average (Beckford et al, 2006). Moreover, only 5 per cent of the Muslim population is over the age of 60, compared to 20 per cent of the England average.

Beckford et al's (2006) desk review on faith communities draws attention to the differential impact on the socioeconomic status of the religious communities in the UK resulting from differences in the circumstances of their migration to the UK (as opposed to their particular living circumstances in the UK). Hence, one of the key reasons why Hindus may appear to be more affluent than their Muslim or Sikh co-religionists is because about a third of the Indian ethnic population in the UK are originally middle-class professionals originating from East Africa after the expulsions of the 1960s and 1970s. Moreover, the relatively higher levels of deprivation among Muslims may be explained by their rural peasant backgrounds, especially among those first generation migrants coming from Azad (Pakistan), Kashmir or Bangladesh. These migrants were concentrated in the industrialised areas of England and have remained geographically located in what are now deprived urban centres of industrial decline (Beckford et al, 2006).

Indeed, while Christians continue to be the largest religious group in the more deprived areas, there are also high concentrations of Hindus, Sikhs and Muslims (26, 22 and 40 per cent, respectively) (Beckford et al, 2006, p 38). To be specific, 33 per cent of the Muslim population is concentrated in the 10 per cent most deprived neighbourhoods. This reinforces fears of cultural segregation in Britain, as highlighted by the Cantle Report (Home Office, 2001). Yet even when ethno-religious minorities experience upward mobility, research cited in Beckford et al (2006) also points to the regrouping of ethno-religious communities in the new areas that they move to. This issue asserts the centrality of policy concern with the social cohesion of ethno-religious minorities in the UK.

Beckford et al cite several reasons for the geographical concentrations of ethno-religious groups: (1) chain migration from place of origin to place of destination, which, in the case of Hindus, is also influenced by caste identity; (2) a tendency to live in close proximity to the extended family grouping; and (3) a tendency to live in close proximity to members of the same religious group in order to participate in ritual worship or social functions together, as can be found among Muslims, Sikhs and Jews. Thus, geographical proximity to the religion's place of worship is of key concern here. The issue of social cohesion, while central to the new social policy context of the UK, is nevertheless one of many circumstantial and intrinsic features in the contemporary relationship between religion and social policy, as discussed in the next section. What should be noted here, however, is that the presence of Muslims in Britain has been one of the main triggers for the increased attention paid to religion in UK public policy, leading some critics to argue that this religious group has attracted a disproportionate share of public resources.

Profile of religious welfare organisations

It is useful at this point to consider some basic figures about the estimated size and resources of the faith-based voluntary sector in the UK. According to a 2007 report published by the NCVO, the total income of faith-based registered charities in the UK was £4.6 billion. Ninety per cent of this was concentrated among 10 per cent of organisations whose income surpassed £2 million, indicating that this was a sector largely made up of small informal organisations depending in large part on volunteers (Faith-based Regeneration Network and Dinham, 2008). According to figures cited in the Charities Aid Foundation (CAF) report *Charity trends 2004*, about 12 per cent of all charitable giving in the UK was through the church. In the US it was between 30 and 40 per cent. Faith-based organisations accounted for 14 per cent of the top 500 fundraising charities, and 8 per cent of their total income, worth £163,700,000.[4]

According to the 2004 CAF report, religious charities were in the enviable position of obtaining the greater proportion (two thirds) of their income from investments in comparison to other fundraising sub-sectors. This gives them greater autonomy from government and donors, and is corroborated by information provided by the Charity Commission below. However, this self-reliance also means that religious charities are dependent on their members, which explains the religious motivations and potentially exclusive motivations behind donations. According to the 2004 CAF report, 'These figures show the enormous value of a committed donor community, bound in by beliefs and regular habits of giving and volunteering. This is precisely the model for future relationship-based fundraising which many charities are seeking to build' (see www.scvo.org.uk/tfn/news/the-future-of-giving-caf-column-by-cathy-pharoah/).

A joint report by CAF and NCVO, *UK Giving 2004/2005*, also found that the highest level donors in the UK, which by its definition included the 5 per cent of donors paying £100 or more on average every month, were faith-based donors. Faith-based donors accounted for 11 per cent of the total proportion of high level donors, second only to donations for medical research, at 13 per cent (CAF and NCVO, 2005, p 13). Faith-based methods of donation also had the highest level of cash-based donations (25 per cent of total faith-based giving) among all other forms of payments (CAF and NCVO, 2005, p 13), suggesting that this was an informal and personalised style of giving. At the same time, the highest proportion of direct debit-based giving was done for religious causes.

In terms of the number of religious charities, various estimates exist in the tens of thousands. Christian charities outnumber those from other religions and are among the largest in terms of annual incomes (Charity Trends data for 2011, see www.charitytrends.org). The largest such organisation is The Salvation Army with an annual income of almost £300 million (Charity Trends data for 2011, see www.charitytrends. org). This puts The Salvation Army closely within the range of the top 10 richest charities in the UK. However, if we take into account organisations such as Barnardo's and Oxfam, which have a Christian heritage, then these two organisations would also not be far off having annual incomes of around £200 million each. The largest UK religious charities also include non-Christian organisations, namely, Tearfund, (Methodist) National Children's Homes, Nugent Care, Christian Aid, Islamic Relief UK, Muslim Aid, Muslim Hands, Jewish Care and The United Synagogue.

According to the NCVO (2007) report, 23,832 charities registered with the Charity Commission stated that they were involved in religious activity (NCVO, 2007). This figure is corroborated by the estimate of 22,000 charities for England and Wales cited in *Breakthrough Britain*, a milestone report by the Social Justice Policy Group (SJPG, 2007) that gave recommendations to the Conservative Party on issues of poverty and social deprivation. This is lower than the recent estimate of 41,870 cited by the Charity Commission (email communication with a policy adviser on 19 May 2011). This number is out of a total of 116,000 charities, so it is a significant proportion of the total charity sector. Scotland has its own Charity Register, kept by the Office of the Scottish Charity Regulator, that records a total number of 23,345 charities, 1,000 of which have a religious character.[5]

The work that these organisations are involved in varies tremendously, from emergency relief in poor countries abroad, to social assistance in the UK such as food banks and night shelters. The breakdown of self-reported types of activities of religious charity groups in England and Wales are shown in Table 3.2 in rank order, according to the Charity Commission's register of charities, illustrating that educational and training services are the most common followed by general charitable purposes and relief of poverty. Admittedly, however, some confusion is likely to arise between the categories of general charitable purposes and other charitable purposes.

Table 3.2: Types of activities of religious charities (organisations may offer more than one of these)

Educational/training	18,486 (44.2%)
General charitable purposes	12,992 (31%)
Relief of poverty	9,396 (22.4%)
Sports/recreation	9,129 (21.8%)
Arts/culture	7,198 (17.2%)
Economic/community development/employment	6,206 (14.8%)
Medical/health/sickness	4,808 (11.5%)
Overseas aid/famine relief	4,763 (11.4%)
Disability	3,692 (8.8%)
Environment/conservation/heritage	3,643 (8.7%)
Accommodation/housing	2,313 (5.5%)
Other charitable purposes	1,297 (3.1%)
Animals	669 (1.6%)

Source: Charity Commission, email communication, 19 May 2011

Dinham's (2007, p 9) review offers a much more extensive breakdown of the activities of religious welfare organisations (48 types of activities in total) in the UK, extending from advice and counselling to substance abuse, employment training, crime prevention, social activities and a large array of social work and community development activities. Dinham (2007, p 10) further classifies the work of religious organisations into the following four areas: (1) project-based work; (2) congregational and network-based work; (3) partnership-based work; and (4) leadership and governance-related work. Thus, religious groups are seen to fulfil the twin roles of service provision, but also of representing the interests of their communities in relations with government, particularly at local level. It is also the case that not all religious groups actively seek to influence public policy, as Dinham (2007) notes. Often their goals may also entail ends that are specific to the daily life of their community such as evangelism or community-based worship. In the case of minority ethnic populations, inter-general transfer of cultural identity and moral values is a key aspect of their work.

Further insights into the activities of the religious welfare sector are offered in the NCVO (2007) report, with religious organisations stating that 56 per cent of their activities were spent on grant-making activities and 35 per cent on service provision. Having said this, a report in 2003 by the North West Development Agency (NWDA) (a leader in the debate about the contribution of religious groups to their local regions) found that most religious welfare organisations were self-financing, with only 30 per cent in receipt of some public funding for their work. Over half of these charities aimed to serve the general public and two fifths focused particularly on children and young people. The NCVO (2007) further states that the number of officially registered faith charities underestimates their true number in the UK since many smaller charities were not registered and other well-established ones did not call themselves religious (like Barnardo's, which states on its website that its inspiration comes from Christian values) (NCVO, 2007). In line with Bretherton's (2010) cautionary note about essentialising 'faith' and dichotomising between 'secular' and 'religious', it is important to note that in the UK religious welfare organisations exhibit diverse degrees of 'religiosity'.

Much of the work that religious charities carry out occurs in the context of projects and associations, and not necessarily through a single religious welfare organisation (Faith-based Regeneration Network and Dinham, 2008). Thus, community-based religious welfare action can occur through a Christian diocese, for example, and be open to all members of the community, not just the members of the faith itself (Faith-based Regeneration Network and Dinham, 2008). It is useful to look at the religious welfare sector in the UK as a web of interlinked organisations, networks and strategic partnerships that cut across geographical regions, religious faiths and layers of governance, such as the Inter-church Merseyside Strategic Partnership or the Birmingham Be Programme. This web changes as structures of governance change in the UK, as local, religious and national government policy calls on religious groups to engage in service provision or policy implementation (Weller, 2009). Thus, what exists at present is an array of 'groups', 'forums' and 'councils' which may be 'inter-faith' in that they involve an initiative between two religious groups, or 'multi-faith' in that they involve a variety of religious groups drawn from the nine main faiths in the UK (Weller, 2009). In total, there are around 25 national inter-faith organisations in the UK with the Faith Communities Inter-Faith Council bringing together religious organisations, government minsters and civil servants to discuss a range of policy issues (Weller, 2009).

An important source of information for and on religious organisations in the English context are the regional faith forums or particular faith units in the regional development agencies, of which the NWDA has been a leading player in commissioning research on the contribution of religious organisations to social welfare and also to local economic development. The regional faith forums cover all the nine regions of England (except the North East), and their role is to engage with regional assemblies, regional development agencies such as the NWDA and other regional bodies (Dinham, 2007; Weller, 2009). Scotland, Wales and Northern Ireland (Weller, 2009) also have their own inter-faith councils or forums.

Although the regional faith forums collect their own data on the religious welfare sector in the various regions, which may not necessarily be comparable, they represent an important support structure of religious bodies (Dinham, 2007). Again, it is mainly the Christian churches that have the largest spread across the various districts and in many cases can act as a gatekeeper for other non-Christian groups in delivering social welfare services, most notably in the area of prison chaplaincy (Gilliat-Ray, 2008). In terms of what information the different regional faith forums provide about the faith groups operating in their different regions, this includes basic information such as the total number of volunteers, the total number of volunteering hours worked and the different types of services and forms of engagement that religious organisations are involved in. Dinham's (2007) detailed review of English regional faith councils and forums indicates that activities for children and young people are particularly prevalent in London, the West Midlands and Yorkshire and the Humber, accounting for between one third to half of all faith-based activities offered in these regions. This contrasts with the North West, where educational and arts and music activities are more predominant, and the North East, where a broad category of community development encompassing credit unions, homelessness and counselling takes up around 40 per cent of total faith-based activity.

In an effort to develop an evidence base for the contribution of religious organisations to society, and a calculation of the economic impact of the religious welfare organisations to their local communities, the NWDA (2005) calculated that the North West region benefits from between £90.7 million to £94.9 million per year's worth of buildings and volunteers belonging to the various faith groups in the region; 84.8 per cent of this is attributable to Christian denominations in the North West region, followed by the Buddhist and Jewish communities who respectively contribute £3.3 million and £3.5 million's worth of volunteer time and building assets per year (NWDA, 2005, p 2). An earlier report in 2003 by the NWDA which offered one of the first official snapshots of the social welfare role of religious groups in the North West mapped out the geographical distribution of religious groups in the region to show that it coincides with the urban areas of highest social need, based on a questionnaire survey using a multiple deprivation index. It is clear from the discussion so far that part of the task at hand is to consider the broader governance structure within which religious welfare action in the UK sits.

Religion and the new social policy context in the UK

In this section, we look at three key areas that map out the current context of policy in relation to religion: the first covers the general political climate in the UK which has made it more 'faith-friendly' (Powell, 2007b); the second develops the discussion by considering the way in which the infrastructure of governance in the UK has changed in order for government policy to take better account of religious concerns within society, but also to create space for religious representatives and bodies to become involved in policy making, to develop inter-faith and multi-faith initiatives; and the third covers the view by government of what religious organisations are seen to contribute to social policy, including the major policy statements that have come out in this regard.

Political momentum for engagement with religion in the UK

The Welfare Reform Act 2007 was accompanied by a string of seminars held by the Department for Work and Pensions around the UK, one of which took place in Manchester City Stadium in February 2007 under the title, 'The role of faith-based groups in welfare provision', where John Battle MP emphasised the key role of religious groups in social renewal and welfare, and a string of organisations from the main religious faiths also gave their organisations' perspectives on social welfare and engagement with the public services.

The public role of religious welfare has a historical association with Conservative politics in Britain, with the Church of England earning the nickname of 'the Conservative Party at prayer'. This association was sorely tested in the 1980s when the Church of England launched the *Faith in the city report* (Commission on Urban Priority Areas, 1985),[6] a harsh critique of the impact of Margaret Thatcher's policies, and had to be reassessed in publications such as *Christianity and conservatism: Are Christianity and conservatism compatible?*, in which Thatcher (1990) herself wrote of the church's innate responsibility for moral oversight over society, and that political life needed to be guided by some moral values. So what is rather striking in the UK is that it was in fact a Labour politician who brought religion to the attention of social policy. This politician was Tony Blair (Prime Minister, 1997–2010), one of Britain's most openly religious leaders and a key architect of Britain's more favourable turn towards religious organisations. Blair had a strong ideological association with his US counterpart, Bill Clinton, and the welfare reforms of the 1990s began in earnest under their leaderships – in both cases, lowering the barriers of government engagement with religious welfare providers. Indeed, Ahmed et al (2009) argue that the real turning point happened in 2002/03, when government funding became available to religious organisations, and having a religious identity became better recognised in government circles.

To this end, Bretherton (2010) identifies the key factors that have led British (and US) social policy down the path towards greater religious welfare provision. The first is the growth of religious diversity in these countries as in the rest of Western Europe due to incoming migration since the 1950s. Minority ethnic groups in the UK have increasingly preferred to identify themselves by their religious identity and have called on government to recognise their religiously based needs and sentiments. For instance, the Muslim population lobbied for the provision of meat and poultry slaughtered in the Islamic *halal* way. Similarly, state funding of faith schools has been a campaigning issue for some minority religions, with Muslims, Hindus and Buddhists succeeding only quite recently in gaining government funding to establish their own faith schools (Tinker, 2006). Related to the issue of integration and multiculturalism, however, is increased government and public concern around the security risks associated with religion, particularly Islam in the post-9/11 world (Bretherton, 2010).

A second issue is the general turn towards communitarianism in British social policy that Bretherton (2010) sees as part of a broader historical trend since the end of the Cold War. Under the present Coalition government and its push towards greater localism and the Big Society, a philosophy of mutualism has returned. This trend sits well with neoliberalism and its push towards decentralised power, participation and personal responsibility, themes that have now become staples for social policy in the UK. They also emphasise the trend of welfare retrenchment, and the need for the state to occupy a smaller role within the mixed economy of welfare. Like its predecessor Labour government, the Coalition government is concerned with issues of social cohesion and civic renewal, and in this climate, religious people and organisations are seen as a force for strong communities. More importantly, they are able to reach individuals and communities with high levels of need, or, in the discourse of policy, that are 'difficult to reach' (NWDA, 2003, p 4). But the extent to which religion is a source of division or solidarity remains a matter for further research.

The third issue is the trend towards the greater prevalence of moral debate surrounding welfare. Bretherton (2010) focuses on the greater degree of moral judgementalism in relation to the discourses of deservingness and personal responsibility for welfare that in the UK began during the Thatcher era (Bretherton, 2010). Religious groups offering social welfare services fit well into this new moral landscape in that they have an emphasis on social relationships and character change, and seek to instil a sense of moral responsibility and social purpose. But equally, the heightened moral and ethical debates surrounding public policy have been expressed as outcries against major events that are having a direct impact on social welfare and levels of equality in Britain. The impact of the 2008 global recession and the related disillusionment with the global capitalist system and the dramatic cuts to public spending in the UK that were announced in 2010 are part of this broadening ethical debate whereby religious leaders, in particular the Archbishop of Canterbury (as expressed in his *New Statesman* article: Williams, 2011), have voiced concerns about the accountability of elected officials to ordinary British citizens.

The final issue is the change in the governance structure of the UK, which has become more decentralised in order to facilitate greater partnerships between state and non-state sectors in welfare provision, and greater local responsibility for decision making. This is an important theme touched on at the beginning of this chapter, and is the focus of the next section as it has important implications for how religious organisations are entering the mainstream of social policy making.

New structures of governance

Changes in the structure of governance and relationships of accountability and policy making have meant that religious representatives and groups now have a formal presence at national, regional and local levels, the latter two being most visible and active. Chapman (2009) notes that there are three main ways in which religious organisations and actors are engaging in the policy-making process, through:

- direct engagement and representation in strategic and serviced delivery partnerships;
- wider consultations with religious communities by statutory authorities;
- increased partnerships with religious groups in the delivery of publicly funded welfare services and initiatives aimed at social inclusion, community cohesion and preventing violent extremism.

A variety of initiatives have come in and out of existence since the 1990s, and it is important to remember that, as major public sector restructuring goes on at the time of writing, what is described below is a snapshot of the current situation as things stand: at the national level, first came the establishment in 1992, under the auspices of the Department for the Environment, of the Inner Cities Religious Council (ICRC), the first national organisation of its kind in post-war Britain to bring religious representatives and government officials together in consultation over social policy. The ICRC had permanent representation by mainstream and majority black Christian denominations, Jewish, Muslim, Sikh and Hindu organisations, but its work was often dominated with concern for meeting the needs of minority religious groups. Linked to its establishment was the provision of funds to minority ethnic faith communities, particularly for building their capacities to deliver local services. For some authors, this constitutes the seed of a new kind of multi-faith establishment in the UK (Taylor, 2003; Bretherton, 2010). Various government funding schemes have also come into existence, most notably the £13.8 million Faith Communities Capacity Building Fund (FCCBF) which ran between 2006 and 2008 and aimed to help faith groups build their capacities in order to be able to deliver services, and a £4 million Faiths in Action government grant that was meant to run between 2009 and 2011 aimed at helping faith groups develop understanding and dialogue.

In 2006, the ICRC was replaced by the Faith Communities Consultative Council (FCCC), housed within the CLG with a similar portfolio of responsibilities to its predecessor but also a mandate focusing on civic renewal and social cohesion. Various funds came into being during this period such as the Capacity Building Fund and the Community Development Foundation, both of which specifically targeted faith communities in providing them with grants to build their resources in order to deliver services and to carry out local social initiatives. Major restructuring of the CLG occurred after the Coalition government took power in the spring of 2010, leading to the closing down of the FCCC, partly as a result of the introduction of the Localism Bill, and partly due to the cut in public spending.

The strategy of the Coalition now entails direct consultation with representatives of the main faith communities, and also through the regional faith forums. For instance, the CLG has invested directly into the Church Urban Fund which has maintained its standing as a beacon of defence for the rights of deprived urban communities. The CLG has, however, retained members of staff in key senior positions whose role is to advise it on faith communities. Other important developments at national level were the establishment of the Home Office Faith Communities Unit in 2003 and the appointment of a 'faith envoy' for the Prime Minister (Bretherton, 2010).

It is more at regional and local levels that governance structures have been most modified in order to make way for religious organisations to cooperate formally with government in social policy in Britain (Weller, 2009). This has been through inter-faith and multi-faith initiatives, the main modes of engagement with religious representatives. In the 1980s, this was part of the Conservative 'rolling back the state' discourse; in the 1990s, this was under the New Labour 'community partnerships' discourse; and in the 2000s, it is the Big Society and volunteering orientation of the Coalition government (Weller, 2009, p 71).

At regional level, a range of inter-faith organisations have come into place although representation remains patchy, and the regional infrastructure of governance is not yet fully developed (Weller, 2009). Some organisations exist at city level, such as the Birmingham Council of Sikh Gurdwaras or the Federation of Muslim Organisations in Leicester (Weller, 2009). Thus, as they have the greatest spread and resources, the various Christian church denominations can help facilitate regional representation for minority ethnic religions. Various ecumenical church bodies have been formed at regional level such as the East Midlands Churches Forum and the Churches Regional Commission in the North East. Weller argues that the fragility of religious representation at regional level will need to be addressed. In the meantime, the most important regional bodies in England are the faith forums or councils alluded to in the previous section that represent all the English regions. These forums and councils deal directly with the regional assemblies and regional development agencies in consultation over policy design and implementation. Issues of representation and membership preoccupy inter-faith activity at the regional level, as they do at the local level. On the one hand are questions regarding whether to include pagan and humanist organisations, although increasingly inter-faith bodies are having to expand their definitions of spirituality; on the other hand are questions surrounding gender and generational representation which have to do with the participation of women and young people (Weller, 2009).

It is at the local level that the involvement of religious groups in governance has been more widespread and diverse (Weller, 2009): religious organisations have been active in greater numbers and with much more direct involvement in the implementation of social policy. In rural areas, the formal presence of religious representation in local governance has remained strong due to the Church of England's well-established system of parish councils (Weller, 2009). Under New Labour, City Partnerships, Local Strategic Partnerships (LSPs) and local compact agreements were key forms of engagement for religious groups with local authorities in urban areas (for a more detailed discussion, see Chapman, 2009 and Weller, 2009). LSPs are non-statutory partnerships found in most local authority areas in England that bring together local councils, other public sector agencies, the business sector and the third sector to design and deliver local services. They often include local inter-faith forums. The Coalition government has not commented significantly on LSPs, although in principle it supports the idea of partnership. In view of the current restructuring of the public sector, however, some LSPs have had to be closed down due to the cut back in staff and duties (Weller, 2009).

Escott and Logan (2006) carried out an extensive and informative review of the role of religious representatives on LSPs. From the outset, they lament the fact that official guidance from the Department of the Environment, Transport and the Regions (DETR) on the role of religious groups was often confused with ethnicity and conceptualised in the narrow terms of accessing hard-to-reach groups, often from minority ethnic communities, as opposed to a broader vision of social change to which all religious groups could contribute. Nevertheless, Escott and Logan's review offers a mixed assessment. On the one hand, in opening up space for greater interaction between religious groups and secular officials, LSPs have helped enhance mutual understanding and trust and a greater sense of common purpose among these groups.

But the authors note that the greater availability of resources in a local area and the pre-existence of organised religious action are important factors in explaining the success of LSPs that have included faith representatives. Indeed, LSPs helped to strengthen these previously existing relationships. But strong relationships were harder to cultivate between religious groups, meaning at the multi-faith level. Faith groups are also more likely to keep their focus on helping the poor, and Escott and Logan see this as a strength in their contribution to LSPs. They also identify different gaps in resourcing that need to be addressed in order for faith communities to be able to contribute well: on the one hand, religious groups may have time and volunteers to offer, but they often lack relevant training or indeed basic resources and funding. However, their presence on LSPs ensures that the faith dimension is not neglected in local public services and that faith organisations themselves represent large segments of local communities that may otherwise not have their voices and needs heard. Moreover, it also means that strategic policy discussions are able to take into account spiritual and ethical dimensions of life that normally go neglected (Escott and Logan, 2006).

More profoundly, Weller (2009) sees the inter-faith and multi-faith initiatives as a successful model for the new shape of state–church relations. It tempers the predominance of any one religion in society, opens up a forum for dialogue and common ground among various religious and secular worldview traditions and allows a more balanced rapport between religious traditions and the state, whereby neither is totally detached from nor totally incorporated into the other. Weller (2009, p 79) thus concludes that the best way forward is one whereby local inter-faith councils and initiatives are legitimated and supported by the state and public bodies.

Under the Coalition government, the Localism Act 2011 is set to allow greater freedom for private and voluntary sectors organisations to directly take over the provision of public services in their local areas if they have the relevant capacities. The 'right to provide' and the 'right to challenge' clauses of the Act would make such provision possible. Religious organisations that can provide public and welfare services may therefore directly take over services or bid for government funding through prime contractors. Social finance bonds are also a new initiative, and a new 'Faiths in Social Finance Bond' was launched in 2011 involving all nine faith communities, aiming to include 500 congregations, each contributing £500 (talk by Francis Davis, 2011).

Current status of policy on the role and place of religion in social policy

Although UK policy has made significant strides in facilitating the engagement of local and national government with religious actors and organisations since the late 1980s, the discourse surrounding the contribution of religion to society has not been clearly pronounced. Dinham and Lowndes (2008, p 6) argue that 'rationales for faith group involvement have rarely been spelled out; they have been implicit, sometimes contradictory and often opportunistic'. A major obstacle in this respect has been the issue of religious literacy on the part of government and policy literacy on the part of faith groups.

Before looking at the official government stance in relation to the role of religious organisations in social policy, it is useful to note that in the background, various pieces of legislation have come into place in Britain which not only seek to prevent discrimination against religion but actively endorse the freedom of religious practice (or none), depicting this as a vital component of human welfare (Furness and Gilligan, 2010).

Article 9 of the European Convention on Human Rights (included in Schedule 1 of the Human Rights Act 1998) enshrines religious freedom; the Children Act 1989 for England and Wales as well as the Children (Scotland) Act 1995 and the Children (Northern Ireland) Order 1995 require due consideration of the religious background and needs of 'looked after' children (Moss, 2005); and the UK's Department of Health 1991 Patient's Charter stipulates 'respect for privacy, dignity and religious and cultural beliefs' (Gilliat-Ray, 2003, p 335). Most recently, the Equality Act 2006 makes it unlawful to discriminate against anyone because of their religion or belief (or lack of religion) in a variety of areas such as in their workplace or in the provision of goods and services to them (Furness and Gilligan, 2010, pp 20-1). Furness and Gilligan also discuss in more detail specific guidance by the CLG relating to the Equality Act 2006 on the provision of social care and social services. These require public authorities to ensure that members of the public are not prevented from accessing services on the grounds of their religious faith and that local authorities may fund care homes run by religious organisations for people of their own faith provided that people of other faiths are able to access similar services elsewhere (cited in Furness and Gilligan, 2010, p 21).[7]

This legislative context inevitably also has a bearing on social policy. Policy statements made so far under the Coalition government do not depart significantly from New Labour's approach of encouraging religious groups to deliver welfare services and support social harmony. Indeed, the Coalition government has yet to match the intense activity of the New Labour government in this respect. However, the political discourse has moved from one based on concepts such as civic renewal and social capital to one based on localism, volunteering and the Big Society: religious groups are, in this view, independent social entrepreneurs. Government policy remains heavily preoccupied with knowledge development and capacity building to enhance collaboration and dialogue between faith groups and government agencies. There is an implicit assumption that religious groups are an untapped source of social action and welfare from which nothing bad can emanate. The enthusiasm of central government may not always be a feeling shared by local authorities, however.

Since 1997, an array of national guidelines for local councils to consult and collaborate with faith-based organisations were published under New Labour, for instance, the 1997 handbook and later in 2002, the Local Government Association's (LGA) good practice guide for local authorities. In 2004 the Home Office Faith Communities Unit published a major document, *Working together: Co-operation between government and faith communities*, which starts with the important statement of 'faith – not just a personal issue'. The report stressed the value of public authorities at all levels working in partnership with faith communities and gaining 'faith literacy'. To this end, it highlighted examples of good practice to increase knowledge of religion among staff members and to consult better with faith communities among key government departments and agencies such as the Department for Trade and Industry, Jobcentre Plus and the Crown Prosecution Service. The report went some way in asserting that faith communities were a 'distinctive' part of the voluntary sector and that they had a special link with minority ethnic groups. It also noted that there was a need to evaluate at a later stage how effective religious organisations were as partners for government. In 2006, a White Paper, *Strong and prosperous communities* (CLG, 2006) also emphasised the role of inter-faith work in local communities.

Another important document during the New Labour era was CLG's *Face to face and side by side* (2008), which offered further evidence of the activities of religious actors and organisation and provided further guidelines for local authorities on how to integrate faith communities into their policy planning and delivery. The report proposed 'building blocks' for improving collaboration between local authorities and religious communities, these being: (1) developing confidence and skills to 'bridge' and 'link' faith communities and local authorities; (2) creating shared spaces for interaction and social action; (3) putting in place structures and processes to enhance communication and collaboration among faith communities and between faith communities and local authorities; and (4) creating and using opportunities for learning which can build better understanding.

Chapman (2009) offers a detailed review of various documents that the LGA and CLG published in the 2000s under the New Labour government. These emphasised the social capital, resources and social cohesion components of religious organisations with much less consideration of what the faith element itself means for social welfare and the common good. Space does not allow deeper consideration of New Labour's policies here, but one key issue to raise is that the term 'social capital' became especially popular within New Labour policy discourse and was seen as a deliberate move to depoliticise debates on social justice and poverty. Thus, bringing religious organisations into the equation was a way of fostering social harmony but at the same time preserving principles of multiculturalism and diversity in British society (Bretherton, 2010). This underpinned a philosophical motive of renewing civil society as the bulwark of a healthy liberal democracy.

Dinham and Lowndes (2009) categorise the various types of arguments for state–religious partnership in the UK in three ways:

- a resource-focused rationale that emphasises the material resources that religious organisations own and which they can put to the use of their local communities. For example, buildings can be rented out and used as venues for meetings and service provision, and volunteers are at hand to maintain contact with service users and to deliver services. The resource approach tends to be favoured by national policy makers;
- a governance-focused rationale that emphasises the capacity of religious groups to represent their community interests to government and facilitates the implementation of policies among their local communities. Participation in LSPs is a key example of this. The governance approach tends to be favoured by local stakeholders;
- a normative focus, which has gained least presence in policy rhetoric and in some ways is the least understood since it emphasises the way in which the moral values and vision of religious welfare organisations can help improve social welfare. The normative focus tends to be emphasised by religious groups themselves. However, tokenistic appreciation of it by policy makers may be seen in the use of concepts such as social capital and civic renewal.

Nevertheless, various authors caution against a rosy view of partnership between the state and religious organisations. Lukka and Locke (2000), Farnell et al (2003), Davis et al (2008) and Bretherton (2010) warn against a variety of challenges, namely that:

- government underestimates some of the difficulties that religious groups face in accessing government resources since they do not necessarily have the expertise and resources for making grant applications, nor are they always comfortable with the ethos of competitive commissioning which can create greater social conflict among religious organisations as they find themselves forced to compete for funds;
- government does not quite yet fully understand the way in which religious organisations work or what the impact of their services are; this includes recognition of the role of spirituality and faith in social welfare at a time when the focus of government is on the cost-efficient and administrative effectiveness of religious organisations in delivering social assistance services. Religious groups themselves

may not quite appreciate what government expectations are of them or what is entailed in the regeneration partnerships they enter into with local government;

- in the process of developing closer links with the state and accepting their new functions of service delivery, religious organisations may become more alienated from their local membership or have to change their identities and methods of work.

Bretherton (2010) concludes, therefore, that a new form of establishment may be emerging in the UK whereby religious groups including the church are subordinated to the state and have to substantially compromise their religious missions in order to meet the efficiency goals of social welfare provision. This contrasts with the older forms of church establishment in the UK where the church maintained its identity and cooperated with the state on a more equal footing. There is a process of secularisation and instrumentalisation at play here that is counter-productive for the agenda of social transformation and respect of diversity (Bretherton, 2010).

Under the Coalition government, the Big Society rhetoric is offering opportunities for religious organisations to access government funding more directly. The 'right to challenge' and 'right to provide' clauses mean that any private or community-based organisation may be able to take over the provision of services from local authorities if they have the capacity. Research conducted for this book with key advisers and spokespeople from central government show that faith groups are considered to be part and parcel of the voluntary sector. This may have both positive and negative dimensions as it may be that the issue of ignoring specific contributions by faith groups in social welfare will continue to be missed in policy-making circles. The establishment of more faith schools and city academies that are often run by faith groups have also featured in the Coalition's legislative programme.

It is useful to note that Iain Duncan Smith, present Secretary of State for Work and Pensions, is sympathetic to faith-based social welfare provision. The *Breakthrough Britain* (SPJG, 2007) report that involved policy recommendations to the Conservative Party dedicated a section of its sixth volume on the third sector to faith-based organisations. The report calls on statutory bodies to judge religious welfare organisations by the 'effectiveness of their results'. It argues that government needs to create a level playing field for religious organisations by creating appropriate legislation which protects religious organisations against discrimination; providing funds directly to religious welfare organisations, 'even if they conduct religious activities, as long as these activities are optional' (SJPG, 2007, p 71); and establishing with commissioning authorities a common minimum standard of governance to which religious organisations would adhere to while maintaining their distinctive religious character. The report advocates the adoption of a charter proposed by the leading Christian charity, Oasis, called the Faithworks Charter, which establishes standards of faith-based welfare provision and commissioning (see www.faithworks. info/about-us/faithworks-charter).

Thus, under New Labour, we saw a preliminary phase of introducing religious organisations into the social welfare sphere with an array of formal publications and national guidelines that began to set the terms for better engagement with statutory bodies. Under the Coalition government, we are seeing faith-based organisations being mainstreamed like their secular volunteer counterparts through national legislation such as the Localism Act. David Cameron himself is quoted as telling church groups they are right to claim that Jesus invented the Big Society 2,000 years ago (House of Commons Report, 2011). And, as a senior member of his administration remarked in an interview to me in 2011,

> 'New Labour was perhaps accused of taking a more instrumental approach towards faith-based organisations whereas for this government, we are just letting them do what they have already been doing.'

Conclusion

This chapter has discussed the contemporary social and political profile of religion in Britain. First, it examined the religious profile of British society drawing on 2001 Census data that highlighted that three quarters of the British population considered themselves to belong to a particular faith tradition. Furthermore, a variety of surveys show that religion remains of deep significance to believer, especially among minority religious groups. In Britain, Christianity has a strong cultural character that allows it to be both latent and pervasive in the national British identity.

Second, available data from the 2001 Census were explored on the religious profile of social deprivation and poverty in the UK. This showed that Muslim communities were the worst off in terms of educational achievements and self-reported health, and in terms of levels of employment.

Third, the current position of religion in UK government policy was examined – so far, the New Labour government was much more active than the present Coalition government in publishing guidelines and frameworks for government engagement with faith groups. In part this may be explained by the preoccupation of the Coalition with public sector reform. Hence, while the Coalition government may be downsizing public agencies, it is opening up direct routes for faith communities to participate fully in special welfare provision through, for example, the Localism Act 2011. Thus, while the Big Society rhetoric bodes well for religious organisations to participate in social welfare provision, big questions continue to loom over the capacity and desire of religious organisations to engage with government and to deliver services, the understanding and critical evaluation on the part of government as to what religious organisations can deliver and how far faith itself can be factored into this critical evaluation of what religious organisations can achieve. The deep concern of the Coalition government with the moral health of the nation, evident during the riots in England in August 2011, are likely to strengthen the role of the churches and religious groups in upholding community peace and harmony.

In a sense, then, social policy in the UK has come full circle. In the mid-20th century, the Church of England gave up its dominion over social welfare and oversaw the establishment of a secular and comprehensive state-led welfare system. In the early 21st century, the state is looking again to the church and new minority faith groups to play a part in social welfare provision.

In the second part of this book, a group of chapters offer an overview of what religious organisations are achieving in the key social welfare sectors.

Questions for discussion

1. How religious is the British population?
2. How does religion map onto social deprivation and poverty in the UK?
3. What are the strengths and shortcomings of government policy in relation to religious organisations in the provision of social welfare?
4. Should religious organisations be eligible for government grants?
5. Do all religious organisations want to engage with government? Why or why not?

Useful websites

Church of Scotland, Church and Society Council: www.churchofscotland.org.uk/about_us/councils_committees_and_departments/church_and_society_council

Department for Communities and Local Government: www.communities.gov.uk/corporate/

UK Interfaith Network: www.interfaith.org.uk/

English Regional Faith Forums Network: www.erffn.org.uk/

Faith Communities Forum (part of the National Welsh Assembly): http://cymru.gov.uk/topics/equality/rightsequality/faith/faithforum/%3Bjsessionid=nJhvLsyFhQs5CDwqdkhRPKC17sQpZm2HXGyRy95bh8t41GB3kyHv!-1718541967?lang=en&status=open

Inter-Faith Council for Wales: www.interfaithwales.org/index.php?pageid=15

Local Government Association: www.lga.gov.uk/lga/core/page.do?pageId=1

Northern Ireland Inter-Faith Forum: http://niinterfaithforum.org/index.php?option=com_content&view=frontpage&Itemid=65

Scottish Inter Faith Council: www.scottishinterfaithcouncil.org/index.html

The Church in Wales: www.churchinwales.org.uk/index_e.php

Notes

[1] This figure was cited in a speech by Baroness Warsi and is discussed further as more precise estimates do not exist.

[2] The 1851 Census of Religion was carried out separately to the national census. In Northern Ireland, a question about religious affiliation has been present in the census since the Census Act 1969 as well as the need to monitor more closely the situation of religious communities.

[3] As McAndrew (2010, p 99) notes, the 19th-century Liberal Party was part of a non-conformist movement, and popular discourses describe the Labour Party as owing more to Methodism than Marxism, with the Church of England once famously being dubbed the 'Conservative Party at prayer' (Thatcher, 1990).

[4] Cited in the Scottish Council for Voluntary Organisations (SCVO) (www.scvo.org.uk/tfn/news/the-future-of-giving-caf-column-by-cathy-pharoah/). See also the Charity Trends website (www.charitytrends.org) for the 2004 trends report.

[5] Based on a website search of the Office of the Scottish Charity Regulator on 29 July 2011 (www.oscr.org.uk/).

[6] Subsequent to the report, the church also established the Commission on Urban Life and Faith (www.churchofengland.org/media-centre/news/2004/02/new_commission_on_urban_life_and_faith_launched.aspx) as a way of continuing to engage with issues of urban regeneration.

[7] Furness and Gilligan (2010) provide a detailed discussion of legislation in relation to various vulnerable groups such as older people, people with disabilities, children, young people and asylum-seekers. All these emphasise the need to take the religious views and identity of clients into account, particularly in the field of social and health care.

Part II

Sector-specific religious welfare
provision in the current UK context

FOUR

Social work and social action

Summary

- Social work has religious roots dating back to the 19th century but has shed them in favour of social scientific methods that have resulted in religion becoming a taboo subject.
- Social work research in the UK has made great strides in the last decade in raising awareness among social work teachers and students of the significance of religion and how to assess it in the lives of clients. Social policy research could learn valuable lessons from this.
- Social work and social action are deeply connected and this is evident among religious organisations that see themselves as offering more than just a service to their clients, and are part of more fundamental processes that enhance and empower their local communities.
- Religious welfare organisations need to be conceptualised as offering both a social welfare *service* and *services*. The former refers to a spiritual act of selfless help for the common good, deeply rooted in theological teachings about the purpose of human life; the second is a functional exercise of transferring that help in a material way through resources and activities in order to solve social problems and satisfy apparent needs.

Introduction

We start our review of the contribution of religion and religious organisations to social welfare by looking first at the social work profession. It is also apt to begin with social work because the empirical research which this book draws on will help illustrate fundamental characteristics about the nature of religious welfare provision and social action which will help illuminate the concept of *ways of being* proposed in this book.

Together with education, social work is a central plank of religious welfare activity. In the British academic literature, it is the subject of social work that has surpassed its cousin, social policy, in engaging with the implications of religion and spirituality for human wellbeing. In part, this may be explained by the physical proximity of social work to people's lives and the increased need to pay attention to minority ethnic populations, some of who are among the poorest and least well-integrated populations in the UK. The previous chapter has already outlined that there are high levels of deprivation among the Muslim population, so it is not a surprise that one of the more recent social work publications in the UK is in relation to Islam (see Ashencaen-Crabtree et al, 2008).

The term 'social work' is used here in the broad sense of the profession of social work which began to take shape in the 19th century, and also in the more generic reference to a wide variety of social services which seek to offer help to individuals and communities dealing with various social problems ranging from bereavement, imprisonment and resettlement as an immigrant or refugee. In many ways, the term acts as a catch-all phrase that helps to define the emerging role of religious organisations in social welfare. Social action is another way of referring to the work of religious organisations (Wallis, 2002), which stems from the deep tradition of community organising and solidarity with the deprived that can be found in all the religious traditions. Indeed, Bowpitt (1998) notes that, originally, the term 'social work' and the development of the profession began as a notion of social action which was different to two other spheres that have an impact on human wellbeing: individual spiritual regeneration and state intervention. This new conceptualisation is linked to the work of the Charity Organisation Society and in particular, the writings of Helen Bosanquet, who described a new form of social action aimed at helping other people and not at personal spiritual benefit, like Victorian philanthropy (Bowpitt, 1998). Crucially, this new form of social action depended on the use of methods of social scientific enquiry that were rational and practical in nature. Hence, as Bowpitt (1998, p 683) puts it: 'a secular approach to charity produced a professional approach to social work'.

It is interesting to note that in countries where social policy and the welfare state are not well developed (such as in Africa or the Middle East), religious organisations often refer to what they do as social work, which they also closely correlate to the concept of social service (Jawad, 2009). These issues highlight the deep affective elements that drive religious welfare which are not necessarily amenable to rational exploration, much in the same vein as the argument by Hay (2006) and Gilligan (2010) that the issues which explain human action may not be easy to articulate or analyse empirically – hence the usefulness of a baggy term like social work for religious organisations.

A diversity of issues are explored in this chapter. On the one hand, the chapter looks at how social work as an academic subject and professional field is re-engaging with issues of religion and spirituality in the UK. To this end, there is a focus on two case illustrations: prison chaplaincy and bereavement counselling. On the other hand, it looks at a much broader notion of social action which is very pertinent to how religious organisations often define what they do in the UK, and it expands the term of social work to reflect on ways in which religious organisations see themselves as having a broader impact on society beyond service provision. In some ways, therefore, this chapter overlaps thematically with the chapter on social care (Chapter 6), and it is difficult to disentangle the community action orientation from the caring orientation of religious organisations.

Social work, religion and spirituality: re-engaging the profession

The social work literature in the UK has become quite engaged with the role of religion and spirituality in the last decade (Bowpitt, 1998, 2000; Moss, 2005, Zahl et al, 2007; Ashencaen Crabtree et al, 2008; Whiting, 2008; Mathews, 2009; Furness and Gilligan, 2010; Holloway and Moss, 2010; Coleman, 2011). Many authors begin with the neglect of social work professionals to consider the role of religion in the lives of the children, adults, families and the communities they work with. This neglect has been both intentional, with social workers either not comfortable with discussing religion or dismissive of its impact, and also latent, due in large part to the secular orientation of the profession since its emergence. Holloway and Moss (2010) describe mainstream social workers as having a 'tick box' approach to religion, whereby it is one aspect of their client's identity that they ask about but never delve into more deeply. Indeed, in many cases social workers have also treated religion as part of the problem, finding it difficult to engage with, especially if religion is mixed with culture and there is some form of suffering that results from particular religious/cultural values (Ashencaen Crabtree et al, 2008).

Various surveys have taken place in the UK recently, following the North American trend on how accepting social workers are of the role of religion in the lives of their clients and how actively they engage with issues of religiosity in their work (for a fuller discussion, see Furman et al, 2005; Zahl et al, 2007; Furness and Gilligan, 2010; Holloway and Moss, 2010). Furman et al's (2005) small study of professional social workers in Britain found that 47 per cent of respondents thought it was appropriate to include considerations of religion in social work practice. In the Zahl et al (2007, p 303) study, 56 per cent of the British social workers surveyed responded they were Christian out of a total of

63 per cent who professed to having a religious affiliation. Almost 80 per cent of respondents agreed that spirituality was a fundamental part of human nature, although it needed to be engaged with sensitively and critically (Zahl et al, 2007). Furness and Gilligan (2010) also report back on findings of a survey they conducted in 2002 with social workers in the UK regarding the role of religion in their lives. This corroborates the findings of previous research highlighted above, but more importantly shows social work education and training to be lacking in sufficient attention to these topics.

The concern of social work researchers with the extent to which religion forms a part of social work practice is the source of heated debate surrounding the education and training of social workers in Britain. Moss (2005) and Furness and Gilligan (2010) discuss the findings of various studies that report students seeing religion as a taboo topic (Furness and Gilligan, 2010, p 8), even if they might be personally sympathetic to religion. Social work education in the UK has not yet achieved a level whereby it is able to train students adequately to do '"spiritually competent" social work practice', according to Furness and Gilligan (2010, p 7), and there is disagreement over what to include in the social work curriculum regarding religion. However, some attempts have been made since the late 1990s to improve the curriculum for social work on matters of religion and spirituality (for more detailed discussion, see Moss, 2005; Furness and Gilligan, 2010).

Yet historically, matters were different. Bowpitt (1998, 2000), in his review of the roots of social work in Victorian Christian philanthropy and its emergence as a secular profession in the UK in the late 19th century, notes the often-cited phrase of social work being intrinsic to the identity of the church and inseparable from the message of the Gospels (Whiting, 2008). Indeed, Bowpitt (1998, p 689) notes: 'there are three areas in which the revival of explicitly Christian *methods* is visible: Christian counselling, neighbourhood work and residential communities'. Likewise, in other Abrahamic (Judaism and Islam) or Dharmic faiths (Buddhism, Sikhism, Hinduism, Jainism), social work is seen as fundamental to notions of social justice and social care (Gilligan, 2010). Indeed, Gilligan alerts us to the fact that, as in the US, the UK has a long-standing professional social work organisation for practitioners who are of Christian faith, called the Social Work Christian Fellowship (SWCF) (www.swcf.org.uk/), established in 1964 'to encourage Biblical reflection on social issues, social work theory and practice'.

Gilligan (2010) proposes a typology of faith-based social work that he denotes as 'fundamentalist or exclusive' and 'liberal or open'. An organisation like SWCF would be classed in the first type because its religious faith (Christian) is part and parcel of the social worker's professional ethics and identity and is applied directly to the solution of social problems being dealt with. According to this view, Gilligan (2010) argues, religious faith is not merely the route to salvation but also the source of a fulfilling life on earth.

Box 4.1: Two types of faith-based social work

1. 'Fundamentalist or exclusive': religious faith is essential to the identity and professional ethics of the social worker and to the methods they use in solving social problems and dealing with clients; clients are encouraged to take on board aspects of the faith in order to move on with their lives, hence in many cases the social workers and the clients are likely to share similar if not the same religious views (example: SWCF).

2. 'Liberal or open': religious faith is primarily a source of inspiration for social workers and religious welfare organisations but it does not form a determining part of the work that the organisation and the social workers do. Clients and members of staff do not need to share the same beliefs of the organisation (example: Barnardo's).

Source: Gilligan (2010)

The research conducted in the UK for this book would indicate that the typology offered by Gilligan exists in a much more nuanced and intertwined manner. Many religious organisations combine both approaches in Box 4.1, depending on the types of services they offer. The Faith Regen Foundation (Muslim) and The Salvation Army (Christian) are two such examples. Both operate an array of services including employment contracts for the government's Work Programme. Here, junior members of staff, for instance, the staff directly in charge of work placements or training, may not necessarily share the same religious creed as the organisation. Indeed, the clients come from all walks of life; in a sense this is expected as these are government contracts that Faith Regen and the Army take on. At the same time, both organisations run other social work services or religious activities that are more targeted at their own religious communities and require some religious element in them.

It is also quite commonly the case that religious organisations may have dual identities: most senior staff and policy directors who lead a religious welfare organisation tend to share the same religious conviction, but personnel further down the ladder in the organisations may be more diverse in terms of their religious beliefs. Again, this might make sense in terms of safeguarding the ethos of an organisation but keeping it open and in touch with outside society. Thus, we find that religious organisations are varied in terms of how they locate religion in their identity as an organisation and how they communicate their religious convictions to the outside world.

Why should social work take religion into account?

Basic precepts of ethical social work practice point to the need to take religion into consideration. The basic premise of casework, of dealing with each individual as a whole person taking into account the person's background and needs, and respecting their basic human dignity, emanates from basic Judeo-Christian precepts, according to Bowpitt (1998). Increasingly, authors are arguing for a new kind of approach to social work that focuses on the strengths of service users, rather than the traditional focus on isolated needs and problems (Moss, 2005; Ashencaen-Crabtree et al, 2008; Furness and Gilligan, 2010).

At the most basic level, legislation requires this of them (Furness and Gilligan, 2010). The prevention of discrimination is a central concern in social work, and legislation has mirrored this concern, but more recently it has sought to actively protect religious freedom as a factor contributing to human welfare (Furness and Gilligan, 2010).[1] Furness and Gilligan (2010, p 5) cite the General Social Care Council's 2002 Code of Practice for social care workers which requires social workers 'to protect the rights and to promote the interests of service users and carers' as well as 'treating each person as an individual' and 'respecting diversity and different cultures and values'. Moss (2005, p 47) reminds social workers of Article 9 in the Human Rights Act 1998 about protecting the practice of religious freedom, as well as legislation in England and Wales for 'looked after' children, such as section 22(4) of the Children Act 1989, which requires that the religious background of children be taken into account by social workers. Similar statements can be found in the Children (Scotland) Act 1995 and the Children (Northern Ireland) Order 1995, which also state that the child's religious views must take priority (Furness and Gilligan, 2010). Gilliat-Ray (2003, p 335) cites the first Standard in the UK Department of Health's 1991 Patient's Charter, which stipulates 'respect for privacy, dignity and religious and cultural beliefs'.

Indeed, Mathews (2009, pp 8-10) notes that social work is increasingly concerned with health care and the promotion of healthy lifestyles. Much research in North America, and increasingly in the UK, argues that religious belief and practice are good for personal health (Moss, 2005; Mathews, 2009). According to Mathews (2009) and Moss (2005), these are further reasons why social work needs to take religion and spirituality seriously since they can lead to better health outcomes, and a more holistic assessment of clients' needs.

The latter point is essential to social work practice as highlighted in Holloway and Moss (2010). There are two key issues here which these authors raise: that there is a spiritual dimension to human needs and that addressing these is part of the task of making social work not just person-centred but able to help individuals and families achieve a sense of 'wholeness' in their lives. This is a key difference in the interpretation of 'holistic practice' in current Department of Health guidance, according to Holloway and Moss (2010). Holloway and Moss (2010, pp 47-8) argue that social work practice has tended to take a narrow view of need, understood as a problem or an *unmet need* that requires a particular service to be provided. They advocate an approach whereby needs are defined jointly by service users and social workers, but in order for spiritual needs to gain legitimacy as a field of intervention for social workers, it is the service users themselves who should express this need, as has been the case in mental health services. Acknowledging that this is a very difficult concept to define, Holloway and Moss offer the following definition for spiritual need:

> ... the need to find meaning and to experience peace and reconciliation in life in general and in particular circumstances and relationships. (Holloway and Moss, 2010, p 48)

Holloway and Moss (2010) also note that social workers should follow the lead of service users in defining spirituality and *spiritual need* in their own ways. Spiritual needs vary from purely religious ones such as attending church and praying, to the need to have a sense of meaning and purpose in one's life, to issues of love and lack of belonging, to the desire for moral standing and credibility. Box 4.2 sets these out clearly.

At the heart of spiritual need, Holloway and Moss (2010, pp 49, 50) argue, are other symptoms commonly referred to in the social work literature as *spiritual pain* or *distress*, also expressed as *existential pain* or *distress*. The defining feature of these is 'a sense of alienation, dissonance or deep conflict in the inner self' (Holloway and Moss, 2010, p 51).

Thus, problems of social and economic deprivation, combined with experience of abuse or discrimination, can typically lead to this kind of spiritual distress. The task of the social worker is, therefore, to 'maintain the spirit' (Holloway and Moss, 2010, p 51) of the client so that the latter does not lose hope completely and give up.

Box 4.2: What is spiritual need?

1. Religious needs, for example, going to church or praying
2. Making sense of one's life and having a sense of purpose
3. Lack of love or belonging
4. Distress related to death and dying
5. Moral standing and credibility

Source: Holloway and Moss (2010)

Related to the idea of need, we look at the aspiration to 'wholeness' that social workers aim to help service users achieve. Ashencaen-Crabtree et al (2008, p 41) also corroborate this idea of wholeness, noting the ultimate spiritual status within Islamic teaching of *al-insan al-kamil* (whole human being), which is achieved by following *al-sirat al mustaqim* (the straight path). Holloway and Moss (2010) argue that the social work profession needs to resist the move towards fragmented and unit-based monitoring and evaluation, which is now the predominant work culture in health and social care. Instead, it needs to adopt a 'systems' approach that takes into consideration the way in which external social structures are shaping people's lives and the services they use. Thus, a focus on spirituality allows for more holistic evaluation of needs because it operates at personal, social and political levels. Wholeness is more than the sum of the part in the person's life; it has a transcendent quality since it allows those receiving social work assistance to move beyond their situation and rebuild a new life for themselves (Holloway and Moss, 2010, p 105). It is a new *way of being*.

This leads to the strengths-based approach that many social work commentators are now advocating as a motivating factor for looking at religion (Moss, 2005; Ashencaen Crabtree et al, 2008; Furness and Gilligan, 2010). Social work has traditionally focused on needs and social problems, with the social worker acting as the expert coming to help a person solve their problem and get back on track. But factoring religion into social work practice helps to identify potential sources of strengths in people's lives, moral values they may hold dear or beliefs and practices that matter to them which can help them cope with a difficult situation. Religion is very often one such source of hope and meaning.

Besides moral and value-related issues, religion is a basic demographic indicator of social circumstances that matter a great deal for social work (Furness and Gilligan, 2010; Jolley and Moreland, 2011). For example, the ONS notes the strong correlation between there being a Muslim head of household and children living in the same household (cited in Furness and Gilligan, 2010, p 17). Moreover, religious faith is connected to attitudes about important social issues such as adoption, sex, abortion and euthanasia – these emphasise the importance of religion as a source of self-identity to a greater degree than ethnicity or 'race' (2001 Home Office Citizenship Survey, cited in Furness and Gilligan, 2010, p 17). So how can better appreciation of the role of religion in human life and identity be put into practice?

How can social work take religion into account?

Social work is an applied field of practice and various practitioners/ authors have put forward frameworks and models to aid social workers in assessing the religious and spiritual dimensions or needs of the lives of their clients, as well as integrating better awareness of religion into their practice. Furness and Gilligan (2010) refer to this exercise as equipping social workers with better 'cultural competence', and emphasise a standard argument in social work practice that even if some social workers are not sympathetic to religious belief and practice, they need to be able to engage with religious issues in order to offer their clients the best support possible. Holloway and Moss (2010) focus on integrating spirituality into social work practice and equipping social workers with ways in which they can properly assess the positive and negative aspects of spirituality in the lives of their clients. Moss (2005) proposes what he refers to as a PCSS analysis that basically outlines the personal, cultural, structural and spiritual dimensions to the social worker's assessment of a client's situation.

All of these authors offer a version of the basic approach within the North American tradition of assessing the spiritual aspects of service users' lives revolving around the following questions, shown in Box 4.3.

Box 4.3: Spirituality assessment questions I

1. I was wondering if spirituality of religion is important to you?
2. Are there certain spiritual beliefs or practices that you find particularly helpful in dealing with problems?
3. Are there any spiritual needs or concerns I can help you with?

Source: Ashencaen Crabtree et al (2008, p 61)

These questions emanate from the strengths-based approach mentioned above since they are intended to explore the service user's own view of religion and how service users may potentially call on it as a positive resource in their life. Holloway and Moss (2010, p 56) discuss a North American variant of these questions used by family doctors, called the HOPE questions. These are outlined in Box 4.4 and differ from the types of questions in Box 4.3 in the sense that they do not directly ask clients about the role of religion in their lives, but allow for a more 'natural' progression of discussion into issues of religion if the client takes the conversation that way (Holloway and Moss, 2010, p 56).

Box. 4.4: Spirituality assessment questions 2: HOPE questions

1. H: Sources of hope, meaning, comfort, strength, peace, love and connection
2. O: Organised religion
3. P: Personal spirituality ad practices
4. E: Effects on medical care and end-of-life issues

Source: Holloway and Moss (2010, p 56)

Religious organisations that are involved in social welfare work also devise their own assessment models. In the research conducted for this book, The Salvation Army was one such organisation that is now piloting a new form of assessment of the needs of clients and how they have progressed through the services provided to them. This takes into account the service user's spiritual progression. Jewell (2004, p 23) also gives the example of the Methodist Homes for the Aged (MHA), which uses a spiritual model called 'Nourishing the Inner Being' that helps social workers categorise aspects of wellbeing and ill-being in older people's lives and helps them progress through Christian spirituality to the spirituality of different faith traditions to more universal expressions of human spirituality (Jewell, 2004).

We end this section by returning to Furness and Gilligan's (2010) 'cultural competence framework' in order to sum up the various ways in which the spiritual sensitivity of social workers may be achieved as well as gaining a better sense of the actual role that religion plays in the lives of their clients. These authors remind us that social work can make a very important contribution to human wellbeing in the cultural domain, as opposed to the economic domain, by highlighting how issues of social recognition and cultural values have a dramatic effect on personal and social wellbeing. They also note that much of the emerging literature on frameworks for assessing cultural and spiritual needs emanate from the healthcare literature, and it will become evident in Chapter 5 how instrumental mental health issues have been in highlighting the importance of religion and spirituality to human wellbeing.

Furness and Gilligan (2010) discuss a variety of models that they categorise into *reflective* models aimed at enhancing the practitioner's professional competence and *assessment* models (examples of which are in Boxes 4.3 and 4.4) that are tools that social workers can use for collecting information about the clients. Different types of reflective and assessment models are discussed in more detail in Furness and Gilligan, and highlight the importance of 'religious literacy' among social workers, which is an issue that has also been referred to in the previous chapter. Furness and Gilligan (2010, p 44) propose a more comprehensive framework which is a combination of both reflexive and assessment-type models which they argue can be applied at all stages of social work practice (assessment, planning intervention and evaluation) and crucially, can be integrated into the existing frameworks of assessment advocated by the Department of Health. This model rests on nine principles such as that assessments should be person-centred and strengths-based. These principles need to be underpinned by personal reflection on the part of social workers about how sensitive they are to the religious and spiritual matters raised by their clients. We now move to two illustrations of the way in which religious organisations are active in various types of social work activities, looking at prison chaplaincy and bereavement counselling – the vulnerable groups in question are prison inmates and bereaved older people.

Illustration 1: Prison chaplaincy, the case of Muslim chaplains

Prison chaplaincy has gained the attention of researchers since it offers some important insights into the role of religion in social work, and the changing effect of religious and ethnic diversity in the UK on the primacy of the Church of England as the established church. The case of Muslim chaplains has been especially researched in the last decade, partly since Muslims prisoners are substantially larger in number in comparison to their proportion of the British population, and also because Muslim chaplains are seen as a new breed of professional Muslim clerics, with the potential to act as positive leaders of Muslim communities, both in terms of their capacity as theologians and also in terms of their social position in British society (Beckford, 2001, 2005; Gilliat-Ray, 2008).

The Church of England has had a privileged position for the last 200 years of being responsible for prison chaplaincy services in England and Wales (Beckford, 2001, 2005). Its role involves active engagement with policy makers and also the provision of chaplaincy services to non-Christian inmates by acting as a 'broker' to facilitate their access to non-Christian chaplains (Beckford, 2005, p 291). The lead role of the Church of England was established legally through the Prison Act 1952, which stipulates that an Anglican clergyman must be present in every prison. Combined with the fact that nearly half of all Anglican clergy are full-time prison chaplains (and therefore civil servants), thereby outnumbering clergy from other Christian faiths, they have tended to be seen as the 'natural' representatives of the prison chaplaincy service. Until the late 1990s, the involvement of minority faiths in prison chaplaincy was haphazard and poorly organised, with the title of 'visiting minister' being used to refer to individuals carrying out these services who were from other faiths. This situation created some dissatisfaction among the visiting ministers and non-Christian prisoners who felt that their religious needs, such as for prayer or religious worship, were not being met (Beckford, 2001).

In the Muslim case, the situation changed with the appointment of a Muslim adviser to the Prison Service Chaplaincy Headquarters in 1999, who was able to focus more attention and resources on the religious needs of Muslim inmates (Gilliat-Ray, 2008). Access to religious support, *halal* meat as well as adherence to Islamic prayer and ritual practices were therefore facilitated as full-time and part-time posts for professional Muslim chaplains were created. As Gilliat-Ray (2008, pp 148-9) recounts, in 2003, the title of Muslim chaplain was officially conferred on Muslims involved in prison chaplaincy; by 2007, there were in total 34 full-time and 15 part-time Muslim chaplains looking after the welfare of 8,789 Muslim prisoners across the 138 prison establishments in England and Wales. At the same time, Muslims themselves were becoming better equipped with language and training skills to be able to perform their chaplaincy roles in a more professional capacity. In the Qur'an (the Muslim Holy Book), the sayings of the Prophet Mohamad give ample guidance for chaplaincy work, such as 'Help your brother whether he is oppressed or an oppressor' (cited in Gilliat-Ray, 2008, p 146).

As a result of these developments, the structure of prison chaplaincy in England and Wales has changed and now includes national committees and resource groups that have active input or, in some cases, represent the Muslim chaplains. Gilliat-Ray (2008) offers an important assessment of the broader sociopolitical significance of Muslim chaplains in Britain. She argues that as well as fulfilling the important social work function of supporting Muslim inmates, especially when family ties break down, and helping them reintegrate into society when they leave prison, the role of Muslim chaplains as a new professional breed of theologically trained British Muslims will be important for articulating a new discourse of Islamic identity in Britain.

Illustration 2: Bereavement counselling

Death and dying are important dimensions of social work practice (Holloway, 2006). As well as the grief and sense of loss that are felt, the incidence of death and dying raises perennial questions about the meaning and purpose of life — fertile territory for issues of spirituality and religion. This illustration considers bereavement counselling using the example of older people who have lost their spouse or partner, based on Coleman's (2011) innovative longitudinal research. Coleman notes that the loss of a loved one is a crisis point that can either strengthen or weaken religious faith, and this is a matter that has become increasingly concentrated in the later stages of life as people live longer.

Bereavement counselling is an activity that many faith-based organisations are involved in. It is especially important to be sensitive to cultural practices and values in relation to issues of dying and loss as there are obvious practical implications for how people are buried or how family or social relations pan out in different cultures. In the UK, religious belief is most common among older people; indeed, as mentioned in the previous chapter, there is an inter-generational gap in religious belief in the UK. Coleman (2011) and Furness and Gilligan (2010) provide some useful discussion of the role of religion and spirituality among older people. According to the 2001 Census data, around 60 per cent of respondents saying they belonged to Christian faith were in the 35–64 and 65 and over year groups (Furness and Gilligan, 2010). Coleman (2011) reports on other surveys which estimate that people over the age of 60 report themselves to be around 66 per cent Christian. It should be noted that people of this generation would be likely to have attended Sunday schools. Among minority ethnic populations, the elderly population is much less smaller, partly due to patterns of immigration and larger proportions of a younger minority ethnic generation (Furness and Gilligan, 2010).

In the context of bereavement, religion can be a very important coping mechanism (Spreadbury and Coleman, 2011, p 79). Spreadbury and Coleman (2011) cite a variety of studies in the last decade which show that older people with moderate or low levels of belief, whether this was of a religious or atheist nature, were more likely to suffer from depression after losing their loved one. The authors discuss four different ways in which older people use their religious faith to cope with spousal loss: benevolent religious cognition, which are the core religious beliefs that people have such as that death is part of God's will to which they must submit; biblical assurances, which refers to the reference to passages or verses in the Bible as sources of inspiration to cope during bereavement; religious ritual, which refers to the actual practice of various religious activities such as prayer, using rosaries or lighting candles; and spiritual capital, which is especially pertinent to the role of faith-based organisations.

Here, Spreadbury and Coleman (2011) argue that participating in activities on behalf of one's church is a therapeutic way of dealing with bereavement and rebuilding lives after the loss of a spouse or close family member. Spiritual capital is thus defined by Spreadbury and Coleman (2011, p 91) as 'a source of community wealth or capital that all church members can part own through investment of personal time in performing jobs, roles of activities on behalf of or related to the church'. These activities may include being a welcomer, sacristan or lay pastor and very often they would be in a volunteering capacity where the bereaved person may come into contact with others less fortunate and help themselves spiritually by helping other people.

Religion and social action: social work as 'more than a service'

The two illustrations above show that the boundaries between service provider and service user are not so clear-cut in the sphere of religious welfare. As the case of bereaved older people shows, volunteering in a faith-based organisation has a potential positive impact on both the volunteer and the person being helped.

The engagement of social work practitioners with their local communities and the attachment of the social work profession to aims such as social transformation are important factors in understanding the social action of religious organisations. Here, the chapter draws on new empirical research conducted during 2009–10 with religious organisations in England and Wales about what their social engagement meant to them from their religious perspective. The key idea as expressed by one leading Sikh organisation was that religious organisations were delivering more than just a service; they were transmitting positive values about human respect, dignity, fellowship and social harmony.

Several concepts emerged as important to the religious welfare organisations that took part in the research. First was the idea that values were important. Whether they ran something simple like a soup kitchen or were a sub-contractor in the Work Programme, religious organisations saw themselves as doing more than just delivering a service. They were serving society selflessly, often through the direct sacrifices that they made of their own personal time and resources. The quotes below illustrate these. Moreover, religious groups pointed to other non-material and spiritual dimensions of human wellbeing such as human dignity and self-worth. To this end, the strength of their approach to human wellbeing was in focusing on the whole person:

> '… the people [who use our services] take away more than the service, they take away values. Our philosophy is based on *seva*: selfless service.' (Senior manager of a Sikh centre)

> '… service is an act of corporate worship … the building that you are sitting in here has come mostly from people's pockets … there is a high degree of personal sacrifice for the benefit of others.' (Church leader)

A practical example of the way in which religious organisations sought to transfer something more fundamental than the functional delivery of a service is illustrated by the example below, which juxtaposes statutory services in relation to teenage pregnancy to religious groups:

> '… we're touching hundreds of children and talking to them about rearing and raising children. Now we don't do the healthcare visitor type stuff: how to change a nappy, how to feed a child, how to keep them warm. It's more to do with the emotional, mental, security, development of the child. The role of the father and the role of the mother.' (Church leader)

> '... we are very concerned with the whole human being;
> this does not mean that we force our views on them or
> anything but we would pray for them and so on and we
> would be interested in them as whole not just the problems
> they come with.' (Christian counselling group)

Key to these understandings of service were 'relationships' and the
emotional bonds religious welfare organisations developed with the
people they served by living among them and with them as part of the
same community. This sense of belonging to the local community was
seen to be lacking in statutory services, as illustrated below:

> 'The strengths of faith groups are in the relationships
> that they build. They pay more attention to detail.' (Local
> authority officer)

> 'We are not professionals being brought in. We live here,
> we know the neighbours ... we are home-grown stuff.'
> (Church leader)

This deep commitment to the local communities that they served
and the emotional ties that religious groups developed and sought to
nurture must be understood in terms of the religious motivations that
drove them. These illustrate how notions of social justice and truth are
closely intertwined in the mindsets of religious welfare organisations,
meaning that the desire to help others is not simply because others
are in need of that help but because believers are commanded by their
religion to be socially active: "service is corporate worship", as noted
above, and below:

> 'We have this sprawling of estates, an increasingly challenging
> environment yet there seems to be no strong church there
> that (a) was of a contemporary nature that could connect
> with the unchurched people, and secondly that has a
> strategic intenationality about it to identify local needs,
> partner with others, and seek to serve its community....
> So that was the understanding and the rationale of why
> we moved here, combined with that the sense that we felt
> God was in it and there was this sense of personal calling
> as well.' (Church leader)

For religious groups of immigrant backgrounds, such as Muslims, Hindus or Sikhs, involvement in social action and social welfare provision took on the added role of a social statement and a chance to gain social standing. Indeed, several of the organisations and individuals involved in this research had gained awards or prizes for their work from the Queen. For them, this gave credence to their mission of showing to the wider society that their communities were no longer guests in the UK but contributing and integrating positively. These minority ethnic religious groups were often the first port of call for newly arrived immigrants and many of them offered the English language proficiency qualification, ESOL (English for speakers of other languages) and citizenship training, for a small fee.

> 'As a Muslim-inspired organisation, we want to show that we are giving something back, not just taking.' (Leader of a Muslim organisation)

> 'We want to give a good image of the local area. There were riots here in the 1980s.' (Leader of a Sikh organisation)

These citations echo various poignant arguments in the social work literature. For example, Mathews (2009) notes that social work emphasises values such as empowerment, choice, dignity and respect that form a spiritual foundation for the social work profession. To this end, spirituality forms the basis of human relationships as well as individual conduct (Mathews, 2009; Holloway and Moss, 2010). Moreover, the concern with human relationships and community is mirrored in the Christian notion of the Holy Trinity – God the father, the son and the Holy Spirit – according to Bowpitt (2000, p 357). What is also significant from the citations above is how religious organisations are directly implicated in the communities they work in. Their religious motivations give them a strong sense of identity and purpose that goes beyond the mere act of providing a service. Moreover, Holloway and Moss (2010) also identify a key debate for social workers around the definition of human nature and the pursuit of wholeness, as discussed above. The pursuit of 'human fulfilment' and 'life in all its fullness' is integral to our understanding of quality of life (Holloway and Moss, 2010, p 76) – people seek these in a variety of religious and secular experiences, from prayer to sports, to artistic expression, to drug taking. This links back to the presence of a spiritual need in human beings and to the broader notion of *ways of being* as an all-encompassing term for social policy analysis.

Nevertheless, the idea of social action is multifaceted and varies according to the size and socioeconomic background of the faith community in the UK. The research conducted for this book indicates that some minority faith groups, typically the Baha'i and Zoroastrian faith groups, were much more involved in sociocultural activities than they were in poverty alleviation or the treatment of social problems such as unemployment or substance abuse. Indeed, the concern to preserve cultural identity and heritage was common among many minority faith groups in the UK, even if they were also involved in charitable social work. Thus, even if an organisation undertook poverty relief work, it might still organise cultural, social and leisure activities, such as festivals to celebrate religious events like Diwali (Hindu) or Norooz (Zoroastrian and Baha'i), outings or holidays for community members or language, religion and dancing lessons for younger children.

The physical premises that the faith organisation occupies can also often play a part in this cultural role that the organisation fulfils. The Zoroastrian Centre in Harrow, North London, for example, is based in a Grade II★ listed Art Deco building which it restored to its former glory when the Zoroastrian community acquired it. According to a senior member of the centre, the local council was pleased since the cost of renovating the building was borne by the Zoroastrian community but the building continued to have a public character as it was open on certain days to the wider public and was also often hired out for various functions from people outside of the Zoroastrian community. Most notably, the Zoroastrian Centre in London is the European headquarters for this community.

In this interpretation of social action, religion is an extension of ethnic and cultural identity and helps to keep new generations of minority ethnic descendants connected to their culture of origin. This concern with identity preservation is especially strong among small faith communities in the UK such as the Zoroastrian and Baha'i, who number only a few thousand each and generally tend to be fairly comfortable socioeconomically. In the Zoroastrian community, the first newcomers to the UK were wealthy merchants in the mid–18th century, attracted by new industrial opportunities in Britain. Prominent members of the community were among the first Asian immigrants to the UK to be elected to the House of Commons. In the case of the Baha'i community, this is a relatively newer faith community in the UK (as a religion it is only 150 years old), and in some ways is still developing its understanding of community action. Thus, cultural and leisure activities as provided by such organisations emphasise another dimension of social welfare which has received less attention in the social policy literature but in the context of religious organisations and welfare in the UK, it helps to emphasise the importance of personal identity and its multifaceted nature.

Conclusion

This chapter has looked at how religion and social work intersect. It began by reviewing the place of religion in the social work profession, showing that although the origins of this profession are rooted in Christian philanthropy and charity, social work gradually shed its religious character as it sought to rely more on secular social scientific methods of enquiry. Two broad arguments were made: there are a variety of valid reasons and ways in which social workers can take into account more seriously the role of religion in the lives of their clients which follow the ethos of holism and strengths-based approaches to social work; and this helps to revive the socially transformative role of social work and its connections to social action. Here, the chapter reports back on empirical research conducted for the book, confirming the way in which religious organisations see themselves as offering more than a finite transactional service to their clients and are intricately rooted in their local communities. This refers to a spiritual act of selfless help for the common good, deeply rooted in theological teachings about the purpose of human life. It is the emphasis on human fellowship and the holistic approach to social needs that supports the concept of *ways of being* as a much broader view of the final end of social welfare provision.

Questions for discussion

1. How does religion intersect with the history of social work as a profession?
2. How can the various models of assessment make social workers more sensitive to the religious and spiritual needs of their clients?
3. What are the strengths and weaknesses of the activities of religious organisations in the area of social work?
4. What is the broader significance of social action for the study of the role of religion in social policy?

Note

[1] See Furness and Gilligan (2010) for a detailed discussion of legislation relevant to social work.

FIVE

Health

Summary

- All world religions emphasise the importance of health and physical wellbeing through, for example, religious teachings to visit the sick, rituals of cleanliness and the metaphysical power of religious practices and beliefs such as prayer and faith to heal mental and physical ailments.
- Religious and spiritual perspectives on health emphasise holistic approaches to wellbeing that look beyond the physiological symptoms of illness, thereby challenging the narrow biomedical approach to healthcare. The NHS systems in the devolved nations of the UK have produced guidelines for integrating religious and spiritual considerations into patient care, with Scotland being clearer and more successful than England. The Sussex Partnership Trust is one of the few examples of an NHS 'spirituality strategy' in England.
- NHS hospital chaplaincy has become formally institutionalised and publicly funded since it is seen to contribute to better patient care. But experiences vary with regard to the extent to which chaplains see themselves as constituting a formal part of healthcare provision. Better understanding among healthcare professionals of the religious background of patients, especially of less well-known non-Christian faiths, could help reduce health inequalities.
- Religious organisations undertake a variety of health support, palliative care and health provision services such as the hospice movement or the Jewish Haredi community in North London whose childbirth programme has been formally adopted by the local primary care trust (PCT).

Introduction

In this chapter, we look at the issue of illness and the maintenance of health – the meaning and purpose of the human body in daily human affairs as well as in medical intervention is a matter of perennial importance to all the world religions.

First, there are the teachings and principles in virtually all of the major world religions. The missionary religions (Judaism, Christianity and Islam) call on believers to tend to the needs of the sick and infirm, such as the Jewish principle of *bikur cholim* (visiting the sick) (Kohn, 2010, p 121), the saying of the Prophet Muhammad in the Islamic faith, 'Give food to the hungry and pay a visit to the sick' (cited in Mavani, 2010, p 95) or in Christianity, the significance of Jesus Christ's healing ministry, which inspired the establishment of Christian hospitals worldwide, not to mention the hospice movement in the UK which began in 1967 (Bursey, 2010).

Second, the various religious traditions are fundamentally concerned with the nature of disease and wellness. In the Chinese religions, there is a medical ethic of 'benevolence for all humanity' as well as a fundamental principle of balancing the twin forces of yin and yang in order to produce physical and metaphysical harmony (Park, 2010, pp 67, 69). Chinese medicine has a worldwide reputation as an alternative to Western medicine and is based on the use of natural remedies such as acupuncture, moxibustion (a form of fire heat treatment) or herbal drinks (Bursey, 2010). This is echoed in Hinduism, which has a well-known medical system for the promotion of health and longevity called Ayurveda, entailing an holistic overview of health based on a balance of mental, physical, spiritual, social and environmental wellbeing (Shah and Sorajjakool, 2010, p 40). In Judaism and Islam, physical cleanliness goes a step further with the practice of circumcision on male new-borns (Kohn, 2010; Mavani, 2010).

Third, the world religions also offer a view of the causes of ill health and suffering, which often draws on the metaphysical factors that emphasise the psychological or spiritual state of the individual as having an impact on their physical health, or indeed that there might be an outright supernatural cause such as divine punishment and possession by spirits or the devil (Bursey, 2010). Buddhism is fundamentally focused on the notion of suffering (dukka) and how the 'eight noble paths' lead out of it, as expressed succinctly in the following interchange between the Buddha and his student monks: '"And that which is transient, O monks, is it painful or pleasant?" asked Buddha. "Painful, Master", came the reply' (cited in Sorajjakool and Naewbood, 2010, p 53). In Buddhism, suffering is the basic condition of human existence – from birth, to death, to all matters of human cravings and wants. The solution is to temper the passions and the ego and free oneself from material wants and attachments. This broader view of ill health is shared in Sikhism, which views disease not as the physical source of illness but as a state of disjuncture and disharmony between the individual and the forces of nature, also resulting from the presence of the ego (Mandair, 2010). These ideas are encapsulated in the following saying by Guru Nanak, founder of the Sikh faith, 'Ego is given to man as his disease ... without the Guru sickness never stops' (cited in Mandair, 2010, p 77).

Mandair (2010, p 83) reminds us that the World Health Organization's (WHO) definition of health is also broad, and bears deeper metaphysical connotations as implied above: health is 'a state of complete physical, mental and social well-being and not merely the absence of disease or infirmity'. Equally, we have already referred to the UK Department of Health Patient's Charter, which stipulates 'respect for privacy, dignity and religious and cultural beliefs' (cited in Gilliat-Ray, 2003, p 335). So, healthcare legislation is cognisant of the role of religion and the broader social–psychological dimensions of health, although mainstream medicine tends to have a narrower focus on physical symptoms and vital statistics as the main indicator of health (Mandair, 2010).

This variety of perspectives sets the scene well for the discussion in this chapter. First we consider the basic role of religion in the promotion of health, both physically and mentally. In British scholarship, it is the latter which has gained the attention of researchers, particularly those working in the fields of nursing, community care, psychiatry and social work, such as Swinton (2001), Rumbold et al (2002), Gilliat-Ray (2003), White (2006), Coyte et al (2007) and Gilbert (2011). Thus, the first section looks at how researchers have come to view the role of spirituality in health. In the next section, we consider how researchers recommend that healthcare practitioners integrate recognition of religion and spirituality into patient care and treatment. Then, based on research among the Pakistani community (Mir and Sheikh, 2010), we look more closely at how lack of recognition of a patient's religious beliefs and values can worsen health inequalities. This is countered by a positive example of Jewish healthcare chaplaincy and direct involvement in decision making among female patients suffering from breast cancer (Coleman-Brueckheimer et al, 2009). In both cases, the role of healthcare chaplaincy is taken into account, and the need for health professionals to be sensitive to the religious and spiritual needs and values of their patients. The fourth section focuses on the health-related activities of religious organisations that took part in the research for this book. Based on three case illustrations from Jewish Haredi, Christian and Sikh communities, it shows how such organisations are particularly strong in health support and palliative care services. They therefore play a key role in raising awareness among their communities about good health practices, and also appeal to the more spiritual dimensions of health, such as in the difficult experiences of death and dying. This is a good illustration of the spiritual and pastoral dimensions of wellbeing, as well as the recreational and physical exercise elements.

It is argued here that while we cannot negate the role of natural science in advancing public health, and while some religious practices and beliefs about health and bioethics (such as blood transfusions among Jehovah's Witnesses or euthanasia) may cause controversy, religious communities and organisations are able to achieve two important initiatives: (1) they can promote better health awareness among their local communities by offering health advice and appealing to their spiritual needs; and (2) they can introduce positive health innovations which their local public services providers may benefit from. There is also the more general issue of mainstreaming awareness of religious and spiritual needs and care practices within the institution of the NHS and the work of professional healthcare teams across hospital and community settings. Hospital chaplaincy is only one facet of this endeavour; some researchers argue that the nursing profession itself can and needs to become better equipped to deal with issues of religion and spirituality (see Gilliat-Ray, 2003).

Religion and good health: beyond the biomedical model

In this section we look at the arguments put forth with increasing force in the past decade by healthcare researchers about why religion and spirituality can make a difference to the status of a person's health and the medical treatment received. We use the example of mental health by way of illustrating the need to move beyond the narrow biomedical view of healthcare provision, focusing the technical and physical elements of illness and healthcare on more holistic approaches.

Lynch (2008) argues that the proliferation of health and lifestyle magazines that claim to help readers achieve a higher state of physical wellbeing and personal fulfilment is an indicator of a deeper spiritual search in a secular world.[1] This echoes Anderson's (2008, p 118) argument that patients in Western societies are seeking to move beyond the traditional biomedical model of care to a bio–psycho–social one which takes a broader view of the causes of illness beyond basic physical symptoms, causes and treatment. Similarly, White (2006, p 1) notes the increasing interest in holistic medicine which is made up of three tiers of relationships: the person with themselves, their sense of purpose and code of practice and attitudes towards the wider world; the person with nature, whether they feel at one with nature and feel awe or wonder; and interpersonal or therapeutic relationships such as the relationships between the person and the healthcare practitioner.

White (2006) argues that the NHS is based on the principle of offering clinical care to those who need it on a comprehensive and universal basis. The biomedical approach to healthcare at the foundation of this system focuses on the physical elements of health. This has meant that metaphysical ideas like hope, meaning and belief are outside the scope of healthcare. Healthcare professionals are focused on acute healthcare where technological resources are paramount, leaving little room for partnerships with patients and a more human interaction (White, 2006, p 29). White (2006) recounts a near dehumanising effect where patients are reduced to their symptoms (such as referring to a patient as the 'pancreas in bed'; see White, 2006, p 29). This means that simple and effective aspects of care and treatment may be overlooked, especially in terms of long-term illness and mental health, where the cost of medical technology is becoming exorbitant.

But since the 1960s, concern with the cost and side effects of an overly 'medicalised' health system that ruled out the role of community in healthcare provision has come to the fore (White, 2006, p 30). Also, the nature of disease has changed, especially in the richer Western countries – diseases are becoming more long term and chronic such as cancer, HIV, diabetes and coronary heart disease, raising new questions about the nature of health and posing new challenges of how to manage them. There is, therefore, a greater emphasis on self-care and self-help, with the individual having to draw on their own personal emotional and spiritual resources to cope with their long-term conditions.

This change in healthcare orientation is mirrored in the NHS; concern for quality of care, quality of life and lifestyle are expanding the remit of healthcare into more holistic approaches. The Department of Health has stated in its own guidance that a patient needs to be treated 'as a whole person, and not as a collection of symptoms' (cited in White, 2006, p 24). Moreover, there is a wider appreciation now of the role of social and environmental factors in health. The Greek root of the word health is *holos*, meaning whole, and signifying that health is made up of spiritual, moral and mental wellbeing (White, 2006, p 25). So there is a key hypothesis in holistic care: that a human being's health is made up of both physical/ psychological and social/spiritual elements which are intricately connected and need to be treated together in a healthcare situation (White, 2006, p 25).

Palliative or end-of-life care, where there is no longer a cure for the illness, has been at the forefront of research and practice in the holistic approach to healthcare since it draws on alternative therapeutic approaches (Rumbold et al, 2002; White, 2006). Here, the emphasis on self-help and, therefore, the need for the terminally ill or dying person to find their own way of dealing with illness is especially important (Kellehear, 2002). This, Kellehear (2002) argues, is against a backdrop of competing claims by healthcare professionals and hospital chaplains about who should be responsible for the spiritual care of the patient involved. But, according to Kellehear, palliative care needs to revive its community roots, as in the hospice movement, and refocus attention on spiritual care, which is based on a relationship, and not on a cold analysis of symptoms of spiritual distress or pain. Kellehear emphasises *moral* and *biographical* needs such as visiting people or being visited by them in palliative care.

Box 5.1 below offers a useful illustration that emphasises the importance of community and social identity in offering appropriate spiritual care for dying or terminally ill people. As a result, community care is best placed to undertake palliative care, and Kellehear (2002) advocates community nursing as best placed to undertake the type of spiritual care setting which respects the cultural and community basis of palliative care. This resonates with the work of Anderson (2008) on parish nurses in the North American context – interestingly, examples of parish nursing also exist in the UK and can be found in the work of the Christian charity, Oasis.

Box 5.1: Community, social identity and spirituality – key dimensions of palliative care

1. Moral and biographical needs of the person
2. Importance of self-help and self-care
3. Protecting the social identity and social self-image of the person
4. Care of person-in-community versus care of person-in-bed
5. Community and public health approach versus clinical focus
6. Community-nurse led

Source: Kellehear (2002)

Kellehear's (2002) approach is corroborated by White (2006, p 15) and Swinton (2001), who argue that addressing the existence and role of the human *spirit* in health is important in health situations. For instance, research has shown that religious and spiritual beliefs can be effective coping mechanisms for cancer sufferers as one of the case studies in this chapter shows: relaxation and meditation help to reaffirm feelings of wholeness between spirit and body; motivation, self-esteem and personality can have a positive impact on health as well as a person's 'physical make-up'; and religious practice can also have a positive impact on health. Hence, for White (2006, p 16), these 'intangible aspects of life' need to be taken seriously by health professionals as they matter not just in states of ill health but also in states of good health. Indeed, in this view, spirituality is as much a matter of 'struggle' to find meaning in life as it is a 'warm' feeling of internal peace or happiness (Gilliat-Ray, 2003; White, 2006).

These arguments do not ring with more force than in the mental health literature – Swinton (2001) and Coyte et al (2007) make a forceful argument for the importance of spirituality to mental health. In Box 5.2 below, adapted from Swinton (2001), we see how spirituality can enhance mental health.

Box 5.2: How spirituality enhances mental health

1. *Wellbeing:* through a sense of connectedness to self, others and God, self-esteem and hope
2. *Spiritual support:* through knowledge of God's presence, access to symbols and rituals of spiritual communities, reading of scripture and prayer
3. *Social support through religious communities:* family and support networks, protection from isolation, sense of belonging
4. *Coping and positive cognitive mediation:* having a belief framework through which to explain and understand life events that can provide a coping mechanism
5. *Comfort, hope and meaning:* through feeling valued and cared for, finding comfort in times of distress and feeling that there is hope and the person is not alone

Source: Swinton (2001)

This subject is indeed huge. We end this section on a practical note, however: spirituality and religious belief, as we have seen so far, are deeply associated with the self-care component of medical treatment (White, 2006), which is why, as the research reported here shows, proper communication between religious patients and healthcare professionals can improve understanding of the needs of the patients and support for them to benefit from treatment – 'beliefs, values and expectations' (Anderson, 2008, p 118) play a key role in understanding the ill health a person might be experiencing. Mir and Sheikh (2010) also make this argument.

Integrating knowledge of religion and spirituality into clinical institutional healthcare settings

All of the issues raised above point to a more patient-centred approach in healthcare where personal belief and values will increasingly be needed as a resource that can aid effective treatment of illness. How can healthcare teams begin to practically integrate into this practice such issues of identity, particularly in relation to religion and spirituality?

White (2006) proposes that part of the process of integrating spirituality into healthcare starts with simply talking about it. Multiprofessional healthcare teams are one of the best contexts in which to discuss spirituality, and ideally the healthcare team should aim to develop a shared understanding of spirituality that they can apply to their practice (White, 2006). Because spirituality is still a new and vague topic, it requires a 'safe' arena in which people can discuss it openly and share ideas. White (2006) proposes that focusing the understanding of spirituality on a sense of connection with other people, the Earth or a higher being can help to ground discussions about its meaning and practical application to healthcare settings. Spiritual assessment comes into this process, and the kinds of questions that healthcare writers propose are similar to those outlined in the previous chapter on social work. For White (2006), it is useful to categorise spiritual assessment questions into meaning and purpose, security and hope, religion/ spirituality, as shown in Box 5.3 below.

Box 5.3: Categories of questions for spiritual assessment

1. Meaning and purpose
2. Security and hope
3. Religion and spirituality

Source: White (2006)

White (2006, p 56) advocates a 'multi-professional and whole-team approach' which creates opportunities for talking and learning and sharing ideas about spirituality in the team; at the same time it does not view spirituality as an add-on to be discussed in isolation but as a core part of healthcare provision which has implications for the most mundane tasks, for example, how staff are dealing with a particularly bad death or if they are struggling with diagnosis. Clinical supervision is also another arena for sharing ideas and talking about spirituality. Thus, the basic precepts become ones of effective teamworking and greater levels of team cohesion and support, which also require healthcare professionals to communicate with each other at a more personal level about what spirituality means to them and how it affects them. These may appear high ideals that cannot be applied in practice to a system like the NHS, and, as White (2006) acknowledges, there will also be a need for acute care and technical aspects of health that cannot be ignored. But her argument rests on healthcare teams taking a more holistic approach to care and recognising the potential benefits of having reflective group discussions and even collecting regular updates on the spiritual dimensions of their patients.

Beyond chaplaincy: religion in publicly funded institutional healthcare settings

In the previous chapter we discussed how chaplaincy within the prison service in England and Wales is an innovative development and has been given a boost in the last decade thanks to new training and management structures that are producing a professional class of prison chaplains from minority ethnic backgrounds such as Muslims.

Here, we look at the key role of healthcare chaplaincy and religious intervention in the NHS using examples about long-term illness (Mir and Sheikh, 2010; Coleman-Brueckheimer et al, 2009), but we also move beyond chaplaincy to consider more broadly the importance of mainstreaming religion into healthcare provision. And drawing on recent research in the field of health and ethnicity (Mir and Sheihk, 2010), we argue that taking religious views and spiritual needs into account can have a real impact on the reduction of health inequalities in the UK. We end this section by briefly considering an innovative 'spirituality strategy' implemented by Sussex NHS Foundation Trust Partnership, discussed in Harlow (2010), where a concerted effort has been made to integrate spiritual care into patient care.

Policies on chaplaincy and spiritual care exist in the Department of Health in England, the Scottish Executive and the Welsh Assembly (Edwards and Gilbert, 2007), yet NHS health chaplaincy is both 'marginal' and 'central' to healthcare (White, 2006, p 51). Chaplains are not included in business or normal service monitoring, but they often work in conjunction with healthcare staff to provide appropriate counselling and support to hospital patients (White, 2006). Thus, White (2006) views chaplains as fulfilling a key role in co-coordinating spiritual discussion within a healthcare team. This achieves the dual task of reinforcing the role of the chaplain but also moving beyond it by expanding the importance of spirituality and religion beyond pastoral care to holistic care. Edwards and Gilbert (2007) express similar views.

These arguments are not just prompted by research, but also legislation in the UK, as Gilliat-Ray (2008) and White (2006) remind us, mean that the role of religion in healthcare needs to figure much more prominently in the work of healthcare professionals. Gilliat-Ray's

(2003) argument is that it is the nursing profession that needs to take the lead in this, and we compare this with research in the North American context about parish nurses who administer both medical and pastoral care to patients. In the UK context, Gilliat-Ray (2003) adds that the aspiration within the nursing profession to gain greater professional credibility in the field of healthcare can be well served by better integration of religiously and spiritually sensitive patient care, but that definitions of spirituality should not be 'secularised' by being confined to issues of meaning and purpose in life. Rather, spirituality needs to be adequately connected to religious values and identity in order to meet the needs and concerns of patients of a wide spectrum.

Using the example of care for long-term illness, we now consider the important impact that effective patient–professional communication about religious values and identity has on health outcomes. It has already been argued here that moral values, be they atheistic or religious, play a key role in the coping strategies of people suffering from ill health or going through some kind of personal crisis (Pargament, 1997). Healthcare chaplaincy in the NHS is concerned with these issues: it plays a key role in offering support and solace to patients but also in supporting patients' decision-making processes in relation to treatment. Among the religious organisations involved in the research for this book, most, if not all, offered health chaplaincy, and in some cases, the chaplains were women.

Beyond the issue of chaplaincy is the integration of religious and spiritual concerns into healthcare, especially in the nursing profession. Gilliat-Ray (2003) offers a useful critical review of literature on religion and spirituality in the academic nursing literature and the nursing care profession. She argues that since the 1960s, the nursing profession has increasingly diversified its understanding of spirituality by making a distinction between religion and spirituality, whereas before this era, religion was primarily understood to refer to rituals and beliefs relevant to a person's religious community, which would be mainly Christian in character. In this separation of religion and spirituality, Gilliat-Ray (2003, pp 337, 338) sees the emergence of a specific definition of spirituality which has come to dominate the nursing profession: she describes it as 'secularised, individualistic and humanistic', largely based on concepts such as meaning, fulfilment and purpose – questionable in its real usefulness to patients.

Reviewing a variety of research, Gilliat-Ray (2003) notes that this definition is dominant among nursing academics and educators who are seeking to include spiritual care into the orbit of nursing expertise as a way of adding greater professional status to their profession. On the other hand, research among nursing practitioners in the UK shows that they continue to view spirituality and religion as connected. These ideas are important, argues Gilliat-Ray (2003), since they have real implications for understanding the meaning and role of religion and spirituality in patients' lives and can prevent the instrumental and vague usage of spiritual care and assessment within the nursing profession. Thus, Gilliat-Ray (2003) emphasises Pattison's (2001) argument that spirituality needs to be anchored in communities of practice or discourse, since religious belief provides practical knowledge and insight that can be used meaningfully in healthcare. There is an overlap with cultural bias here in Gilliat-Ray's (2003) view, particularly in relation to minority ethnic religions such as Islam; for instance, Muslim women always prefer to be treated by a female doctor. Indeed, from an Islamic point of view, spirituality is understood in the communal terms of connectedness to the family and the wider religious community, and not necessarily in a personal endeavour of defining meaning for one's own self. Moreover, worship and obedience of God is essential to spiritual satisfaction among Muslim patients. A similar case was found among Hasidic Jews in a case study of breast cancer patients by Coleman-Brueckheimer, Spitzer and Koffman (2009), whereby adherence to Jewish law was essential to medical and pastoral care. Jewish patients feel that they want to fulfil their religious obligations, and by doing this, they gain spiritual satisfaction and are more at ease with their medical treatment.

The lack of voice that minority ethnic faiths experience over healthcare delivery is echoed in Mir and Sheikh (2010), whose research reports back on poor levels of communication between Pakistani Muslims and healthcare professionals within the NHS which is, as a result, leaving the health inequalities experienced by this minority religious group unaddressed. Mir and Sheikh (2010) describe the prevailing conundrum surrounding the approach to minority religions within the NHS setting, echoing Gilliat-Ray's (2003) one-size-fits-all critique:

> ... patient-professional communication and decision-making in long-term illness management reveal the values and assumptions of both patients and professionals. Professional uncertainty and inertia characterise these processes in relation to minority ethnic communities.... Organisational policies are vulnerable to the agency of individual practitioners, who may need support to negotiate cultural difference in contexts promoting contradictory

universalist notions of "sameness". (Mir and Sheikh, 2010,
p 328)

A variety of obstacles to effective communication between Muslim
Pakistani patients and healthcare professionals were found by Mir and
Sheikh (2010), such as poor English skills, absence of interpreters and
a lack of confidence among patients and health practitioners alike
to discuss the importance of religion in affecting patients' medical
treatment decision making. Practitioners felt they did not know enough
about the Pakistani patients' religious values and patients felt that these
values would be undermined if they were to discuss them openly. As
a result, health practitioners relied on stereotypical understandings of
patients' behaviours, for instance, when it came to non-compliance
(patients not following the treatment prescribed by clinicians.) In
the case of women, practitioners assumed that their domestic duties
overrode their personal care. Similarly, fatalistic approaches to illness
among Pakistani patients as a matter of fate that would not really be
resolved with treatment caused problems of communication. Thus,
health risks were not discussed, or treatment was delayed due to
problems of communication about religious faith. Some positive cases
were also reported, however, whereby Pakistani patients consulted
doctors about some religious practices such as fasting and prayer during
illness. Mir and Sheikh (2010) thus conclude that:

> ... [there is a] dichotomy between the significant personal
> resource that faith provides and the discrimination that
> Muslim identity triggers in UK society. Consequently,
> although religious identity can affect communication and
> decision-making in distinct ways, Pakistani patients may
> make this aspect of their identity almost invisible, with
> adverse consequences for treatment and self-care. This
> context for lay-professional communication may undermine
> patients' well-being at both individual and community level.
> (Mir and Sheikh, 2010, p 337)

Some of these arguments are echoed in the more positive example of
Orthodox Jewish patients in research by Coleman-Brueckheimer et
al (2009), exploring how rabbinic authorities or 'culture brokers' are
often consulted by patients who wish to abide by Jewish law in their
treatment, typically, for example, if/how they can have surgery on the
Sabbath, the Jewish holy day. In the case of Hasidic Jewish women with
breast cancer, who were the main population sample for the study by

Coleman-Brueckheimer et al (2009), religious faith played a key role in decision making about medical treatment – rabbis are directly involved in helping female patients proceed with their treatment in ways that conform to Jewish law. For Coleman-Brueckheimer et al, this meant that Jewish chaplains and rabbis had effective communication with medical teams and were given detailed information about the medical cases of the patients so that their decisions were properly made. Thus, Coleman-Brueckheimer et al (2009) make recommendations that are also applicable to the Muslim case above: (1) the involvement of a religious authority or representative can help facilitate therapeutic solutions and reframe treatment options in religiously understandable terms that the patient may accept better; and (2) the involvement of a religious authority can help clinicians assess if the decisions made by patients are religiously sound or can be overturned in cases where the medical treatment provides the only treatment solution for the patient.

These experiences are given added force in the example of the 'spirituality strategy' of the Sussex NHS Foundation Trust Partnership (see Harlow, 2010). Acknowledging that the NHS system, in England especially, has not yet been able to provide clear practical guidance and supporting resources to integrate spiritual care into patient care, and that NHS chaplains themselves tend to be marginalised by their healthcare counterparts or indeed practise self-marginalisation by not fully recognising themselves as an integral part of healthcare teams, the Sussex NHS Trust put in place a 'spirituality strategy' whose aim was to add spiritual care into 'every care worker's skill mix' (Harlow, 2010, p 621). The Trust identified eight key priority areas to develop spiritual care for patients, shown in Box 5.4 below.

Box 5.4: Sussex NHS Partnership Trust – eight priorities for achieving better spiritual care

1. Raise the threshold of understanding and awareness of spirituality
2. Identify and resource staff spirituality advocates
3. Make a visible commitment to spiritual care
4. Employ an appropriately skilled chaplaincy service
5. Involve service users and religious and belief communities
6. Work in partnership with faith communities and charities
7. Recognise and support staff and carers' spiritual needs
8. Expect innovation

Source: Harlow (2010, p 618)

Key to the success of the strategy was identifying and resourcing 'spirituality advocates'; this was, in effect, the 'big idea' that helped translate the vision of better spiritual care into action (Harlow, 2010, p 615). Existing members of staff who already had direct contact with patients, such as nursing or therapy staff, signed up to act as 'spirituality advocates' with the job description of integrating a spiritual dimension into holistic patient care. They received training to enhance their knowledge of religion and belief, and crucially, were able to act as a bridge, linking chaplains to the healthcare teams – referrals to chaplains therefore increased. The role of chaplains was also seen as dynamic and supportive of the care workers, and they were expected to train local members of the community to also offer spiritual care support. Additionally, the Trust holds an annual conference on spirituality. Activities such as meditation, Yoga and Reiki now form part of clinical psychology care services at the Trust (Harlow, 2010). According to Harlow (2010, p 619), 'the strategy uses the word "spirit" to describe the inner life of human beings – their emotions, intuitions, values, desires, and creativity'. This emphasises the importance of the worldviews of patients (Stewart, 2002), which is brought up in Harlow's quotation below and discussed in more detail in Chapter 6 on social care. Sussex Trust's spirituality strategy is now in its tenth year, and Harlow's assessment of it concludes in the following positive terms:

> By refusing to relegate spirituality to a position of low priority and low profile, it invites its staff to offer their personal learning and willingness in this area (thus releasing more resources and maybe contributing to staff retention), it empowers service users to expect their spiritual needs to be understood and actively supported (thus enhancing their recovery), and it indicates willingness to listen to the concerns of religion and belief groups that would like to use our services, if they were assured that we would respect their world view (thus improving access by hard to reach groups). It is a win–win situation which, even in a harsh financial climate, makes sense. As so often in spirituality, you reap far more than you sow. (Harlow, 2010, p 624)

Health support services by religious organisations in the UK: three case studies

This final section focuses on what faith-based organisations in the UK provide in terms of health services. A vast array of services exist, three illustrations of which are presented below. Other examples abound, such as drug and alcohol addiction services, which is an especially common service among religious welfare organisations not just in the UK but also in Europe, and health support services for sex workers. The case illustrations presented below have a strong community dimension – they are tailor-made to the specific needs of particular religious communities, be they strict Orthodox Jews, Christians following the example of Christ's healing ministry or Sikhs seeking to enhance the situation of their at times troubled neighbourhood through positive civic action that combines their spiritual philosophy and values with secular modern-day techniques of health and wellbeing.

Illustration 1:'Birth Buddies' and the Hansy Josovic Maternity Trust, Homerton Hospital, Hackney, the Jewish Haredi community in Stamford Hill, North London

The Haredi community in the Stamford Hill area of North London follows a structured and devout Orthodox Jewish way of life. The community (*kehilla* in Yiddish) is based on a tradition-abiding 'communal and mutual system of care' (Holman and Holman, 2002, p 13) and is thus served by a web of voluntary organisations called Interlink, with the specific ethos of returning £5 to the community for every £1 of the organisation's running costs. Female members of the community are particularly active in voluntary work and the *kehilla's* education system, as evidenced by the research conducted for this book and by research commissioned by the community itself (see Holman and Holman, 2002). The Haredi community has very specific guidelines relating to all matters of life and has sought hard to protect and advance this way of life in harmony with its local area in the boroughs of Haringey and Hackney.

This community has emerged as highly distinctive in terms of some of the health-related provision it has established – indeed, one of the specific aims of Interlink is 'Better health and wellbeing' through the development of the community's own services and a better response by public services to the needs of the community. For instance, the community is served by its own emergency medical service (*Hatzola*), which is better equipped to comply with Jewish Sabbath practices and rules of gender segregation. It also responds to emergency calls by the local non-Jewish community. Senior members of staff at Interlink see their organisations very much as engaging in action which can positively contribute to the Big Society and are positive about the opportunities for more local and independent provision which will be made possible by the Coalition government's new Localism Act.

One such example in the area of health is the Hansy Josovic Maternity Trust (HJMT), a small charity in Stamford Hill supporting mainly Jewish women during childbirth through the provision of a volunteer childcare companion, also known as a *doula*. In the Haredi community, the husband should not touch his wife during childbirth; therefore, new mothers-to-be or women with no family support make use of a doula, alongside the midwife. As a result of this service, Orthodox Jewish women have the lowest rates of caesarean sections or childbirth complications in the Borough of Hackney. HJMT collaborated with City and Hackney PCT to introduce a similar programme called 'Birth Buddies' in order to help reduce the number of caesarean sections and improve childbirth prospects among women from the Afro-Caribbean and African communities. Based at Homerton Hospital and funded directly from the central PCT budget, the 'Birth Buddies' programme is now commissioned to HJMT for £10,000 per year, and has helped the hospital save money by reducing the number of caesarean operations and providing better health outcomes for mothers and new-born babies.

For senior members of staff at Interlink, the HJMT initiative is a way of 'making public services more accessible' to local communities, particularly in the case of the Haredi community, which is quite sheltered and self-contained. Moreover, the HJMT initiative acknowledges, according to the organisation, the right of minority ethnic groups to maintain their own way of life. The added advantage of the HJMT is that it has been able to benefit non-Jewish residents in Hackney. Thus, according to senior members of staff, the ability to self-organise and have a real partnership with the local state authorities in the provision of services for the local area is a key advantage of the Big Society initiative. Universal and standardised public services do not necessarily fit the needs of local people, whereas community and faith-based projects such as the HMJT can be 'universal' and 'distinctive' at the same time. In this view, it is the state that can be hard to reach, not local communities.

Illustration 2: Burrswood Christian Hospital, Kent, 'Seeing the person in the patient' who falls through the NHS

Burrswood is one of the few remaining Christian hospitals that still operate in the UK. Based in Kent, England, it offers fee-paying post-surgical care, rehabilitation, palliative and end-of-life care, counselling and care for stress, and has specialist expertise in emotional and spiritual care as well as support for chronic fatigue syndrome (CFS). According to the medical director of the hospital, the healthcare approach is based on "people, relationships and the impact of illness, rather than just focusing on disease processes and polypharmacy. This is a work of God born out of obedience to God's call". The health philosophy at Burrswood resembles the holistic approach propagated by the various Indian and Chinese religions discussed at the beginning of this chapter, with a focus on the human being as a whole person and the cultivation of a relationship based on listening to them and their needs. The medical director also argues that in the NHS chaplains are not seen as a priority, with the aim of the NHS being to provide a cost-efficient mass service, yet fundamentally, it is a place where the patient or ill person thinks about the meaning of their life and seeks to make sense of their illness. Thus, the medical director emphasises the need to 'see the person in the patient' and to listen to their needs that stem from 'illness and isolation'. Thus, the medical director sees the role of Burrswood not as negating the NHS but as providing healthcare to people who fall through the gaps in the system. Although most of the patients are Christian, like the HMJT above, Burrswood also offers its services to non-Christian patients.

Illustration 3: The Nishkam Centre, health support and alternative therapy in Birmingham's Sikh community

The Nishkam Centre is a Sikh temple and civic centre in Handsworth, Birmingham, an area that has witnessed its fair share of social deprivation and rioting in the 1980s and more recently in 2011. The centre has already caught the eye of senior officials in local government as a beacon of local civic action. Members of staff at the centre have a very strong ethos of self-less service which, like the two illustrations above, is distinctive in that is based on Sikh religious values but universal in that it offers its services to the wider society in a way which can be beneficial to them and does not oblige them to share the same religious faith. As part of its commitment to local community welfare, the Nishkam Centre has recently established a wellbeing and fitness centre that operates very much as a regular gym but incorporates alternative therapy based on a variety of massage techniques including Indian head massage and reflexology. These services are not free of charge but are cheaper than the normal commercial rates, and the centre emphasises the spiritual element in all these services. For instance, the masseurs are volunteers who see the therapeutic techniques they offer as a form of self-less service since they are not paid directly.

A vital community service that the Nishkam Centre offers and which is typical of other minority ethnic faiths in the UK is health support and awareness-raising services to their members. Typically, this involves health screening days or information events on health conditions that are common in the community such as diabetes or heart problems. Health professionals do the check-ups or give their talks free of charge as a form of self-less service that they are offering to the community. This emphasises the personal link between giver and service and is one of the key fault-lines of critiques of the bureaucratic and impersonal welfare states. These services should not be underestimated since they are especially helpful to members of ethnic communities who do not speak very good English or who have differing cultural practices. According to senior members, the centre has an ethos of combining the spiritual with the secular. The spiritual values are the basis of social action and fellowship with all other human beings, but the work of the organisation is to engage with its local context and seek to develop its material resources in order to conduct its spiritual mission in the local community.

Conclusion

This chapter has looked at the important topic of health in relation to religion, raising issues such as the increasing importance of self-care, partnerships between healthcare professionals and patients, better understanding of the patient as a whole person and greater scope for patients to express their voice and choice in their medical treatment. These all provide a context within which the biomedical model of health is being challenged as religious values and identity are being increasingly called on to help patients cope with illness and also to enhance the impact of the treatment they receive. These moves fall within a wider rubric of holistic definitions of human health and approaches to healthcare, which the world religions support. Holistic approaches show how a better integration of religion, belief and spirituality into healthcare may not only respond better to users''moral and biographical needs' (Kellehear, 2002) but can also release greater care resources on the part of healthcare professionals (see Harlow, 2010).

The key challenges remain in the extent to which consideration of religion and spirituality can be mainstreamed into NHS care so that not only do healthcare chaplains play a more integral role in treatment decision making, but health professionals also gain a greater understanding of the spiritual dimensions of healthcare provision. In contrast, the illustrations of faith-based organisations provided here show that these not only have the capacity to respond to health needs, but they are doing this in a way that is harmonious with issues of personal belief and identity.

This helps illustrate the conceptual thrust advocated in this book, which is a view of the human condition as much more than an isolated set of symptoms of wellbeing or ill-being; rather, people are self-aware agents with an identity and moral values. The arguments portrayed in this chapter have shown how important community belonging and social relationships are. Added to this is a focus on self-less service and obedience to religious teachings that have important weighting for the providers of health services. There is also an understanding here of religion and spirituality as more than just the warm feeling that someone experiences, and intrinsically connected to a personal journey that each person takes over the course of their life. This religious perspective is, therefore, about the sense of personal meaning and worth, and the ability to continue to live by the moral values that people consider important to them. It is more than an issue of wellbeing – it is about *a way of being*, an attitude to living that seeks to make subjective sense of one's circumstances as opposed to applying a one-size-fits all of welfare outcomes.

Questions for discussion

1. How can attention to religious and spiritual issues enhance new thinking beyond the biomedical model of healthcare?
2. Why and how should healthcare professionals take religion and spiritual issues into consideration in patient care?
3. How can religious organisations offering health services ensure that they can appeal to people of other faiths?
4. What is the significance of the palliative care and mental health literature for the study of religion in health?

Useful websites and resources

Burrswood Christian Hospital: www.burrswood.org.uk/

NHS chaplaincy careers: www.nhscareers.nhs.uk/details/Default. aspx?Id=532

NHS Scotland (2008) *Spiritual care and chaplaincy in NHS Scotland*, Edinburgh: Scottish Executive (www.merseycare.nhs.uk/Library/ What_we_do/Corporate_Services/Spiritual_and_Pastoral_Care/ NHS%20Scotland_spiritual_care_revised_guidelines.pdf)

Note

[1] See also the 2009 issue of *TIME* magazine that ran a feature on the role of faith in health matters.

SIX

Social care

Summary

- Care is an important moral philosophical concept for social policy that emphasises the moral relations that bind human beings. This ethics of care is juxtaposed with the ethics of justice that stipulates that social welfare is best achieved through the provision of universal social rights and the just redistribution of wealth.
- The ethics of care thus goes beyond social care services to a broader community-based culture of compassion and social trust also denoted by the concept of social capital which shows that individual welfare cannot be separated from the social context within which a person is embedded, or their self-identity.
- Spiritual care helps to develop an holistic approach to human welfare that emphasises the agency of the service users and the importance of their relationship with their care giver.
- Religious welfare organisations provide a variety or residential, community and day centre social care services with residential care for older people being a particularly significant area and most developed in the UK within the Jewish community. Religious teachings generally emphasise family-based care for vulnerable children and adults.

Introduction

This chapter is concerned with social care. It is important to note from the outset that it represents a complementary conceptual progression from previous chapters on social work and health due to the very close conceptual and practical ties between these three domains. Two tasks are accomplished which are consistent with the book's overall aims and the progression of its argument: (1) it develops the discussion of holistic approaches to human wellbeing by honing in on the concepts of 'worldview' (Stewart, 2002) and 'lifeworld' (Grunwald and Thiersch, 2009) in the provision of adequate social care; and (2) it takes the argument to a higher analytical level by highlighting the normative importance of the concept of care to social policy (Daly and Lewis,

2000) and the useful insights that a perspective on religious welfare brings to the perennial debate on the ethics of justice versus the ethics of care unleashed by Carol Gilligan's seminal book, *In a different voice* (1982). There are therefore gender-related undertones in this chapter as we explore empirical findings on the role and position of women in faith-based welfare in the UK. But the chapter goes beyond these narrow confines of the definition of care. It discusses various dimensions of the concept of care in the light of what religion can bring to personal and community wellbeing. These help illustrate further the concept of *ways of being*.

To avoid confusion, it is important to be clear about what we are referring to by the concept of social care here. Daly and Lewis (2000, p 285) offer the following definition of the term which encompasses the broad array of ideas covered in this chapter: 'the activities and relations involved in meeting the physical and emotional requirements of dependent adults and children, and the normative, economic and social frameworks within which these are assigned and carried out'. Social care has generally been viewed as a subordinate corollary of the more fundamental social rights of health and education. 'Curing' is the domain of medicine, while 'caring' is the domain of nursing (Edwards, 2009, p 231). This not only reinforces the gendered division of labour in the healthcare sector but more fundamentally, the relegation of moral and emotional bonds to the private sphere and their exclusion from public political debate.

This situation explains why social care and social services more generally were the missing link in the 1948 Beveridgean-led welfare settlement (Glasby, 2007). Indeed, the term 'social care' is of recent coinage as a result of the changing demographic and health profile of the UK and other rich democracies, which has meant that people are living longer and having to manage various types of illnesses on a long-term basis. This has forced them onto a new and ill-defined terrain at the community level after hospital-based care has attended to their acute conditions. This integration between health and social care is seen by policy makers as a more effective way of attending to members of the population who have 'crosscutting and multiple needs, whether these be frail older people, people with mental health problems, people with learning difficulties' (Glasby, 2007, p 373). Some authors stretch the concept of social care widely, such as Nash and Stewart (2002), to encompass a broad array of activities, from the basic care of dependent or vulnerable people such as children or older people to political mobilisation and social action.

This broad continuum of meanings for social care is also reflected in this chapter in two specific ways that will help illustrate some of the core dimensions of religious welfare: namely, that on the one hand, care is a moral philosophical concept which provides normative parameters for the conceptualisation and practice of social policy (Daly and Lewis, 2000); and second, that care is a specific activity or service that can occur in informal or formal contexts which is historically associated with the role of women in families attending to the needs of dependent, vulnerable or also dominant male members in their family context (Daly and Lewis, 2000). It is helpful to think of the concept of care, therefore, in similar dual terms as the concept of *service*, discussed previously.

It is not by coincidence that the leading sociologist of religion, Robert Wuthnow (2004), refers to religious congregations as 'caring communities', a point also raised by policy makers in the UK and academics such as Greg Smith (2004a), who note that religious organisations are defined by their caring qualities beyond the basic function of delivering social care. This argument is cast against the empirical research for this book which shows that religious social welfare actors in the UK are thinking more along the lines of needs which they recast as social rights and as part of a concern for justice which is intricately driven by feelings of care and compassion for others.

There are four main sections in this chapter: the first explores the debate around the ethic of care as highlighted above; the second considers the debate and practice surrounding spiritual care; the third looks at specific examples of social care services that religious organisations provide in the shape of elderly care which is the most common and significant and also care for people with disabilities; and the fourth section takes this debate on service further by considering the broader care role of religious congregations, taking its cue from the research by Wuthnow (2004), which brings up arguments about social capital and the importance of looking beyond basic service provision to the life of the religious community as a foundation of social protection and support. The chapter makes an important conceptual leap based on the experience of religious welfare provision, by taking the concept of care beyond its female/informal roots to give it broader connotations of public and political concern for justice that are as intrinsic to human society.

Ethics of care versus ethics of justice: significance for social policy

In this section we look at the concept of social care in two key ways. First, as an important unit of analysis for the study of social policy and the welfare state, and second, as a moral philosophical concept guiding social action and public policy whose relevance is highlighted by the role of religious organisations in social welfare, as emerged from the research for this book. These two dimensions of the argument emphasise the importance of care in thinking about social welfare, and, therefore, the relevance of religious organisations to social welfare action since religious organisations also describe their work in terms of care and religious welfare actors are motivated by feelings of care and attentiveness to the needs of others. These ideas will help develop the conceptual shift in terms of *ways of being* that this book is articulating.

Daly and Lewis (2000) make the case for focusing on changes in social care policy as a way of analysing shifting responsibilities for welfare in the advanced capitalist countries. They argued the following at a time when academic research was beginning to engage more fully with the concept of the mixed economy of welfare:

> To represent the changes taking place in welfare states in terms of retrenchment and cut-backs is to stop short of the real qualitative change that is being played out around the activity of and responsibility for caring. For, underlying the alterations that are being made to benefit entitlement is a more subtle shifting of responsibilities among institutional domains.... (Daly and Lewis, 2000, p 282)

Daly and Lewis (2000) noted that within the policy area of social care, the increasing tendency for direct cash payments and cash transfers was arguably the most important way in which the welfare state was in fact enlarging its role in welfare and also exercising greater degrees of innovation. Focusing on social care enables better linking in the study of social policy between in-cash and in-kind services. Welfare states thus continue to play a key role in shaping changes in social policy and social care, just as the consideration of the future financial cost and questions over responsibility for social care are taking centre stage in advanced capitalist democracies. Daly and Lewis linked their argument directly to the moral philosophical debate surrounding the ethics of care. This highlighted the emphasis of ethics of care on social interdependency and interconnectedness instead of individualism and competition. Crucially, they made the important point that social care was no longer confined to women's lives and activities within their family settings but provided by private business and statutory bodies in the public sphere. Yet the ethics of care itself as a moral principle guiding social action has not been transferred out of the private sphere, and continues to be associated with the role of women.

So what is the conceptual significance of an ethics of care for social policy? Concepts such as social justice and fairness are central aims and organising axes for social policy (Fitzpatrick, 2001). In Western moral philosophy, social justice has been a cornerstone for thinking about good political judgement and guiding everyday social action and social policy. Yet increasingly the concept of care as an ethical theory that can guide moral action has become more prominent (Taylor, 1998), and with particular resonance for the social work profession and the professional ethics that social workers have to abide by (Banks, 2003). Various theorists have attributed characteristics to social care: Tronto (1995), for example, identifies four phases, which are, caring about, taking care of, care giving and care receiving. Others such as Thomas (cited in Daly and Lewis, 2000) emphasise elements such as the identity of the providers and receivers of care, the relationship between them and the social content and economic character of care. In the original thesis by Carol Gilligan, the main argument was that a focus on justice led to universal rules and principles which missed more specific needs that human beings might have. In an often cited passage, Gilligan (1982) argues the following:

> In this conception [the ethics of care], the moral problem arises from conflicting responsibilities rather than from competing rights and requires for its resolution a mode of thinking that is contextual and narrative rather than formal and abstract. This conception of morality as concerned with the activity of care centres moral development around the understanding of responsibility and relationships, just as the conception of morality as fairness [the ethics of justice] ties moral development to the understanding of rights and rules. (Gilligan, 1982, p 19)

In a similar vein, Tronto (1995) offers the following definition:

> On the most general level we suggest that caring be viewed *as a species activity that includes everything we do to maintain, continue and repair our 'world' so that we can live in it as well*

> *as possible.* That world includes our bodies, ourselves and our environment, all of which we seek to interweave in a complex, life-sustaining web. (Tronto, 1995, p 142; emphasis in original)

Tronto argues that although this view of human relations may be utopian, it underpins the condition of human nature. The citation above is similar to arguments presented by religious welfare organisations in the research conducted for this book, that human beings are connected to each other, that human dignity is sacred and that religious teachings call on human beings to respect the social bonds between them and their obligation to take care of the environment in which they live. The specific use of the term 'repair the world' in Tronto's (1995) citation above is Jewish (in Hebrew, *tikkun olam*) (Jawad, 2009). White and Tronto (2004) develop these understandings of care further by linking them to the issue of social rights and their relative importance in relation to need, as follows:

> ... a justice perspective, based on rights is inadequate because its presumed universality is belied by the reality of the inaccessibility of rights to many. Second, ... a care perspective, currently formulated upon the assumption that only some people have needs, is also flawed because its presumed particularity distorts the human experience and subsequent policies. (White and Tronto, 2004)

Hence, Tronto (1995) sees the ethics of care as being something innately human and beyond the lives and work of women. Care is an essential attribute of being 'attentive' to the needs of others. Justice, on the other hand, involves the application of formal rules that identify a few key characteristics of a situation as relevant so that a decision may be made quickly (Taylor, 1998). In many ways, this exemplifies the universal basis of rights and entitlements which the welfare state in Western countries including the UK has stood on. Tronto (1995) argues that a moral logic based on care has important implications for notions of desert that are fundamental to social welfare and for how we think about social justice. The ethics of care moves the logic of desert away from the founding principle of the 'work ethic' – the idea that for people to deserve social welfare or help they need to have earned it – to the validity of human need in its own right. This entails being attentive to others, and more importantly, basing an assessment of their needs in the actual lived context they are in and not on abstract principles.

People are entitled to care because they are part of ongoing relations of care and the logic of care defines the human condition since it is rooted in the daily concrete experiences of life. As Tronto (1995) notes: 'The moral question an ethic of care takes as central is not – What, if anything do I (we) owe to others? but rather – How can I (we) best meet my (our) caring responsibilities?' (cited in Edwards, 2009, p 234).

Box 6.1 summarises some of these core differences between an ethics of justice and an ethics of care, using an illustrative example from Taylor (1998) about how to divide a pie. Crucially, a key argument made by Taylor is that the ethics of care works best on a small scale when only a small number of people are involved or at least people who can enter into personal relations with each other and have the time to study the needs of one another. This focus on small groups is also reminiscent of Wuthnow (2004) and is apparent in the small-scale localised nature of many religious welfare organisations in the UK, although not all.

Box 6.1: How do you divide a pie? Justice and rights or care and needs as competing views of moral ethics

- *Ethics of justice:* objective fairness which includes fairness with strangers, universal rights, minimum principles-based, formal abstract, treats equals equally, enables quick decision making on a large scale
- *Ethics of care:* personal responsibility, inter-personal relationships which emphasises people who are in close contact with each other, contextual, narrative, deals with entirety of human needs on an emotional attachment basis as opposed to an urgency basis, time-intensive decision making on a small contact group

---

As Taylor (1998, p 481) explains,

> … care-giving entails the time-consuming identification of individual needs; justice, on the other hand, requires the application of formal rules that often abstract away from the particularity of individual needs…. Consider the task of dividing up a pie among a group of people. An application of the ethic of justice would probably lead to some rule, such as equal division, that the participants could quickly agree upon and implement, but that would probably fail to take into account the idiosyncratic needs of those involved. Applying the ethic of care here, on the other hand, would require more time-intensive communication among the

participants in order to reveal individual needs and tailor the allocation to meet those needs.

Various critiques of the concept of care have also been expressed, that it has a tendency for parochialism and bias by giving preference to emotional relationships and helping people we already know (Tronto, 1995). In many ways, this explains some of the unease about religious welfare provision; after all, religious people are tied by personal contact too. But scholars like Tronto have sought to square the circle by including justice in the orbit of care, and in many ways, this is the orientation of religious welfare organisations in the UK, as discussed below. Yet it is the focus on everyday lived experience that is the key logic in this approach to social policy, what is called 'lifeworld' in the German context (Grunwald and Thiersch, 2009). This stems from the phenomenological traditions in sociology and social research and emphasises the importance of culture in considerations of social welfare, or what Stewart (2002) also denotes as 'worldview', that would suggest that personal identity, self-responsibility and agency matter a great deal for successful welfare outcomes. The 'golden rule' of caring and forgiveness of others also reinforces this (Stewart, 2002).

Spiritual care

From establishing the conceptual importance of care to social policy and social welfare, we now move to a discussion of the significance of spiritual care as a way of better understanding how religion and spirituality can enhance human wellbeing and move beyond narrow biomedical definitions of human wellbeing. In part this also relates to taking an holistic approach to human wellbeing that takes into account service users' worldviews (Stewart, 2002). Appreciation of the worldview of a client or service user helps social care workers understand the 'lifeworld' of the latter (Stewart, 2002). It leads to self-healing and self-determination, in Stewart's view, which is based on valuing difference and commonality, and helping to promote belonging and community. Thus, in Stoter's (1995, p 8) definition, spiritual care involves:

> ... responding to the uniqueness of an individual: accepting their range of doubts, beliefs and values just as they are.... It is to be a facilitator on their search for identity on the journey of life and in the particular situation they find themselves in ... spiritual care can be offered through an attitude of love

and acceptance within the caring relationship ... [it is] a gift of love offered with no preconditions. (Stoter, 1995, p 8)

Similar views were also expressed by members of staff at the religious welfare organisations involved in the research for this book. Researchers offer a variety of ways in which spirituality and religious considerations can enter into the social care relationship. Jolley and Moreland (2011) emphasise the importance of spiritual care in helping service users find meaning and purpose in their lives, as is also argued in Stoter's (1995) definition above. This is especially important in the case of older people or people nearing the end of their lives, as discussed in Illustration 1 later. For Jolley and Moreland (2011), spiritual care has to occur on a one-to-one basis and be based on the service user and their needs. Box 6.2 offers a useful illustration of the way in which spiritual care can and should take account of quality of life issues and how it can take a whole life approach to patient care.

Box 6.2: Spiritual care, quality of life and whole life approaches

1. *Anchorage to life:* living in the present, living at the end of life, accepting and adjusting, reminiscing
2. *Access to significant relations:* staying together, being involved
3. *Conditions of life:* having freedom, having a place which is home
4. *Satisfied body and mind:* participating in life, enjoying life, finding meaning in the day, being independent, being aware of the inevitable, having control

Source: Jolley and Moreland (2011, p 389)

Holloway and Moss (2010) add further transformative dimensions to spiritual care by linking it to structural issues of empowerment, hope, transcendence and emancipation. The theme of empowerment is especially important in religious welfare provision and will be revisited in the next chapter on poverty. Religious welfare organisations claim that they empower marginalised and socially excluded people through the help, support and services that they provide. As Holloway and Moss argue, the importance of empowerment means that spiritual care helps people change their life around and not just take control of their current problem, which is perhaps more the focus of some social work and social care practice. This requires that the carer prioritises the views and agency of the care receiver and works in partnership with them (Holloway and Moss, 2010). Many stories are recounted by religious organisations of how a listening ear and guidance helped people who had found themselves in difficult situations, from young girls falling pregnant, to parents being able to deal with their children, to men experiencing drug and alcohol dependency. The quotes below help illustrate this:

> 'We want to help people flourish. I feel blessed when I help people in need. I feel a spiritual buzz.' (Christian drop-in centre manager)

> 'We want to move people forward on their journey, the next step may not be employment, it may be about helping them regain their confidence first [in order to apply for a job]. We care. We wish people well and want them to have a better standard of living and get back into life. We don't look at targets, we treat them as individuals.... It is a hand-holding exercise right to the end.' (Christian employment programme manager)

> 'It is about care. Enlightening their lives, giving them more of a focus of where they can go in life.' (Christian employment programme consultant)

Linked to the emphasis on empowerment is the possibility that spiritual care can also enhance a feeling of transcendence above the ordinary mundaneness of social problems. In this view, it is spiritual connection with one's inner self that leads to true emancipation and freedom, as in St John's Gospel, 'The truth shall make you free'. Thus, spiritual care can 'move people forward on their spiritual paths' and help enhance their life journey (Holloway and Moss, 2010, p 102). Similar arguments are made of the role of hope and building resilience in spiritual care. The need for social carers to engage with the personal biographical and moral narratives of care receivers is crucial, as already highlighted in a previous chapter on health.

The essential aim of spiritual care is therefore to restore a healthy sense of identity to the service user (Holloway and Moss, 2010) – this supports the thesis running through this book that religious welfare helps reshape the meaning of social welfare into a broader concept based on issues of identity, moral values and belonging, termed *ways of being*. Holloway and Moss (2010, p 114) identify four tasks or stages in the spiritual care relationship, beginning with *joining*, which is the ability of the carer to start where the care receiver is. Then there is *listening*, which involves the assessment of the importance of spiritual issues to the care receiver; this is followed by *understanding*, which is about spiritual empathy and is dependent on the personal disposition of the carer – it requires the carer to be able to take on the sense of vulnerability which the care receiver may be feeling; finally, there is *interpreting*, which relates to the capacity for the care provider and care receiver to engage in spiritual exploration whereby deeper concepts such as transcendence and transformation become relevant. Within a more explicitly religious context, carers may offer to pray with care receivers although views differ as to the extent to which religious organisations should maintain a secular character when engaging in spiritual care (Holloway and Moss, 2010).

Mathews (2009) and Furness and Gilligan (2010) provide insightful views on the relevance of spiritual care to various vulnerable groups such as older people and people with disabilities, which are the two groups of people we look at in the next section.

Social care services by religious welfare organisations

What types of social care activities do religious welfare organisations provide? In this section, we look at two illustrations related to elderly care and care for people with disabilities. To a large degree, the issues are cross-cutting for all social groups. Religious organisations are well known for the variety of social care activities they offer, from childcare, to parent and toddler groups, to day centres for older people and people with disabilities, to fully fledged professional residential care for older people (Dinham, 2007).

Illustration 1: Older people and residential care

Respect and care for older people is a key feature of all the major religions discussed in this book (Morgan and Lawton, 2007). Mathews (2009) discusses MacKinlay's (2004) model of the spiritual tasks of ageing. These are depicted as natural phases of psychosocial development that help the person find a sense of identity and leaning in their life. It would therefore appear that adequate spiritual care rests heavily on *who* we are, and indeed, *knowing* who we are. In this view, the first phase involves finding *intimacy* and *relationships*, whether this be with other people or with God (Mathews, 2009, p 58). Having a sense of hope forms an intricate part of this. Another spiritual task or phase in the process of ageing is the ability to *transcend loss* or *disability*, which relates to the capacity of older people, especially in the Western context, for remaining independent and self-reliant. The final phase is to find *meaning* whereby older people are able to review their lives. Added to these, Jewell (2004) focuses on the importance of affirmation, celebration and confirmation in the lives of older people as ways of reinforcing the validity and importance of their lives. Mathews (2009) argues that what is at stake is the preservation of the human spirit over and above mental and physical impairment. This constitutes the essential worth and dignity of the person. Jolley and Moreland (2011) argue that these qualities are especially important in the care of older people suffering from dementia in residential care settings, and propose various tasks that carers can perform in order to offer spiritual care for such vulnerable adults. These are set out in Box 6.3 below.

Box 6.3: Spiritual care for people with dementia

1. Value and respect the person
2. Celebrate the person's religious heritage where appropriate
3. Embrace spirituality, seeking involvement of the person where possible
4. Use creative arts to support spiritual needs and outpourings
5. Provide spiritual care throughout the person's life, including the end of their life
6. Nourish one's own spirituality to help sustain oneself for the tasks and demeanour necessary to care for a person with dementia

Source: Bell and Troxel (2001), cited in Jolley and Moreland (2011, p 389)

In the research conducted for this book, visits were made to a residential home for older people in Birmingham run by the West Midlands Jewish Association. These were older people in generally good health, although some were experiencing financial hardship. Some members lived in small flats that they rented out from the organisation, while others lived in the nursing home. The nursing home organised luncheons and day trips and acted as a day centre that was well attended by older members of the local Jewish community. All service users were Jewish on the day of the visit, as the organisation prioritised services to the local Jewish community, although there were also non-Jewish residents in the home. A key issue for the older residents was the ability to observe a Jewish way of life that was facilitated for them in the nursing home.

Illustration 2: People with disabilities

As in the case of older people, people with disabilities are also included in the spectrum of social care services offered by religious welfare organisations. Historically, people with disabilities were looked after in institutionalised settings and often subjected to segregation or exclusion. Some religious institutions have also been accused of hiding people with disabilities from the public eye within large institutional settings, and in contemporary times, some are either refused communion or full membership of the church (Mathews, 2009). Indeed, for some religious faiths, such as the Indian religions that believe in reincarnation, disability may be a sign of a previously badly lived life. The provision of adult social care has increasingly moved towards the accommodation of choice and the personalisation of services, and the disability movement in the UK has forged new horizons in recognising the agency and rights of people with disabilities. However, many continue to be excluded from mainstream education and leisure activities. In this case, the task of spiritual care is to help people with disabilities to find a voice and to express their strengths.

Box 6.4 provides a useful typology of spiritual approaches to social care. Much less research has been conducted on people with disabilities relatively speaking to the other vulnerable groups, but as Mathews (2009) highlights, spiritual care can be beneficial to both care giver and receiver.

Box 6.4: Three types of spiritual care approaches in social care organisations

- *New wave:* subscribe to practices associated with supported living within the home and possibly within residential care
- *Pragmatists:* subscribe to new wave policies and practices for what it gives them (for example, funding) but not necessarily because they believe that the model is philosophically better than others
- *The old radicals:* promote collective approaches, providing a mediating influence between clients and the community. They do not subscribe to the supported living model

Source: Jolley and Moreland (2011, p 389)

In the research conducted for this book, the social care organisations that were involved saw religious identity as a fundamental part of their social care plans, although in the Jewish organisation in Birmingham no specific questions were asked as part of a spiritual assessment of clients. It should be noted that not all religious social welfare providers rigorously conduct spiritual assessments of the people in their care, as also evident in the Burrswood Christian Hospital mentioned in the previous chapter. This reflects the fact that such organisations are working within secular settings and need to adopt broad universal approaches that can appeal to a wider variety of social backgrounds among their service users. It would also raise concern with their public sector funders, according to senior members of Burrswood Christian Hospital, who advise a 'light-touch' approach to religion.

Religious welfare providers: 'caring communities' versus 'service organisations'

We now reach the final section of this chapter as we bring together the various threads of argument surrounding the symbolic and functional significance of the concept of care in the role of religious welfare, and more broadly, in the conceptual rethinking of social welfare proposed in this book. These elements are also summed up by Daly and Lewis (2000) who, not referring to religion but to welfare state theory, note that the concept of care has both 'relational' and 'service provision' aspects that require a fundamental reconceptualisation of social policy and welfare state change.

The importance of care raises an important question about the identity of religious welfare generally and religious welfare organisations specifically. John Devine, a leading adviser on faith communities at the CLG, has noted the importance of not conflating the role of religious communities of worship with service-focused religious organisations. Wuthnow's (2004) study on US congregations also highlights this point. The subtle difference is that a congregation is a place of worship (Wuthnow, 2004). People gather together on a regular basis primarily for religious acts such as prayer, celebration of sacraments or to hear preaching. Within this context, two things happen, according to Wuthnow (2004): first, they hear sermons and teachings from the preacher about helping others in need or caring about others and thinking more broadly about the welfare of their community – for instance, the preacher prays for strength for those experiencing natural catastrophes or hunger, and money is collected for those in need.

According to Wuthnow (2004), it is these simple acts of raising awareness among the congregation about the plight of others who may be close acquaintances or strangers that is also important for our thinking about social welfare in a religious context. The second important thing that happens is that social relations are formed among members of the congregation – through the act of meeting regularly, deep friendships and bonds are made which strengthen the cohesiveness of the community and can act as a vital cushion of support in case a member of the congregation should come across misfortune and need the help of their congregation. This is what was already referred to as 'social capital' in Chapter 3, and we have highlighted that such strong group bonds may be both inclusive and exclusive. They may insulate the congregation further from other social groups in society, or they may help them become more active citizens in society. The latter is especially evident when the building space of the place of worship is used for purposes other than worship, such as community events, and by people other than members of the congregation. According to Wuthnow (2004), this sees congregations transform into hubs of civic activity, a healthy ingredient for democracy.

The view of congregations and faith communities as hubs of civic renewal is also fostered by the Church Urban Fund in the UK. In the report *Faithful cities* (Commission on Urban Life and Faith, 2006, p 45), it is argued that 'Change in the political context or urban areas, and in faith communities themselves requires a fresh look at the role of congregations in the public life of British cities and urban areas. We see a vibrant strategically significant role for local congregations in civic life, not least in speaking up and taking action for social and economic injustice'. The report sees such congregations as being able to play a lead role in attenuating urban rioting and unease even if some of their leaders may be inward looking and may compete for worshippers. Thus, the report cites the example of the Citizen Organising Foundation which brings together hundreds of people from all the different faiths as well as secular individuals to discuss issues of common concern to their neighbourhoods and to improve knowledge of each other.

This view of congregations as 'caring communities' does not negate the professionalisation of the ethos of care within third sector organisations that have a religious mission and are staffed by religious people. Such organisations may still be guided by the principle of care and compassion for those in need, but the dynamic through which they operate is different since their work would more likely be project-based and funded either through government grants or through donations from their own members. In the UK, we do not yet have comprehensive surveys of how religious welfare organisations are independent voluntary sector organisations and how many are part of a congregational or temple set-up. In the research conducted for this book, there was a mixture of organisations. Generally, the large faith groups, such as Christian, Jewish and Muslim groups, were more likely to have independent voluntary organisations that were service-based and not joined to a place of worship although they would still have contact rooms or halls for prayer. Smaller faith groups, such as Buddhists, Sikhs, Zoroastrian or Hindu groups, were more likely to have twin operations whereby social welfare activities developed around the temple of worship that would have been built first as a focal point for the local community.

Conclusion

This chapter has considered the importance of the concept of social care in the work of religious organisations and for thinking more specifically about the significance of care for social policy. It has argued that social care has a dual meaning, like the concept of service discussed earlier: not only is it an act of looking after somebody else who is vulnerable or disabled, it is also a philosophical ethic for all human behaviour which can guide moral action by emphasising the moral relationships that bind human beings together. These moral relationships are emotive in character and are focused on helping those in need. For the individual who cares, their prime concern is how they fulfil their moral responsibility towards other people. This orientation has been juxtaposed to the more traditional focus on justice in social policy and political philosophy that advocates an abstract universal approach to human wellbeing by focusing on equal entitlements and rights. This chapter has shown that 'caring' is a defining feature of religious congregations and religious organisations. It is also not confined to women, but deeply connected to the human condition in general.

In this sense, the chapter has also looked at social care as a service and the importance of spiritual care within this. Religious organisations offer a variety of residential, day and home-based social care activities for vulnerable groups with particular emphasis on elderly care. Spiritual care is a key function of social care in this sense, and helps enhance the holistic approach to care receivers while also helping the spiritual wellbeing of the care giver. A key caveat highlighted by the ethics of care approach is its tendency towards parochialism and bias, and this explains why care relationships may work better on a small group scale – religious organisations may thus be criticised on this front.

But we end this chapter by considering White and Tronto's (2004) argument that although rights are universal, they are not accessed by all citizens or by those who need to access them the most; and although needs are specific to all individuals, only the needs of some are made visible in social welfare policy and not others, which distorts the ability for self-responsibility and care for others by all members of society, including those who are materially well-off. This is an important and continuing challenge for social policy – White and Tronto (2004) square this circle by arguing that an ethics of moral action based on care advocates the following approach:

> What is most important, then, is that there be democratic processes by which rights can be asserted for and by all, and needs understood and frankly explained by and for all. There should be, in the end, a duty to care about public care, which requires a recognition of collective responsibility for all needs. The goal is to start from these three presumptions:
>
> 1) everyone is entitled to receive adequate care throughout their lives;
> 2) everyone is entitled to participate in relationships of care that give meaning to their lives;
> 3) everyone is entitled to participate in the public process by which judgments about how society should ensure these first two premises are framed. (White and Tronto, 2004, p 449)

The implications of these arguments for the conceptual shift in this book towards the notion of *ways of being* lie in the focus given to human relationships and the need for society as a whole to identify with a set of moral principles that uphold the rights and personal dignity of all. Within the religious context, care is not confined to female members – it is a driving force for the men as well who are engaged in religious welfare action. It may be argued that the care felt by these religiously motivated individuals is purely missionary in nature and seeks to convert them to the religion of the organisation doing the social work. But the research data indicates that religious welfare organisations are primarily preoccupied with delivering a service in a self-less manner in the hope that their actions may have a larger ripple effect within society. They share their religious belief by the example of how they are towards other people.

Questions for discussion

1. What are the relative strengths and weaknesses of an ethics of care versus an ethics of justice?
2. How does a religious or spiritual perspective on social care enhance an holistic approach to human wellbeing?
3. In what ways does religiously oriented social care differ from secular social care provision?
4. Are women potentially disadvantaged by the emphasis on family-based care in the various religious traditions?
5. What is the difference in the dynamics and effect on social welfare between a religious congregation and a service-oriented religious welfare organisation?

Useful websites

Jewish Care: www.jewishcare.org/home
Methodist Homes for the Aged: www.mha.org.uk/HomePage.aspx
The Big Care Debate: www.govtoday.co.uk/index.php/Social-Care/the-big-care-debate.html

SEVEN

Poverty reduction and financial assistance

Summary

- Religious organisations have a discourse of economic justice which complements their discourse of social care although it may not be as visible or as effective since they are restricted by government economic policy and globalisation. In this sense, church groups are the leading voices in campaigning against social and economic inequalities.
- There is spiritual poverty and economic or material poverty according to religious groups. The former is concerned with the individual's sense of inner peace, self-knowledge, self-responsibility and virtuous character. The second is concerned with the absence of key material needs such as adequate income, housing, food, clothing and education.
- Religious welfare actors often speak in the language of social exclusion and empowerment when they are referring to poverty, and see themselves as having a direct impact on the alleviation of poverty.
- Religious welfare organisations are engaged in a variety of economic poverty reduction services including credit unions, cash collections and emergency cash assistance, Islamic or ethical banking, soup kitchens, clothing and food banks, international humanitarian relief and being subcontracted to the government's Work Programme.
- Religious welfare organisations are a supportive, emergency relief resource alongside the formal welfare system in the UK. Their involvement in the Work Programme as subcontractors sees them taking on a highly secularised and professionalised role. But the added 'benefit' is that they are better equipped than statutory bodies such as Jobcentre Plus to effectuate psychological renewal in unemployed people to get them 'ready for work' and not just 'in work', as expressed by the present Secretary of State for Work and Pensions, Iain Duncan Smith himself at a Christian Socialist conference.

Introduction

This chapter takes us into the realm of poverty, broadly defined, and economic justice, both of which are discourses of prime concern to religious groups and actors in the UK. It builds on the previous discussion of social care and ethics of justice in Chapter 6. Poverty is the perennial social problem of human society, and the bread and butter of social policy, but how do we define it? Indeed, our definition of it will determine what solutions we are able to find for it. In this chapter we look at poverty in a variety of meanings, first, as a state of socioeconomic deprivation that is manifested in a variety of material ways such as a low level income, limited ability to access basic social services or limited personal capabilities such as knowledge and skills or political freedom (Jawad, 2009). Secondly, poverty also carries within its definition the more spiritual connotations of moral humility often associated with religious faith (Rahnema, 1997). Thus, spiritual poverty may be taken to mean poor self-knowledge that leads someone to lose control over their life, perhaps through crime or drug addiction or personal self-harm. Hence, the chapter takes a multidimensional view of poverty (Spicker, 2007), and by bringing social, ideational and cultural elements into the definition of poverty, it helps clarify the conceptual shift towards the more holistic notion of *ways of being* proposed in this book. The key idea here, as the research with religious groups shows, is that what matters is *who* we are, and *knowing* who we are.

The terms 'economic poverty' and 'spiritual poverty' are used as these are the two key concepts driving the discourses and practices of religious welfare actors and their organisations in the UK, and indeed other countries in the Western world where religious groups are active in the social welfare sphere. The chapter also draws attention to the advocacy and public critique role that the Church of England has taken in the UK on debates surrounding economic poverty, supported by other prominent church groups such as The Salvation Army.

Indeed, perhaps one of the questions raised here is that the church may be quite vociferous about the plight of the poor and economic inequalities in Britain, but how much structural change or political leverage do they have to change these conditions? Are some of the churches, as Pacione (1990) has argued, too close to the middle classes and ruling establishment in the UK to effectuate a real impact on the capitalist system and the needs of the poor? This chapter draws attention to the fact that poverty reduction is the broad banner under which religious organisations in the UK would place their work. However, the key question the chapter seeks to explore if not answer completely is how effective these religious welfare groups are in helping people out of poverty into long-term prosperity and personal flourishing. Thus, the chapter explores the types of services offered by religious groups that are of a specifically economic character that seek to relieve material and income-based poverty.

Work and unemployment forms an underlying subtheme in this chapter: they have been a core concern for the social mobilisation of the established church both in the UK and in other European countries such as Germany; and for the first time in an academic social policy text, this book reports on research that has been carried out among religious welfare organisations in the UK that have government contracts to provide employment and training services.

The chapter is organised as follows: the first section looks at how poverty is understood from a religious perspective. It draws on the work of Wallis (2002), who identifies three dimensions of poverty. The second section develops this conceptual beginning by looking at some of the key documents produced by churches in the UK that deal with the issue of economic poverty and prosperity for all. These are the following reports by Churches Together in Britain and Ireland (CTBI): the 1996 *Prosperity with a purpose* report (CTBI, 1996); *Unemployment and the future of work* (CTBI, 1997) and *Prosperity with a purpose: Christians and the ethics of affluence* (CTBI, 2005). The third section then looks at the types of social services offered by religious welfare organisations, focusing in particular on the research done with organisations contracted out to deliver employment services. The chapter concludes by arguing that in the arena of economic poverty reduction, religious organisations do well at speaking out against economic injustices but they are less effective in bringing about transformational change in the economic structures of the UK. Some success has been achieved with the campaigns for the just wage by Citizens UK (as discussed in Chapter 8). Some of the more prominent religious welfare organisations in the UK tread a fine line in critiquing the impact of neoliberal policies on the UK but continuing to rub shoulders with members of the government. It is their ability to remain financially independent from government that allows religious welfare organisations to protect themselves and to preserve their prophetic missions.

Defining poverty from a religious perspective

Poverty has a potentially confusing and paradoxical meaning in the religious traditions discussed in this book – it can be understood as both good and bad in itself but can also be used as a symbolic signifier of human life and its final destiny. This makes it a very tricky concept to pin down in the work of religious welfare organisations, that (sensibly perhaps) often refer to social exclusion or disempowerment as a way of denoting people experiencing some form of material deprivation or deficiency in their lives. This confusing picture is aptly summarised in Wallis's (2002, p 51) three-dimensional definition of poverty that he derives directly from the Christian Bible:

> Blessed are you who are poor. (Luke, 6.20)

> One does not live by bread alone. (Mathew, 4.4)

> Then you will know the truth and the truth will make you free. (John, 8.32) (cited in Wallis, 2002, p 51)

Different messages emanate from the citations above; they appear to exalt the status of poverty on the one hand, or indeed argue for a non-material dimension of human wellbeing. They also appear to suggest that poverty is something that is bound to occur within human society. After all, all religious traditions call on believers to help the poor and needy – such misfortune will exist as part of human society even if this may be created by a loving God. This leads to the second sense in which poverty also has a broader symbolic meaning in the religious texts which is intrinsic to human history and destiny. Abrahamic religions view mass poverty and human suffering as a sign of the end of times – the time of Tribulations, which is also marked by the frequency of natural disasters, or as the fall from grace of mankind after Adam and Eve's dismissal from the garden of Eden. In the Indian religions, rebirth as a poor or unwell person may be a sign of a bad previous life. In some Christian Pentecostal faiths, poverty, or its inverse affluence, are a sign of God's blessings, harking back to 16th-century Calvinist interpretations of material affluence being a sign of salvation.

Wallis (2002) argues that poverty has three dimensions: material, spiritual and civic. The material sense has to do the satisfaction of basic physiological needs of survival such as access to an adequate income, food, shelter and clothing. But Wallis gives a particular meaning to this understanding of material poverty in terms of social marginalisation and exclusion. This is a common way of understanding poverty among religious welfare organisations in the UK which emphasises the socio–psychological dimension of material poverty. Wallis argues the following:

> Marginalized people of all ages are the most vulnerable of God's children. They are, indeed, the focus of religious concern in the Torah, the New Testament and the Koran. It is always the treatment of 'the other' that is the test of faith. But why is that? Why are our religious traditions so strong in commanding us to care for the widow, the orphan, the stranger, the forgotten and the poor? The weak, vulnerable and excluded become the standard for what the rest of society really means by 'community'. Who is part of the family and who is not? Who's in and who's out? Who is 'us' and who is 'them'? (Wallis, 2002, p 57)

The problem of marginalisation and social exclusion is heightened by ever-increasing social and economic inequalities in society. Wallis (2002) discusses the case of the US, but equally we may argue that the UK is one of the most unequal societies in the Western hemisphere. Deeply linked to this is that society has become increasingly consumer-focused. Religious traditions have much to say about helping those who are in material need or respecting the property of others (see Jawad, 2009, for a fuller discussion). The same categories of vulnerable people named in Wallis's (2002) quotation above are also those most commonly named in the main religions.

> 'We work with hard-to-reach groups, but in reality it is the state which is hard to reach.' (Jewish organisation manager)

> 'We need to empower people to take charge of their own lives.' (Baha'i organisation manager)

> 'Our aim is to empower people.' (Zoroastrian manager)

> '… the people we help are neglected by the system.' (Christian manager)

The second core concept identified by Wallis (2002) that is also evident among religious welfare organisations is spiritual poverty, which is also denoted as a form of moral poverty. This afflicts both rich and poor people alike and signifies a lack of social bonds and family ties, an attachment to superficial and material elements of life as exemplified by the consumer culture of modern society. This culture of materialism, individualism and competition is affecting families and their children, leading people to commit crimes and children to grow up without any positive or caring adult role models to support them. Cosedine (2002), in support of this view, argues that mainstream modern Western society has largely lost its spiritual sense of life and is driven by technological innovation, material accumulation and values such as individualism and competition. Thus, he asks:

> ... when are we going to recognize this spiritual bankruptcy and place it alongside unemployment, institutionalised racism and poverty as being a principle cause of crime and alienation and a primary need to be addressed? We should be pursuing the 'common good' and not elite interests. (Cosedine, 2002, p 33)

Cosedine (2002, pp 37-46) then proposes four key social principles that would form a just and spiritual society: 'the common good, sustainability, wisdom, holistic spirituality'. These are described in Box 7.1 below. Like Tronto's (1995) secular view of the ethics of care that employed the Jewish moral principle of 'repair the world' (as discussed in the previous chapter), Cosedine's view of the good (spiritual) life employs Catholic social principles; namely, the subsidiary principle which involves devolving social responsibility in society for the vulnerable to most local levels possible, hence the community and the family would be a core provider of care and social support in times of need, but the state would remain the source of help of last resort.

A second Catholic social principle that is evident in Cosedine's (2002) framework for the common good is the principle of the 'option of the poor'. As Kahl (2005) also discusses this at length, the option for the poor leads to the provision of specific social assistance programmes for those identified as the most vulnerable in society. In modern social policy terms, this could facilitate a residual notion of needs-based social assistance rather than a universal rights-based approach to social welfare. But in Cosedine's (2002) model, there is still provision for the protection of human rights. The important element in Cosedine's argument is that all four principles of the common good, as shown in Box 7.1, need to be applied together at the same time, otherwise the principle of the common good would be undermined. An essential concern is not to prioritise elite interests that for many authors like

Cosedine have hijacked the wealth of modern societies. The ideas proposed by Cosedine are not new but they are certainly ambitious. The need to balance environmental sustainability with the demands of modern industrial development and economic growth models that are adopted in all countries around the world has long preoccupied development studies theorists and has proved challenging for the biggest global polluters such as the US, which is also the world's richest economy. Cosedine (2002) paints a grim picture of global poverty, climate change and debt that has been intensifying since the 1960s.

Box 7.1: Four cornerstones of the good spiritual life

- *The common good:* principles of subsidiarity, social solidarity, protection of human rights, option for the poor
- *Sustainability:* protecting the resources of the natural environment for future generations and against further deterioration of the earth's climate
- *Wisdom:* retaining the historical and experience-based roots of knowledge and not the rampant commercial production of information – this entails greater respect of integration of elders in society
- *Holistic spirituality:* recognising the interconnectedness of humanity and of the poor and powerless – together, the sacred character of life and humanity may be recognised

Source: Adapted from Cosedine (2002)

The third kind of poverty that Wallis (2002) identifies is the civic kind, and this really follows on from the deterioration of moral and spiritual bonds that have already been discussed above. Its prime manifestation is in the political apathy and apparent trivialisation of political processes that can now be seen in many democratic societies. It is signalled by the polarisation of political life to a blaming game between Liberal Democratic and Conservative camps that emphasises dichotomous choices. An example is the debate between care and justice. Such theorists would argue that both are connected and much depends on the quality of democratic life and the active will to include the voice of citizens and not prioritise those who rule the economy and oversee the production of social knowledge. Such expressions of indignation are evident in the stances that the churches in the UK, and the Church of England in particular, have taken when they have spoken out against social and economic injustices. We review these debates in the next section and explore how effective they have been in having an impact on social policy in the UK.

Church discourses on poverty and economic injustice

The Church of England has remained a vocal public figure in the critique of poverty and social inequalities in the UK. Its first major report in 1985, *Faith in the city*, against Margaret Thatcher's neoliberal policies, created a major uproar and was mirrored by other similar reports in Europe such as *For a future founded on solidarity and justice* which was released by both the Evangelical Church and Catholic bishops in Germany in 1997 (for more details see Fischer's [2001] helpful review). In the German case, argues Fischer, the churches were not seeking to dictate government policy, but merely to reiterate moral standards of solidarity and social justice as a reminder of the social ideals of German society. But in Britain, similar publications have gone a step further in seeking to assert the role of the church in helping reinforce moral standards in society. We have referred several times already to the *Faith in the city* report published in 1985. In Box 7.2, a snapshot of the key recommendations in this document is presented. These clearly show that the church is giving a clear statement on how public policy should be modified to take better account of poor urban areas and what the church should do to show that it still has an active role to play in poverty reduction in Britain.

Box 7.2: Faith in the city (1985)

- A report of the Archbishop's Commission on Urban Priority Areas (UPAs) launched as a critique of Margaret Thatcher's policies and the plight of the urban poor in inner cities and outer council estates affected by economic decline, social disintegration and environmental decay
- The report produced 33 recommendations to the church and 26 to the nation at large, calling on government to take action in a variety of areas, such as:
  1. increases in social security and more investment in youth services and training
  2. greater investment in public housing
  3. greater community involvement in local authority urban strategies
  4. addressing institutional racism in legal, criminal and public services
- Recommendations to the church included:
  1. Diversion of resources to UPAs
  2. Undertaking audits and more ministerial training in UPAs

3. Establishment of a caucus for Black Anglican concerns
4. Establishment of a Church Urban Fund

Source: Adapted from Commission on Urban Life and Faith (2006)

As a consequence of the *Faith in the city* report, a joint decision was taken between state and church in the UK to establish the Church Urban Fund, which would have a lead role in advising government on social policy, and which continues to operate to this day. Later ecumenical reports by Churches Together in Britain and Ireland, *Unemployment and the future of work* (CTBI, 1997) and *Prosperity with a purpose – Christians and the ethics of affluence* (CTBI, 2005), have continued to tread this fine line between seeking to merely express the voices of the poor and socially excluded but also influencing public policy in the UK (Fischer, 2001). Fischer notes this ambiguity and provides a full discussion of *Unemployment and the future of work*, which was, of course, concomitant with the German report mentioned above. Thus, the 1997 Churches Together in Britain and Ireland report expressly stated:

> God is not above battle.... We are therefore bound, as we think our readers inside and outside the Church will see, to grapple with the detail of policy options. Our own aim is not partisan. It is to help the agenda, to prick the national conscience, by raising the saliency of unemployment as an issue, and to ask the public as a whole to accept the responsibility for effective practical remedies which will be costly to themselves. (CTBI, 1997, cited in Fischer, 2001, pp 157-8)

Senior members in The Salvation Army who took part in the research for this book echoed these:

> 'We are a thorn in the side of government.' (senior Salvation Army official)

Social justice was expressed as being a spiritual issue, and the 1997 CTBI report highlighted the problem of large intergenerational deprivation and the demise of earnest political activism (Fischer, 2001). The report criticises neoliberal economic policies and they way in which they have fragmented society, leading the poor to become dependent on welfare, with women having become a large part of the labour force. But the report does not reject the capitalist system, arguing for a balance to be struck between the workings of the market and the power of the government to regulate it, and that the church has insight and wisdom to help the development of policy, as noted above.

Hence the 1997 CTBI report is very clear on how Christian spiritual values can be the basis of a just economy and the common good. Particular emphasis is placed on the availability of 'good work for everyone' and on 'full employment'. This would involve enlarging educational and training opportunities and reformulating the priorities of the economy to become more long term. Fischer (2001) assesses the emphasis on national social responsibility as a call for civic renewal.

In the subsequent 2005 CTBI report, *Prosperity with a purpose – Christians and the ethics of affluence*, explicit recommendations are provided as to how economic growth may be brought more in line with Christian values. These are outlined in Box 7.3 below.

Box 7.3: Aligning economic growth with Christian values: *Prosperity with a purpose – Christians and the ethics of affluence*

- Humanity is one family bound by universal solidarity
- Wealth creation and the pursuit of social justice are inextricably linked, thus, economic growth is valid but must be regulated in order not to undermine community interests
- Poverty also leads to and is a marker of moral decline
- Shareholders should be more ethically concerned with how the companies they have invested in work, thus demonstrating a more long-term sense of stewardship
- Work has a broad vocational character; it is theologically wrong to depict people as lazy or to even use the term 'unemployment'
- All people should have access to good work without ring-fencing particular trades for themselves, thus rich countries should take into consideration their terms of trade with poor countries and not have protected industries

Many of these ideas are brought together and further developed in the 2006 *Faithful cities* report, published by the Commission on Urban Life and Faith. It paints a bleak picture of increasing prosperity but widening socioeconomic inequalities in Britain. It expressly refers the problem of social exclusion and marginalisation as defining the situation of poor people, in part because of the geographical nature of poverty in the UK – for example, whole neighbourhoods like South Oxhey near Watford in Hertfordshire are described as 'islands of deprivation', and also coastal communities in the UK, which are particularly suffering from economic degeneration and low self-esteem (Commission on Urban Life and Faith, 2006). The report thus argues that in order to address issues of poverty and prosperity, it is not sufficient merely to question the means of economic exchange but also the very purpose of economic life. This brings to the fore a strand of the argument which is of concern in this book about moral values, purpose and identity. Hence, the 2005 report *Prosperity with a purpose* explicitly seeks to include the marginalised and the excluded into economic growth.

Interestingly, *Faithful cities* (2006) argues that the UK could learn from anti-poverty strategies in developing countries that centre round sustainable livelihoods and community regeneration. These build anti-poverty initiatives on the existing strengths and assets of the communities involved by soliciting their knowledge and priorities regarding the problems they are facing and how to solve them. A similar recommendation in the report is for 'participatory budgeting' to be promoted, based on the example of Manchester Pride, a joint initiative between Salford City Council, Oxfam UK Poverty and Church Action on Poverty (Commission on Urban Life and Faith, 2006). The aim of this is to allow poor and marginalised groups to have a say in how public expenditure that affects local communities is spent. Thus, the report subscribed to a wellbeing manifesto presented by the new economics foundation (nef) which focuses on social policy that promotes human flourishing through a variety of ways such as: the education system, better measures of happiness and psychological well-being, less materialism, the strengthening of civil society and greater flexibility with work hours in order to accommodate childcare, family and community commitments.

The *Faithful cities* report again emphasises that these are moral choices and the onus is on the political and economic elites to prioritise the common good before their own interests. There is a need to rethink the capacity of capitalism to achieve wellbeing and happiness. Thus *Faithful cities* sees a key role for local leadership and congregations in public policy, stating, 'The language of renewal, regeneration and renaissance speak of the spiritual dimension in the reordering of our cities' (Commission on Urban Life and Faith, 2006, p 88). It offers specific recommendations on poverty reduction to the government, as highlighted in Box 7.4 below.

Box 7.4: *Faithful cities* recommendations to the government on wealth and poverty

1. Implementing a living wage
2. Expanding measure of economic success by using the new economic foundation measure of domestic progress
3. Further involvement of marginalised local deprived communities in participative public policy decision making such as participatory budgeting and sustainable livelihoods
4. The church must be more vocal in confronting selfish and greedy lifestyles, both within its own membership and in the wider population

The important question for the church, as Pacione (1990) states, is how far it is able to really bring about more fundamental change to economic injustice. In the face of corporate power and secular government, these questions deserve further investigation. But it should not be forgotten that the church has been at the helm of important movements for social justice at a global level, such as the Jubilee Debt Campaign and the Make Poverty History campaign which were launched in 2000 and 2005 respectively by mass coalitions of non-governmental aid agencies, trade unions, churches and other faith and secular campaign groups such as the British Humanist Association and some of the UK's largest religious charities. These mass campaign coalitions were primarily focused on the problem of public debt in poor countries around the world and sought to raise awareness of the need for the richer countries to honour their pledges to achieve the Millennium Goals that are social development targets for the year 2015. The term Jubilee itself is of Judeo-Christian origin and has a specific connection to the ancient practice of periodical cancellation of debt (every 50 years) and the returning of land to its traditional owners. This was in order to promote social and economic renewal and to restore a community's capacities of self-sustenance that would have been hampered by the accumulation of debt or the loss of property due to debt (Hudson, 1993). This was the Law of Jubilee which stems from a fundamental biblical view of man's stewardship of the earth, and that nature is a gift from God; it is the idea that private property is a sin and natural resources should be enjoyed equally by all human beings (Temple, 1942).

Poverty reduction services by religious welfare organisations

We come now to the final section of this chapter which looks at what kinds of poverty alleviation services religious welfare organisations are providing, and in particular what role they are playing in the retraining and employment contracts that they have with the government. A full appreciation of the extent and impact of these services is difficult to ascertain due to a lack of accurate and comprehensive data. The Northwest Regional Development Agency, the Faith-based Regeneration Network and a number of faith forums have produced various documentation that give an overview of the kinds of activities that would fall under the categories discussed here. Future research in the area of religion and social welfare would do well to consider these issues. For the present purposes, these services are split into four strands: in-cash assistance, in-kind assistance, retraining and employment services, and international poverty relief. We look at these below as four illustrations.

Illustration 1: In-cash assistance

Charity collections are an important part of the work of religious temples and faith communities in the UK. Typically, they make charity collections for a wide variety of good causes, especially during religious occasions such as Christmas or Ramadan. This is very much a congregation-based activity that asserts religious identity and revolves around religious worship and participation in the religious life of a community. For Muslims, it is the principle of *zakat* that involves an act of money transfer symbolising solidarity, and also a religious purification of a person's wealth (Jawad, 2009). For Jews, it is the principle of *tzedakah*. As well as financial collections that are made during congregational meetings, religious organisations also give financial assistance to needy members of their communities. For example, the Birmingham Jewish Federation helps members of the community with one-off payments to cover everyday expenses such as bus passes or utility bills. Similar practices are organised by other religious organisations.

Admittedly, the number of people involved is small and the sums of money are also small. The number of people may vary from a mere handful to a few thousand over the life course of an organisation's services. More organised methods of cash assistance involve credit unions (see, for example, the *Faith in action* report by the East England Development Agency [2003]), such as the *Gemach* in the Haredi community of North London. Members pay a fixed sum of money which is loaned out to one of the members if needed, but at no extra interest. This falls in line with Jewish law, and also requires that the person borrowing the money names two guarantors. Such activities are common in developing countries and have been institutionalised inmicro-credit organisations that target the poor such as the Grameen Bank and BRAC in Bangladesh.

Illustration 2: In-kind assistance

Food and clothing banks, as well as soup kitchens, are a common and widespread way among religious organisations to deliver vital emergency supplies to people in need. Typically food offerings from harvest festivals and Christmas may be divided into parcels and given to families in need or used in communal meals. Some organisations focus on giving food to asylum-seekers and refugees awaiting decisions on their applications and who have no other source of support. A variety of other activities, such as negotiating the supply of food to a night shelter or organising subsidised luncheon clubs for older people, are typical activities. In any one gathering there may be tens or hundreds of people. Some organisations such as The Trussell Trust operate as food banks, sending out thousands of food parcels to families around the UK. According to the Trust, 13 million people in the UK are living below the poverty line and are thus socially vulnerable. Food banks help prevent crime, housing loss, family breakdown and mental health problems. Vouchers are issued to public sector care professionals such as doctors, the local police, social workers and Citizens Advice Bureau staff. They identify people in need and give them the food vouchers to go and collect food and other vital household needs. Redundancy, illness, benefit delay, domestic violence, debt, family breakdown or paying for heating during winter are all cited as reasons for people going without food in the UK. The Trussell Trust also operates in countries outside the UK, such as Bulgaria. It states clearly that it is a Christian organisation inspired by Jesus Christ's teachings on feeding the hungry but that it remains open to helping people of non-Christian or no faith.

Illustration 3: Retraining and employment services

The larger and more professional religious welfare organisations such as The Salvation Army and the Faith Regen Foundation take on government-funded contracts with the Work Programme to find training and work placements for unemployed people. These organisations note that sometimes they are allocated people from minority ethnic backgrounds or 'difficult cases' such as people who have been long-term unemployed. The Salvation Army has an Employment Plus Programme (see below) that employs staff who are not religious or Salvation

Army members. This is also the case with Faith Regen, and the members of staff in charge of running the employment and training programme are not Muslims. The service users are also from a wide variety of backgrounds and know hardly anything about the religious character of the organisation offering them employment and career advice and training. This was certainly the case for the service users interviewed during the research for this book. Members of staff involved directly with clients spoke of the culture of 'humanity' within the organisation that meant that clients were properly listened to and members of staff enjoyed a good work rapport. Secular members of staff were aware that the organisation might have other services specifically directed to members of its own faith community but this was seen as a separate strand of activity that the organisation was involved in. In a recent speech at a Christian Socialist event, Iain Duncan Smith noted that voluntary sector organisations could perform the difficult task of preparing unemployed people psychologically for work and changing their attitudes so that they could stay in their jobs. The involvement of religious welfare organisations in the Work Programme saw them acting like their secular counterparts, although they might stress that their attentiveness to the needs of their clients and their dedication to making the work placements a success was a distinctive feature. Being able to get involved in such programmes gave a chance to minority religious organisations to prove that they had come of age as British citizens in the UK.

Faith Regen is a Muslim organisation and works with many deprived minority ethnic populations. When such organisations enter into government contracts, they are, in effect, delivering public services and need to abide by criteria set by government. Inevitably, such services take on a secular character and are used by clients who have specific needs. Religious organisations do not change the rules of social policy or the way in which the Work Programme operates. Indeed, service users who were interviewed noted that they had no choice in which organisation they were referred to, and often found their contact with Jobcentre Plus to be impersonal and superficial, whereas with employment consultants working in the religious organisations, lengthy conversations could take place and in some cases, the clients themselves ended up either volunteering or working for the religious organisations, as in the case of several interviewees at The Salvation Army.

Illustration 4: International poverty relief

Our final example takes religious organisations further afield in the international development effort. Some of the most important international relief organisations are British and religious in character, such as Islamic Relief UK, Tearfund and Christian Aid. These organisations focus their efforts on emergency relief services in disaster zones such as earthquakes or famine, and may spend longer periods of time involved in development projects. For minority ethnic religious organisations such as Jewish and Muslim ones, these organisations may help organise visits or pilgrimages to the Middle East. At this level, such organisations are active civic actors in the field of global humanitarian aid and global politics. Readers may recall the Jubilee Debt Campaign to wipe out poor country debts, referred to earlier. This clearly shows how religious and secular discourses of social justice become intertwined. But perhaps what is also striking is that whereas the efforts of religious organisations in international humanitarian relief have been well-known and better publicised for a while, it is only more recently that their work within the UK is beginning to catch attention. Organisations that have the experience of working in developing countries, as mentioned in the *Faithful cities* (Commission on Urban Life and Faith, 2006) report, are now arguing that lessons may be learned in the UK for how to tackle long-term poverty from the experience of development policy in poor, low-income countries.

Conclusion

This chapter has looked at the realm of economic justice in the work and discourse of religious organisations in the UK. It has explored three dimensions of the meaning of poverty: material, spiritual and civic. It has been highlighted that religious welfare organisations are also concerned with issues of economic justice, although it is the churches that have taken a lead position in this regard. Like their counterpart churches in Europe, the Church of England and other smaller church groups have produced various documents which have sought to engage directly with the analysis of the causes of poverty in the UK and the policy options that may be pursued in achieving greater social inequality. This sees church groups seeking to directly influence policy and make the church an active member in the formation of a just society.

A key theme running through the church is work and employment. This is of key concern to the Church of England, that all people should have good work and that all work should be seen as vocational, with no one being branded lazy, and no such category as unemployment. Equally, the church has raised the issue of globalisation and the unequal terms of global trade. The chapter ended with a review of the types of services offered by religious welfare organisations, which have been classed into four types: in-cash assistance, such as charity and credit unions; in-kind assistance, such as food and clothing banks; employment and training services, which are part of government contracts and see religious organisations operating very much as secular organisations; and international poverty relief, which sees religious organisations diverting their attention to poverty and disaster relief outside of the UK. In some ways, this chapter has raised more questions or pointed the direction towards new areas of research, as this topic is poorly researched in the UK. What it does make clear, however, is that religious organisations, and the Church of England, have the right discourse but not sufficient political leverage or the resources to make a greater impact on social and economic prosperity in the UK.

In terms of how this chapter furthers the argument about the concept *ways of being*, first, we see this in broadening the concept of poverty to spiritual matters which have to do with human nature and moral values; second, there is a broader critique of the capitalist system by the church in particular. This emphasises that the basic principles underpinning the social order matter, and religious traditions perhaps offer alternative visions of society that value different modes of behaviour that would be less individualist and materialistic.

Questions for discussion

1. How is poverty understood from a religious perspective?
2. How effective has the stance of the Church of England been in the fight against poverty in the UK?
3. What lessons might the UK learn from poorer countries about how to tackle poverty?
4. In view of the types of poverty reduction services that religious organisations provide in the UK, do they treat the causes or the symptoms of poverty?

Useful websites

British Humanist Association: www.humanism.org.uk
Faith Regen Foundation: www.faithregenuk.org/
Islamic Relief Worldwide: www.islamic-relief.com/
Jubilee Debt Campaign: www.jubileedebtcampaign.org.uk/
Make Poverty History campaign: www.makepovertyhistory.org/ takeaction/
The Salvation Army Employment Plus Programme: http://admin. salvationarmy.org.uk/uki/www_uki.nsf/vw-dynamic-arrays/ A4C06596F5F34B0E8025729500566743
The Trussell Trust: www.truselltrust.org/foodbank-projects

EIGHT

Housing, urban governance and regeneration

Summary

- Faith-based organisations have figured prominently in the urban regeneration agendas of consecutive British governments. The city itself has deep symbolism in Christianity, and although church groups are best placed to engage with government with regeneration projects, minority religions are increasingly coming on board as well.
- Although deeply motivated by an ethic of service to fulfil social needs, faith groups in the UK also engage in political mobilisation, as evidenced by the example of Citizens UK that follows the community organising principles of the US activist, Saul Alinsky (see Alinsky, 1973). This alliance of religious and non-religious organisations seeks to challenge the structures of global capitalism and has successfully campaigned for initiatives such as a just living wage.
- Religion shapes housing needs and aspirations. Strict Muslims and Orthodox Jews are especially significant in this regard due to the various religious requirements they have.
- The UK is quite unique in that state funds have gone towards minority ethnic housing associations and more recently, faith-based housing associations that provide social housing to members of their own faiths. The impact of these housing associations is ambiguous – they do not foster social segregation, but neither do they differ significantly from secular organisations and debates abound regarding the extent to which the needs of religious communities may be met within mainstream social housing provision.
- A further key dimension of housing services relates to emergency relief services for homeless people, as epitomised by nightly soup runs, over 80 per cent of which are either run by religious organisations such as The Salvation Army or local churches. Despite hostility from government and other homeless agencies, soup runs continue to go strong and are a key arena for the development of ethical citizenship aimed at serving the needs of the homeless, with no religious strings attached.

Introduction

This chapter takes a spatial lens to consider the role of religion and religious welfare provision in the areas of housing and urban regeneration that are related to a broader constellation of issues such as homelessness, social cohesion and social exclusion, and urban poverty. In both housing and urban regeneration policies, the UK government has increasingly begun to take into account the needs of religious communities and also what part they play in the development of harmonious and socially cohesive communities. In addition, religious organisations offering social welfare services in Britain have themselves catered to the housing and social needs of deprived people, in informal long-established ways such as soup runs and night shelters, or more formalised temporary housing provision such as paid-for accommodation in The Salvation Army's lifehouses, like Booth House, alluded to at the beginning of this book.

The concept of 'love thy neighbour' is perhaps the most famous teaching of the Christian Bible and one that finds universal resonance among people of other religions and indeed of no religion (Greg, 2004b). The connections between expressions of love, charity, altruism, social action and philanthropic action in relation to those who are in need or living in deprivation has been made evident in the preceding chapters. What we now focus on in this chapter is the notion of a 'neighbour'; without overstating the obvious, the concept of a neighbour refers to other people who live in close geographical proximity to us, people with whom we share living space and a geographical environment made up of natural resources. In Wuthnow's (2004) research on faith-based organisations in the US, he uses 'neighbourliness' to describe the social motivations and work ethos of religious social welfare organisations. So the core idea is that where we live matters a great deal for how we live, and therefore our wellbeing (Holloway and Moss, 2010). This is not a new idea for social policy. It raises concerns about geographical localities that lose out in the process of economic urbanisation, the particular association of poverty to urbanisation and the inner city, and thus, the geographical segregation of poverty in advanced capitalist societies such as the UK (Beaumont, 2008). These issues directly concern the social action and social welfare service role of religious organisations. Cities are therefore the main arena for interaction between religion, politics and a post-secular society (Beaumont, 2008).

So the social and geographical environment is the focus of this chapter and how faith organisations interact with their local environment. There is a social and geographical dimension encapsulated in the two concepts of 'community' whereby people living in a particular place share a sense of identity, belonging and life, as well as the idea of 'stewardship', which is that, within the religions discussed in this book, nature is given to them as a gift that they should take care of and not as a commodity to own and use without accountability (Holloway and Moss, 2010). The idea of social relationships bounded by a shared space, defining themselves according to the place where they live and sharing its physical resources comes together in the concept of the 'city'. We cannot overstate the significance of urbanisation and city life to human civilisation and modern life. Cities are engines of economic activity, seats of political power and hubs of cultural diversity. More importantly, rich and poor live in them, and often in very contrasting ways.

In Christian thought, the idea of the city has symbolic force for humankind's purpose on earth, and a dual meaning that is at the heart of Christianity's spiritual mission. The 'heavenly city' and the 'earthly city' are two philosophical concepts in Christian thought, propagated by St Augustine, the 5th-century Christian theologian and philosopher, in his book *City of God*. Both cities are 'two spatial realms – two cities – coexisting in single time – *saeculum*. However, the citizens of both cities are inextricably interwoven and cannot be told apart until Christ returns' (Bretherton, 2010, p 83). The earthly city is visible and the heavenly city is not visible. Both are made up of true Christians and Christians who have gone astray. The heavenly city is the ultimate reality that unites the true church but in the meantime, Christians must live in the earthly city while they await the coming of the heavenly city, and therefore have to find a way of reconciling their Christian faith in a geographical space (the earthly city) that does not abide by the same Christian ethos. Hence, they must find ways of maintaining peace and common understanding with other citizens. This, Bretherton (2010) argues, is symbolic of the need for Christians to engage with non-Christians in order to exercise some influence on political institutions and public policy. A fundamental part of Augustinian thought was that Christendom had not undermined the superior political power of the Roman Empire, and in fact that Christians needed to abide by the ruling secular powers that governed them.

So there is, to some extent, a Christian focus in this chapter that is not coincidental, particularly in the discussion of urban regeneration. As Smith (2004b) notes, church groups, and the Church of England, have the largest geographical spread and politico-economic clout in order to engage with government-funded community regeneration projects on a large scale. Urban social welfare action has a deep association with church groups in the UK, from Glasgow to London, as also evidenced in various Church of England publications such as *Faith in the city* and *Faithful cities* and the formal establishment of the Church Urban Fund which works closely with government to oversee resolution of inner-city deprivation (Taylor, 2003). But there is also an increasingly popular labelling of Britain by commentators following the work of Habermas (2006) as a post-secular and post-Christian society (Judge, 2001; Beaumont, 2008). This is certainly the case in terms of housing needs and social provision, as will be highlighted in this chapter, whereby there is a greater presence in the UK for religious housing associations catering for the needs of their religious communities and a greater recognition within government policy in the UK of the housing needs of minority religious groups (Flint, 2010). Equally, there has been a growing expectation since the Blair government that minority religious groups could play an active role in fostering social cohesion and contributing to their neighbourhoods and communities (Farnell et al, 2003).

Thus, there is a focus in this chapter on the extent to which religious welfare organisations move beyond mere social service provision to more fundamental moral and social transformation. We look in the final section at political mobilisation among religious welfare organisations, some of which were involved in the research for this book. This chapter thus allows us to come full circle. It extends some of the arguments presented in Chapters 3 and 4 on governance and social action and offers the possibility of thinking differently about space and being (Dewsbury and Cloke, 2009).

The chapter is divided as follows: the first section looks at some of the key conceptual and policy issues underpinning the relationship between religion and housing in contemporary Britain; the second develops this focus by looking at the services provided by religious housing associations and also the particular role of religious charities towards the homeless, making use of examples such as soup runs and night shelters. Here, an argument proposed by Cloke et al (2010) about religious organisations contributing to a new form of ethical citizenship and civic action is developed further in the third section, where we look at the role of religious groups in community organising and political mobilising. The chapter ends with a review of the challenges and opportunities facing urban regeneration policy and its engagement with religious organisations.

Religious identity and housing processes

British housing policy has traditionally focused on the importance of ethnic and racial identity in identifying community needs and planning for housing provision (Flint, 2009). Nevertheless, significant changes have begun to take place since the mid-2000s: first, The Housing Corporation, the public agency which funds and regulates housing associations in England, has commissioned various studies into the housing needs of Orthodox Jewish and Muslim tenants and has added a religious classification into the national surveys it conducts (Flint, 2010). The Corporation's Black and Minority Ethnic Action Plan 2005–08 also states that faith will be now be considered in its housing plans, like 'race' (Flint, 2010). Second was the holding of the first national Faith and Housing Conference in November 2005 that focused in particular on the 'Muslim dimension' and was addressed by the government Minister for Housing at the time (Flint, 2010).

This section considers the historical role of religion in shaping housing policy, processes and social conduct in relation to housing. The purpose is to link issues of culture and home life to broader patterns of housing, what Flint (2009, p 419) refers to as 'practical conduct in housing processes'. These ideas are important for thinking more broadly about the challenges of social cohesion and urban unrest that face Western societies, and the geographical segregation of socially deprived populations in poor housing estates. The debates were re-ignited by the 2001 riots in the northern towns of Bradford, Burnley and Oldham, and have been revitalised by the 2011 riots in various English cities that started in London. These policy debates are framed within the context of immigration, national identity, civic values and, more specifically, the position of Muslim populations in European societies in relation to these issues (Flint, 2010). Focusing in particular on the English case, as illustrated in research by Flint (2009, 2010), these issues are especially salient for 'the role of faith as a particular dimension of cultural identity and urban institutional organisation is increasingly being recognised in English housing policy' (Flint, 2010, p 257). Flint argues that housing policy has traditionally focused on how ethnic and racial identity shapes social segregation and housing aspirations, and in particular, it has a secular orientation to Christian faith which is not adequate for responding to other minority faiths, such as Islam and Judaism, where religious belief assumes the status of a way of life and it is harder to separate private space from public space or the sacred from the secular.

On the basis of this assertion, it is important to recall preceding discussions in this book about the role of religion in shaping human behaviour, social conduct and social order – which were central to the work of the founding fathers of sociology, Max Weber (1930) and Emile Durkheim (1915). Weber (1930), in particular, emphasised the influence of Calvinist interpretations of moral duty, moral behaviour and salvation in shaping everyday life after the Reformation. In *The protestant work ethic*, his central thesis revolved around the internalisation of social norms, with individual members of society linked to psychological process, which eventually produced the social order that we know today as capitalism. These ideas are well known. What is less well known is how Calvinism shaped our modern notions of housing. Flint (2009) reminds us that religious institutions have provided various forms of housing and accommodation since the Middle Ages, but furthermore, Weber (1930, p 171) posits that Calvinism also shaped the notion of the 'clean and solid comfort', as epitomised by the 'middle-class home' (Flint, 2009, p 420).

The flip side of these is that religious minorities find protection from wider social discrimination in living together. This issue is especially acute among Muslims, as Phillips (2006) argues, who now appear to have replaced the White deprived population as the new underclass. There is partly an issue of self-segregation here that was also pointed out in the Ouseley Report on the city of Bradford, just prior to the 2001 riots (cited in Flint, 2010). The Cantle Report (Home Office, 2001) had also identified the issue of 'parallel lives' whereby religious and ethnic communities were geographically segregated and shared very little cultural or leisure interchange with members of other faiths or religious communities (cited in Flint, 2010). These forms of self-segregation are taken to extremes, such as in the study by Valins (2003) cited in Flint (2010, p 262), whereby a member of the Jewish Ultra-Orthodox community referred to the area where she lived as 'my beautiful ghetto'. Nevertheless, such communities remain open to outsiders, as Flint (2010) highlights, and are not strictly drawn in the term 'parallel lives' suggests. Equally, other studies show that members of religious communities are seeking congregation, not segregation, and would not object to living in a mixed religion neighbourhood (Flint, 2010). Sellick (2004) also describes areas in North London, where, for instance, communities of different faiths, in this case Muslim and Jewish faiths, co-exist harmoniously.

The ways in which religious identity shape housing aspirations and preferences are manifest in a variety of ways: in the Jewish and Muslim contexts, examples can be found in the Ultra-Orthodox Jewish requirement for geographical enclaves (*eruv* or *eruvin* plural), marked by posts and fine wire within their normal residential localities which they can use during the Sabbath (Milmo, 2002), the Muslim need to respond to the call to prayer from a nearby mosque (*adhan*) and access to *kosher* and *halal* meat outlets for Jews and Muslims respectively (Flint, 2010). Indeed, Flint further notes that some social housing in the UK was built with low sinks and separate bathrooms in order to accommodate Muslim ablution practices before prayer. Various studies show that Muslim and Jewish populations tend be concentrated at neighbourhood and not district ward levels, such as particular streets in Bradford which have over 80 per cent Muslim residents, or Ultra-Orthodox Jewish neighbourhoods in Manchester or North London, with 100 per cent Jewish residents (Flint, 2010).

In conclusion, the key argument here is that, as in other areas of social policy, religion has climbed up the agenda of housing policy as a key demographic variable which defines housing needs, aspiration and provision (Flint, 2010). Flint notes that for minority religions such as Islam and Judaism, religion is a way of life and a significant factor of social and personal identity, which means that it has implications for housing process and needs. The next section explores the practice of service provision in the area of housing and its implications for social welfare and human beings.

Religious housing associations and homeless services

Very little research has been conducted on the role of religious groups in housing service provision. To date, research by Cloke et al (2010) and Flint (2009, 2010) provides some of the most comprehensive research illustrations. In this section, we look at two key areas of housing service provision by way of illustrating the impact of religious organisations on housing needs and also their potential for broader social transformation.

There is a long history of religious philanthropy and intervention in housing as well as in the development of housing policy in the UK. As Kosmin (2005), cited in Flint (2010), notes, Christian philanthropy was especially influential in inspiring the development of social housing, including the Shaftesbury, Peabody and Guinness Trusts. Jewish social housing also has a long history, such as the Industrial Dwellings Society (Kosmin, 2005). During the Victorian era, programmes for improving sanitation and drainage were held on days of national prayer for the resolution of the cholera epidemic (Burleigh, 2005, cited in Flint, 2010). In this section, we review two case illustrations, one looking at the role and impact of religious housing associations (Flint, 2010), and the second looking at more traditional emergency relief services provided by religious groups, such as soup runs and night shelters (Cloke et al, 2010).

Illustration 1: Religious housing associations

Flint (2010) offers some insightful research on religious housing associations in England: most have Anglican, Roman Catholic, Methodist or evangelical origins, and this may still be inferred from their organisation's ethos and name. But since the 1970s, more non-Christian housing associations have come into being, particularly Jewish and Muslim. Flint notes that the presence of religious housing associations in England is part of a longer tradition of Black and minority ethnic (BME) housing associations from the 1970s, with very few international parallels anywhere else in the world. These associations are funded directly from mainstream government budgets. The Housing Corporation played a key role in the establishment of BME housing policy through its 1986 BME Housing Needs Strategy (Flint, 2010). In terms of basic facts and figures, 64 BME housing associations are registered with The Housing Corporation, established mostly in the 1980s, and around half own less than 200 housing units. Regulations of registration stipulate that 80 per cent of the governing members of BME housing should be from BME backgrounds. The 23 largest BME housing associations manage 20,000 homes, and have an annual turnover of £82 million (Lupton and Perry, 2004, cited in Flint, 2010). 'BME housing associations are an example of state-funded institutionalised diversity on ethnic or religious lines' (Flint, 2010, p 267), but there has been very little public debate about their role. On the one hand, they are not seen to have the same impact of national identity as faith schools, for example, and are much less visible, accounting for only 1.5 per cent of housing association sector activities (Flint, 2010). Moreover, several research studies, including some commissioned by The Housing Corporation inspection reports, have found that BME organisations have similar performance to mainstream housing associations. These studies found no evidence that BME housing associations produce social segregation or weaken civic identity.

Religious housing associations are a much newer development but follow the path of BME associations. Flint (2010) notes that many BME housing associations have religious roots or are the result of smaller religious organisations combining to form one housing association. Examples of such associations include the North London Muslim Housing Association, established in 1986, although other BME housing associations have a majority of Muslim tenants. The North London Muslim Housing Association caters for the housing needs of the Muslim community and provides homes for large families. It manages 500 homes, mainly in the London Borough of Hackney, and like other religious organisations cited in this book

---

from non-Christian backgrounds, it seeks to give a positive impression of Islam by engaging with society at large (The Housing Corporation, 2007 cited in Flint, 2010). Apart from this Muslim example, there are also Jewish housing associations in various English cities, notably in London, Birmingham, Manchester, Liverpool, Sheffield and Leeds.

Flint (2010) notes that, like BME housing associations, religious housing associations have received little official policy debate in relation to their effect on community relations. A series of inspection reports by The Housing Corporation state that these organisations are generally performing well, and have appropriate financial, governance, management and service delivery processes (The Housing Corporation, cited in Flint, 2010). Indeed, although The Housing Corporation inspection reports note that these Muslim and Jewish housing associations need to keep close tabs on ensuring that they respect equality and diversity in their service provision, none failed The Housing Corporation's regulatory code. Various pieces of research also note that some religious housing associations have seen a decline in tenants from a Christian, Muslim or Jewish background (Lupton and Perry, 2004; Kosmin, 2005). There is also increasing cooperation between some religious housing associations from different religious backgrounds such as close relations between the North London Muslim Housing Association and Agudas Israel Housing Association, which is also a sponsor of Interlink, the umbrella non-governmental organisation for the Hasidic Jewish community in North London (Flint, 2010). Flint also cites the example of the Manchester Methodist Housing Association that developed large family homes in Oldham, Manchester for the local Asian population in 2005. These housing units include kitchens to facilitate *halal* food preparation and bathrooms facing away from Mecca (Flint, 2010).

Flint argues that this kind of cooperation has a positive effect on social cohesion since it can enhance dialogue between housing associations such as in the Muslim and Jewish cases in London, referred to above, or in the Manchester case, such provision may enhance more mixed religion and mixed race residential communities. Thus, even though such cooperation may be small scale, there is a possibility of expansion through housing associations providing consultancy services to other housing associations in delivering community cohesion and housing services. The impact of this may have ripple effects beyond the housing association sector. But, Flint argues, the future of these associations is uncertain. Since 1998, The Housing Corporation is increasingly supporting the provision of religiously and ethnically sensitive housing through its mainstream social housing provision. Flint (2010) argues that there is a good 'business case' for BME and religious housing associations since they can offer community cohesion consultancy and development activities. However, due to commercial constraints on the social housing sector, some BME associations have opted to merge with larger social landlord groupings as they fear for their future prospects. In recent years, government policy, as pronounced, for example, by the CLG and also as noted in the Cantle Report (Home Office, 2001), has stated that it will move away from the previous model of funding minority ethnic or religious communities directly as these are seen as undermining social cohesion (Flint, 2010). Since housing is deeply connected to urban segregation, there is a fear in housing policy discourse that housing associations might reinforce this.

In Flint's view, religious housing associations do not lead to urban segregation; their contribution to promoting cohesion is not conclusive. For example, the government's national priorities in relation to community cohesion and the prevention of 'parallel lives' are not necessarily communicated or shared by local organisations. It is not clear, in Flint's view, if religiously based housing needs are best met through mainstream secular organisations or 'specialist and autonomous' religious organisations. In many ways, this conundrum mirrors much of the debate on religious welfare provision. It is certainly refuted in Chapter 6 on social care, which shows how religiously based residential care is paramount for meeting the needs of people in whose lives religion is a significant factor. Thus, Flint (2010, p 271) concludes, 'given that most religious minority tenants are not in BME housing associations, the greatest contribution that faith-based housing providers may make to cohesion is through advising other landlords about accommodating the diverse needs of their tenants in relation to faith. This could facilitate ethno-religious diversity within urban spaces of social housing.' The research that was conducted for this book looked at the lifehouses run by The Salvation Army. These offer temporary accommodation, offered for a period of up to six months for a monthly fee. The people who use them may be on benefits and often seek advice and information at the lifehouses on their statutory rights. Service users are not affected by the religious dimension of the staff running the lifehouses. There is a sense in which these are commercial enterprises that do not dramatically differ from other secular organisations.

Illustration 2: The 'extra-ordinary ethic of care' in emergency relief services for the homeless

Research by Cloke et al (2010) highlights the key role of religious organisations in more traditional emergency or outdoor relief homelessness services such as night shelters, soup kitchens, hostels and day centres. Cloke et al argue that these form alternative, informal and less well-documented spaces of urban activism whereby services to the homeless are provided on the basis of a logic of 'compassion and care', in contrast to the conventional logic in urban policy of social control, containment or punishment. Key to their argument is that religious groups offering services to the homeless are not exclusive to religious people but often incorporate people of no faith and activities that have no religious character. Cloke et al see in this a 'rapprochement between public secularism and private religion' and 'a new form of ethical citizenship' (2010, p 2) that promotes the agency and autonomy of homeless citizens.

Soup runs and emergency relief services for the homeless are traditional territory for Christian philanthropy, and today, in Britain, most services for the homeless are provided by Christian organisations (Cloke et al, 2010). Without these non-statutory organisations, homeless people would quite simply die, as a volunteer worker in the research commented. These volunteers are acting out of the principle of charity (caritas) and love (agape), most often giving services with no strings attached. Soup runs are the most active of these emergency services and entail not only the provision of food to people sleeping rough, but also clothing, someone to talk to and advice on where to go next for help. Cloke et al identify three types of motivation which prompt volunteers to become involved in these types of homeless services, as illustrated in Box 8.1, but the key issue they highlight is that Christian groups offering these services are operating within the context of humanist values and partnerships with other organisations, and volunteers who do not necessarily share the same religious faith. Very often, these partnerships are intentional and it is hard to distinguish between Christian and secular homeless services (Cloke et al, 2010).

Box 8.1: Three ethical frameworks for working in emergency services for homeless people

1. *Christian caritas:* traditional Christian love/agape; evangelism and open sharing of Christian faith; aim to alleviate spiritual needs and not just emotional and physical needs
2. *Secular humanism:* reason-based altruism; social justice and human rights-based notions of charity; no emphasis on the spiritual dimension of recovery
3. *Post-secular charity:* rejection of universalist notions of justice; construction of notions of ethics and justice based on the interaction between the service provider and the homeless person; care is taken not to impose an ethical view on the homeless person but at the same time to remain caring of their needs

Source: Adapted from Cloke et al (2010)

Soup runs can run on very low budgets, for example, £500 per year, and depend entirely on charitable donations (Cloke et al, 2010). Cloke and his colleagues argue that this is proof that people living in urban areas still care about homeless people and have not been consumed by the urban politics of social control and punishment. They estimate that 55 per cent of soup kitchens are run by Christian charities such as The Salvation Army or the St Vincent de Paul Society. A further 37 per cent of soup runs are run by local churches. Seventy-four per cent of soup runs are operated by unpaid volunteers and generally, there is one paid coordinator; 66 per cent depend on donations in kind such as clothing and bedding to give to homeless people. Thus, 70 per cent of soup runs provide food, clothing, bedding, soup, hot drinks and sandwiches. Seventy per cent offer advice and information on statutory services that helps to counter the claims that soup runs deter homeless people from seeking government services. Soup run coordinators in the research by Cloke et al (2010) estimated that 36 per cent of service users were indeed homeless and sleeping rough; 17 per cent were in night shelters and hostels; and 23 per cent were part of the hidden homeless, staying in bed and breakfasts, squatting or staying with friends or family. Many of them were banned from night hostels, so soup runs really were the final legal resort for help.

Ironically, Cloke et al (2010) note that soup runs have faced much criticism and attempts to close them down. They face a challenging existence to survive in the face of hostility from both government and other homelessness agencies. Thus, they tend to keep a low profile. The most common critiques of soup runs are that they are condoning street life and addiction by making food and basic supplies available to people on the streets, and that they do not distinguish between 'deserving' and 'undeserving' street sleepers and squatters. They also operate with very little connection to other homeless agencies and lack properly trained staff. Attempts were made in London in the 2000s to reduce the number of soup runs with the help of The Salvation Army. Cloke et al (2010) see soup runs as an expression of the ethics of care for strangers based on the simple premise that they are in need. Cloke and his colleagues argue that the key motivating factor in practice in the British context is not a desire for evangelism, but for *serving* others in need – this is an expression of extra-ordinary care for strangers, a form of ethical citizenship which is beyond the ordinary relations of family and friendship ties that underpin social care relationships. This is a central ethic of religious welfare provision that the UK shares with other countries of the world (Jawad, 2009). It exemplifies the post-secular ethics highlighted above, which is an unconditional form of generosity given on the basis of a 'sense for the other' rather than any desire to change them.

Community organising and political mobilisation

At the other spectrum of urban mobilisation is the example of full-blown community organising and political mobilisation that the UK is beginning to see more of. It was the Blair government that adopted a very overt communitarian turn in its politics as part of the broader quest to deal with social cohesion and to combat social exclusion. Flint (2010) notes that the community cohesion agenda under New Labour also propagated the notion of religious organisations as repositories of social capital (illustrated in Box 8.2 below) and, therefore, as prime contenders in urban regeneration initiatives (Furbey et al, 2006). The agenda represented an attempt to move away from multiculturalism in the UK for fear that this was bringing about geographically segregated communities. Nevertheless, the concept of community cohesion has faced much criticism: some claim it de-politicises 'race'; that it fosters a limited notion of cohesion and tends towards assimilation; and it is also argued that the community cohesion agenda has ignored the existence of self-segregation among middle-class populations within the UK housing and education markets (Flint, 2010).

Box 8.2: Social capital

1. *Bonding capital:* promotes strong ties within a group
2. *Bridging capital:* promotes ties between groups
3. *Support capital:* ability to get by when there is a problem
4. *Leverage capital:* ability to get ahead
5. *Developing networks*
6. *Establishing norms of conduct and shared values*

Source: Adapted from Putnam et al (2004)

For Smith (2004a), this view is slightly naive and overly optimistic, since it neglects the darker side of inner-city life where there is sometimes conflict and competition between faiths, and faith-based organisations themselves can be informal and lacking in resources. Nevertheless, commentators agree that the strong adherence to social and moral values that we find among faith-based organisations make them strong contenders for civic renewal and urban regeneration initiatives (Fischer,

2001; Hepworth and Stitt, 2007). Examples of this mobilisation for the service of those in need and in protest at the stark social and economic inequalities that now plague the UK can be found in the Church of England's *Faith in the city* and *Faithful cities* reports. These were explored in more detail in Chapter 7 on poverty reduction, a theme closely connected to urban social deprivation in the UK.

The argument that faith groups promote civic renewal and are champions of the cause of the poor finds further support in Warren's (2009) extensive study of the community organising and political mobilisation alliance, Citizens UK. Illustration 3 below gives a snapshot of the alliance, after which this section engages with more detailed discussion of its merits and achievements.

Illustration 3: Citizens UK

Origins

Neil Jameson, a Quaker social worker, established Citizens UK, formerly known as the Citizen Organising Foundation, in 1989 after undertaking training in the US in the methods of community organising. Saul Alinsky established this approach to politics in Chicago in the 1930s (see *Rules for radicals*, 1973). There, he organised poor people in a Black neighbourhood to fight for their jobs that were under threat. Citizens UK established citizens groups in Liverpool, North Wales, the Black Country, Sheffield, Bristol, Milton Keynes and London. Twenty years later, London remains the most successful initiative of all, having started in East London in 1996. The main reason for this is due to the presence of trained and experienced organisers, and London is now the training ground through the Guild of Community Organisers. Churches, mosques, schools, trade union branches and voluntary agencies, religious and non-religious, form an alliance in each city with a view to working together for the common good.

Local action
- Fighting to stop factories polluting neighbourhoods with noise and smell
- Making roads and schools safe for children
- Tackling drug dens and closing them
- Persuading public transport companies and retail stores to change policies which threaten local neighbourhood centres
- Seeking a closer relationship with the police to participate in plans to contain crime in communities
- Opening over 200 safe havens in shops and public buildings in neighbourhoods across London

National level campaigning

- Reform of the way the asylum system treats families and children
- Promotion of the living wage as a norm for public contracts and procurement
- An anti-usury requirement putting a cap of 20 per cent on commercial interest charges
- One per cent of the £1 trillion used to bail out the banks for mutual lending in deprived areas

Source: Adapted from www.citizensuk.org/about/history/

Warren (2009) argues that the alliance has accomplished some important achievements in creating a more socially just and inclusive society, particularly in the context of increased cultural diversity in the UK. Weary of the drain of the 'nanny state' on social welfare, Warren (2009) notes that the alliance has been healthy for democratic life in Britain. The success of the living wage campaign needs to be reinforced by the ability of the alliance to entrench the culture of community organising and political mobilisation in Britain. Its faith-based strategy that combines strong partnerships with secular agencies is as much a source of strength as it is a weakness due to the hostility against religion and the ever-looming spectre of religious extremism.

Urban regeneration: challenges and opportunities of engagement

So what are the implications for urban regeneration policy in the UK? First, it is important to recognise the diversity and disparities within the faith sector in terms of resources, capacity and desire to engage with government (Farnell et al, 2003). Many fear being consumed by the government agenda to deliver services: that their prophetic missions will be compromised and they will lose their radical or critical edge. Moreover, there is a perception that the push to involve faith communities is coming from politicians in government who are themselves 'people of faith', yet urban regeneration projects are long-term initiatives which should not fall prey to short-term election concerns (Farnell et al, 2003, p 11).

On the positive side, however, Chapman (2009) identifies some new opportunities for faith community engagement in the policy process of urban governance and regeneration areas, as follows:

- direct engagement and representation of faith communities on strategic and delivery partnerships
- wider consultations by statutory bodies of faith communities
- increased partnership with faith groups in delivering publicly funded welfare services and initiatives aimed at enhancing social inclusion, community cohesion and preventing violent extremism.

Nevertheless, Farnell et al (2003) argue that the contributions of faith communities, although significant to urban regeneration, can be overestimated, and questions of capacity and skill loom large. It is therefore important not to privilege the tokenistic involvement of Christian clergy but to extend real opportunities of engagement to members of minority religions. This recognises the value of diverse minority religious groups not just in relation to each other but also in relation to secular organisations whereby they can bring a strong sense of motivation and ethos of social action, a long-term presence in their local communities and the provision of informal settings and activities as well as a commitment to listening to the views and needs of local people (Farnell et al, 2003, p 42). But equally, government agencies must be receptive to the diversity of values and theologies of religious groups. Various government agencies such as The Housing Corporation, the Neighbourhood Renewal Unit and staff in local authorities need to engage seriously with faith groups by taking better account of their values and language.

The key message therefore is that central to the urban regeneration agenda is the capacity for good neighbourliness (Farnell et al, 2003; Wuthnow, 2004). Faith-based organisations, whether driven by evangelism or an altruistic desire to serve those in need, demonstrate ample doses of this.

Conclusion

Prosperity and social cohesion in the urban centres of advanced capitalist democracies is an elusive and challenging goal. In this chapter we explored the contribution that religion and faith-based welfare make to the housing process and urban regeneration more broadly. It is common to hear and read about the threat of self-segregation by religious communities in the UK, and less so by the deliberate self-exclusion of the middle classes from the rest of society, for instance, through gated residential communities. This chapter presented a variety of case illustrations in the areas of faith-based housing associations, homeless services to the poor and political mobilisation by the community organising network Citizens UK to show the variety of ways in which religious organisations contribute to civic renewal and political engagement. Although the Church of England and other Christian denominations have tended to dominate the arena of urban regeneration due to their stronger political and economic leverage, the landscape is fast changing as the UK's religious minorities are organising more effectively. Engagement in urban regeneration policy brings a variety of opportunities and challenges for the faith-based organisations but a key issue this chapter has demonstrated is good neighbourliness – so far research evidence is mixed, however. Some faith communities may segregate themselves as they seek to live within their own congregations and perhaps protect themselves from discrimination, but faith-based organisations are socially active and extend services to their wider neighbourhood, not just their faith communities. This begs the question of how to accommodate religious needs and diversity in liberal democracies. These are the larger questions that will bring this book to a close in the next and final chapter. Where the concept of *ways of being* is concerned, this chapter has shown that urban regeneration is fundamentally about social transformation at both personal and societal levels. These are issues that move beyond transient individualist and materialist definitions of the human condition.

Questions for discussion

1. Why is religion important for understanding housing processes?
2. Should housing associations of a religious character receive state funding?
3. Are the arguments that religious organisations are a source of civic renewal justified?
4. What are the key challenges and opportunities facing urban regeneration policy in its engagement with religious groups?

Useful websites

Agudas Israel Housing Association Ltd: http://apps.hackney. gov.uk/servapps/CommunityDirectories/Details. aspx?OrgID=2994&Admin=0

Church Urban Fund: www.cuf.org.uk/

Citizens UK (TELCO): www.citizensuk.org/

North London Muslim Housing Association: www.nlmha.com/main. cfm

CONCLUSION

Theoretical and practical implications for social policy

As we come to a close in this final chapter, where the main arguments proposed in this book are brought together and a potential future agenda for social policy research and practice is explored, two aspirations deserve articulation: that this book has helped set the scene about religious welfare generally and religious organisations in Britain specifically in relation to their social welfare role; and that a more rigorous academic debate has been etched out that may help students and teachers of social policy in the UK broaden their view of social policy, historically, theoretically and practically.

In both cases, however, what this book may have done is raise more questions than give answers, but ultimately, if this has served to better distil the key issues surrounding religious welfare and to raise critical analytical questions that show the merits of 'dispassionate social scientific' research (Sutton and Vertigans, 2005) on religion and social policy, then this book has achieved a worthy purpose. These new critical questions revolve around such themes as whether or not religious groups are being unfairly excluded from civic and democratic participation, what the real contributions in material terms are that religious groups bring to social policy and social welfare, and how we might rethink the terms of the social welfare debate under this light. Hence, as argued in Trigg (2007) and Sutton and Vertigans (2005), in order for religion not to fester in the 'private' sphere of life and explode sporadically in the public arena, it should undergo 'critical scrutiny', which academic research can offer. This can only be done once religious action in the public sphere is seen as a legitimate activity, and the likely contribution of religious groups to social policy debates is accepted.

But before this final chapter can delve into the concluding discussion about the arguments raised and the relative usefulness of the concept *ways of being*, it is important to address some potential weaknesses and points of criticism in this book, in order to better express the significance of its arguments. The book was restricted by the practical issue of space, and the ambition of this writing project, which was to offer both a broad and deep view of religious welfare in an introductory style. It is hoped that it has been able to offer an empirically broad view by discussing the nine main religions in the UK and the full array of social welfare *service* and *services* that they perform.

First, this book may have veered too far towards a positive view of religious welfare. We are all too aware of the chequered relationship between religion, peace and tolerance everywhere in the world. The main reason for the book's orientation in this regard has been in order to set out what it is that religion and religious welfare organisations bring to the table of social policy interventions. It is good to remember that religious welfare organisations are regulated by the Charity Commission in the UK – this is a secular state agency, so even though proselytisation may happen in indirect and informal ways among religious organisations working in the welfare sphere in Britain, religious organisations that enter the public sphere as charities and public service contractors have to abide by the same laws that regulate the voluntary sector. These formal service-oriented organisations are, of course, different from the religious congregations that are communities of worship and also serve a social welfare function through the more informal daily activities of 'caring', as argued in Chapter 6 on social care.

By bringing together the whole gamut of social welfare discourses and functions that religious organisations carry out in the UK, the book is acknowledging that, to some extent, the collective academic debate within social policy in the UK is starting from a position of very limited knowledge, and may perhaps use this book as a useful starting point – undoubtedly its content will spark criticism but that is the stuff of good debate, and what will move research in this field forward. So this book is in effect throwing the first motion in this open debate on religious welfare within the social and public policy communities: that religious welfare organisations are, or indeed can be, capable of furthering the causes of social care and economic justice. They are also valid public actors and deserve a voice in the arena of deliberative democratic politics. Let us also not forget that our modern primarily secular history since the early 20th century has seen world wars, nuclear bombs and political dictatorships arise across the world. The world is now grappling with the volatility of the capitalist system and the immense social and economic inequalities it has created. The demise of socialism has left a moral gap that religion can fill only in part.

We return to William Beveridge's argument cited in the Introduction to this book that perhaps the power of religious faith needs to be part-revived and part-replaced by an alternative force. What might that force be? The first concluding argument in this book, therefore, is that social policy has been a direct casualty of these events, yet it remains the place for reviving this alternative force but perhaps in a more inclusive manner that takes into account the diversity of the social welfare context of contemporary Britain. The multicultural character of the UK has a fundamental part to play here, and although it may not be possible to speak of a new form of multi-religious Establishment in the UK, there is a need to rethink the UK's welfare settlement (Bretherton, 2010).

Bretherton (2010) calls this a Christian practice of hospitality based on the principle of the 'Good Samaritan': humanity is one family, but people have an affiliation to the place where they live, hence they need to be hospitable to strangers coming from outside. In this logic, Christian politics can rise above identity politics and parochial nationalism but also needs to protect itself against the distorting influence of 'global citizenship, liberal cosmopolitanism and reductive universal capitalism' (Bretherton, 2010, p 221). This harks back to the perennial issue of how to preserve the distinctiveness and universalism of religious identity that has been a constant theme of this book.

One possible answer is to recall that religious traditions each represent one route to the human spirit, which is itself a universal condition. But what the issue of a multi-faith Britain does highlight is how the welfare state is being reconfigured at a time of diverse religious and cultural demands on it. As Flint argues:

> In addition to the growth of Islam and other minority faiths, the arrival in the UK of large numbers of migrant workers from the European Union accession states has resulted in a substantial increase in the size, presence and activities of Catholic congregations and there has been a similar rapid and substantial growth in predominately black Pentecostal urban congregations. In reality, the accommodation between state and faith in Western Europe, most notably in the UK and to a lesser extent in Germany, has often been ambiguous, inconsistent and characterised by compromise and pragmatism. (Flint, 2010, p 259)

To redress this situation, this book argues that empirical applied social policy research can help develop critical and constructive debate and the role of religious organisations and congregations in British society.

Second, the book may have focused more on certain religions than others, although its aim has been to include a broad discussion of all the main religious faiths, including minority faiths such as Zoroastrian and Baha'i, which rarely appear in contemporary British social science research, if at all. The relatively higher degree of focus on Islam in the book partly reflects concerns in the current state of policy and debate in the UK: Muslims are numerous in number, and they are perceived as posing greater political and cultural challenges to life in Europe than other religious groups (Modood, 2009). The book may also have focused relatively more on Christianity – this is to be expected, as Christianity is the majority religion of Britain, and in the welfare sphere, churches have the upper hand, both historically and in terms of material resources to engage at national level and in leading positions such as in education, urban regeneration or the prison service. After all, the church has long-standing access to Parliament and forms part of British national identity. But the book has also shown that other major faiths, the Dharmic and Indian religions in particular, are a dynamic civic force to be reckoned with. It is not a coincidence that the first Council of Dharmic Faiths has now been established in the UK in the city of Birmingham – so this is, again, an important dimension of the religious welfare landscape of the UK that has been made explicit in this book.

A third point related to the broad remit of this book was to give a view of the UK as a group of nations. Devolution in the UK is also reflected in the diverse state–church relations of the British nations, from the established churches of Scotland and England, to the absence of an established church in Wales, to the deep geographical segregation of politics and society along religious lines in Northern Ireland. It is the debate on faith schools that can further highlight the differences between the various nations of Britain, but which the book has not been able to engage with. There is a major agenda for further empirical research here that can bring out the impact of the different state–church relations in the UK nations on the role of religious organisations and congregations in social welfare.

Fourth, the book has not been able to cover the sphere of education policy, although various segments of the argument have shown that education policy has been central to the influence of religion more broadly on society, and indeed to the poverty reduction social transformation policies of all religious traditions. There is a fairly healthy literature on the role of religion in school education, although the research for this book has identified the new city academies as a future area of research since they are run by religious groups in deprived areas .

A fifth and final point of contention is the gaps in empirical research that this book has both highlighted and sought to fill. As yet, there are no accurate or comprehensive data that can provide a full mapping of religious welfare organisations in the UK. To an extent, some of the academic and grey literature which has been highlighted may appear anecdotal, although it should be noted that the sector has accumulated sufficient experience and the key challenges are already being pointed out such as the importance of religious organisations in understanding the policy context and policy makers understanding where religious organisations are coming from. To some degree, British scholarship and policy debate have the benefit of a longer history of research into religious welfare in the US and to a certain degree continental Europe, as well as beyond the Western world, if non-Christian faiths are to be taken into account.

This volume has shown that there are some degrees of similarity between the issues that motivate and matter to religious welfare organisations in the UK, and those beyond the UK, Europe and the US. For example, the concept of *service* may truly be understood to be universal and cross-cultural, as is the symbolic and material importance of social care both to religious welfare organisations and to the evolution of the welfare state (see also Jawad, 2009). Moreover, community-based participatory development projects that have been in operation in poor countries in Africa, Latin America and the Middle East have been part of the agenda of international relief organisations such as Islamic Relief UK and Christian Aid, and may well offer insights for the challenges of urban poverty in the UK.

Clearly, then, there is a major research agenda here, and what this book has sought to do is bring together existing and new empirical research from within and outside the UK to begin to shed some constructive light on religion and religious welfare in British social policy. At the heart of this issue is a question that is attracting much discussion among commentators: is there a civic role for religion in liberal societies? This question fundamentally concerns social policy and the study of the welfare state. If social policy academics continue to keep their distance form research on religious welfare, at the very least what the subject matter of this book can point to is that ethics and the pursuit of 'the worthwhile life', or eudaimonia, ought to remain the central focus of social policy research, particularly in the present economic climate.

The aim of this concluding chapter, therefore, is to briefly revisit the key arguments of this book so that a more structured concluding argument may be presented about the concept of *ways of being*, and the implications of the book's discussion for social policy theory and practice in line with the big questions about religious welfare raised in the introduction.

Summary of key arguments

The book began with the importance of empirical research into how religion shapes the content and meaning of social welfare and how religious actors have interacted with political and cultural forces to shape the development of the welfare state. The geographical focus was the UK, where academic social policy research on the role of religion in providing welfare services and also in shaping the institutional configuration of the welfare state has been somewhat poorly developed, in comparison to the rest of Europe and indeed to the US.

It is useful here to go back to the main aims and questions stated in the Introduction to this book, which can be usefully summarised along two interrelated lines of enquiry: is there more to religion than the mixed economy of welfare framework? Can we reconcile being active members of religious communities, and good citizens, in a liberal democratic nation-state? In the introduction, it was argued that religious welfare focuses our attention on human identity, which is intricately connected to the relationship between the individual and their physical/ metaphysical environment. These are intricately moral questions which affirm that the human being is a meaning-making and purpose-seeking species: *who we are matters and knowing who we are matters even more if we are to flourish as individuals and as societies.* The affirmation here that morality and social ethics may be just as important if not more important than individual happiness is an argument that religious welfare shares with other moral philosophical positions, namely utopianism and European idealism. All these debates sought to make real the notion of how to live the good life, and indeed that how an individual lives their life is a reflection of the higher ideals that make up society as a whole. Hence, the book has introduced the concept of *ways of being* as a broadening of the concept of wellbeing or welfare.

This also means that religious welfare organisations may contribute positively to civic life. As Herbert (2003) notes, the major theorists of our times, such as Kymlicka, who have debated at length the compatibility of liberal societies with religious views, argue that identity and culture are fundamental to an articulation of human rights. This parallels the argument made by the Church Urban Fund, that questioning the means of economic production and exchange is not sufficient, but what is required is questioning the very purpose of economic life. These are inevitably moral debates that we can no longer shy away from, and some recent social policy scholarship has already shown an appetite for this (Jordan, 2008; Rowlingson and Connor, 2011; Spicker, 2011). A religious perspective shares in the moral debates in that the measures of welfare outcomes inevitably reflect the normative values of the policies that have underpinned them. If a society values self–responsibility and the 'work ethic' and looks down on single mothers, it will devise welfare policies that reflect these values. Thus, as Clarke and Fink (2008) have aptly argued, social policy is about the identity of a nation and the political order that structures and produces social relations.

These issues were aptly demonstrated in the first chapter on the historical role of religion in social welfare policy. This showed how religious/Christian values shaped the provision of social welfare services to the needy according to records from the early medieval period, as well as the reform of social and educational policy in Britain in the centuries that followed. With the introduction of the Poor Law of 1601, more organised institutional control at local government level began to take shape as poverty began to be seen as a social problem in need of organisation and redress. Prominent religious figures who were also part of the political establishment influenced the emerging liberal political ideas of the day, and by the early 19th century, Christian Socialists would lead the way in social and educational policy. In the early 20th century, religious philanthropy reached its apogee, with the proliferation of Christian social activism and concern for human virtue. But as the demands of industrialisation and pauperisation increased, the church found itself under-resourced, with dwindling rates of Christian membership in Britain. With the end of the Second World War and the massive devastation of Britain, the Church of England, led by Archbishops such as William Temple, argued that the British state was a Christian state and oversaw the handing over of responsibility for social welfare to a secular administration. Some of the most important political leaders and social reformers, from William Gladstone, William Beveridge to Tony Blair, were guided by their religious beliefs; Beveridge himself argued that religion was an unrivalled source of solidarity and social welfare.

Chapter 2 reviewed the main theoretical perspectives on the role of religion in social policy. It argued that British social policy has lagged behind North American and continental European research in factoring religion into social policy analysis, although British sociologists of religion and social work researchers are increasingly engaging with social welfare topics. There is a need, therefore, to address religion from a social policy perspective, particularly when religious groups in Britain are increasingly being called on by the state to fulfil a social welfare function. The chapter gave two broad lines of argument: an institutional analysis of religion which showed church teachings both within the Catholic and Protestant faiths, as well as the role of political cleavages particularly around the interwar period, either expanding public spending or diminishing the role of the state in welfare provision. The specific absence of a consideration of Protestantism in social policy analysis was also noted, with this religious tradition becoming absorbed into secular welfare institutions, as was the case for Britain. In terms of the normative contribution of religion, scholars have considered how religious identity fosters social capital or how it links to happiness, but this literature remains underdeveloped and insufficiently exposed within social policy scholarship. The latter continues to be dominated by utilitarian understandings of welfare as an individual material outcome. The chapter proposed that the degrees of political liberalism and religious pluralism in European countries helped determine how active religious welfare organisations were in the public sphere.

Chapter 3 discussed the contemporary social and political profile of religion in Britain. First, it examined the religious profile of British society, drawing on 2001 Census data that highlighted that three quarters of the British population considered themselves to belong to a particular faith tradition. Moreover, a variety of surveys showed that religion was of deep significance to believers, especially among minority religious groups. It was argued that in Britain, Christianity had an ambiguous cultural character that made it pervasive in national British identity. Second, the chapter explored available data from the 2001 Census on the religious profile of social deprivation and poverty in the UK. This showed that Muslim communities were the worst off in terms of educational achievements, self-reported health and levels of employment. The chapter emphasised the argument made by other scholars that religion was a significant demographic variable for policy making and more research is needed in this area. A brief profile of the religious welfare sector was also offered, arguing that it was largely financially independent and worth roughly £6 billion. Finally, the chapter examined the current position of religion in UK government policy. This showed that so far, the New Labour government had been much more active than the present Coalition government in publishing guidelines and frameworks for government engagement with faith groups. In part this may be explained by the preoccupation of the Coalition with the national debt and economic recession, but while the Coalition government may be downsizing public agencies, its Big Society idea supported by the Localism Act is opening up direct routes for faith communities to participate fully in special welfare provision. Various challenges cloud over the likely terms of this engagement, however, most notably the capacity and desire of religious groups to jeopardise their religious independence and missions in favour of government contacts, and also the lack of adequate mutual understanding between religious groups and the government.

Chapter 4 is the first of the empirical chapters in the book. It looked at how religion and social work intersect, and began by reviewing the way in which religion tended to be viewed as a taboo subject within the social work profession, although social work has its roots in Christian philanthropy and charity. Nevertheless, research cited in the chapter has shown that UK social workers are becoming increasingly open to discussing issues of religion and spirituality with their clients. The chapter was broadly split into two sections. The first explored why religion needs to be taken into account by social work and how. This cited the various pieces of legislation in the UK that require that health and social care professionals take into account the religious needs and identities of their clients, and also that social work and religious values share many intrinsic values, such as respect for dignity and the uniqueness of each individual. The chapter then looked at various reflexive and assessment-type models that social workers could use to increase their sensitivity to religion and also to gather information about their clients in relation to religion. Two illustrative examples were offered: prison chaplaincy among Muslim communities and the role of bereavement counselling for older people who have lost a spouse. This led into the discussion in the second part of the chapter which was how social work was deeply related to social action, and here the chapter reported back on empirical research conducted for the book, confirming the way in which religious organisations saw themselves as offering more than a service to their clients and were intricately rooted in their local communities. This emphasises the dual meaning of service as self-less help and a finite transaction to cover a human need.

Chapter 5 on health is crucial in advancing new ways of thinking about wellbeing, by moving the traditional biomedical and clinical model of health into the realm of identity and values and holistic medicine. First it looked at what the different faiths said about the meaning of health and disease, and the importance of caring for the sick and infirm. The chapter then considered how religion and spirituality had gained the attention of healthcare writers and practitioners and what measures could be put in place to improve consideration of them in institutional healthcare settings. The chapter highlighted the importance of holistic approaches to healthcare, showing how a better integration of religion, belief and spirituality into healthcare could not only respond better to users' 'moral and biographical needs' (Kellehear, 2002), but could also release greater care resources on the part of healthcare professionals. The importance of engaging with the worldviews of patients was highlighted as essential for reducing health inequalities and improving patients' coping strategies and treatment compliance. The chapter used illustrative examples from palliative care and mental health, as well as examples of the work of faith-based organisations in the UK. We saw that faith-based organisations were undertaking a variety of innovative tasks, ranging from health support, health screening and awareness raising to hospital care and maternity programmes that have begun to be integrated into the NHS. The chapter thus showed that life illness should not be seen as an isolated physiological problem, and that social problems should also not be treated in isolation from the person's moral and cultural background.

Chapter 6 considered the importance of the concept of social care in the work of religious organisations and for thinking more specifically about the significance of care for social policy. It argued that care has a dual meaning as both a philosophical ethic for human relationships but also a material service that is offered to people in need. Care is a phlosophical ethic which can guide moral action by emphasising the moral relationships that bind human beings together. These moral relationships are emotive in character and are focused on satisfying the needs of others. In this logic, the prime concern for each individual should be how they fulfil their moral responsibility towards other people. This orientation has been juxtaposed to the more traditional focus on social justice in social policy and political philosophy that advocates an abstract universalist approach to human wellbeing by focusing on equal entitlements and rights. The chapter showed that 'caring' is a defining feature of religious congregations and organisations. It is also not confined to women, but deeply connected to the human condition shared by both men and women alike. In this sense, the chapter also looked at social care as a symbolic form of service and the importance of spiritual care within this. Religious organisations offer a variety of residential, day and home-based social care for vulnerable groups with particular emphasis on elderly care. A key caveat highlighted by the ethics of care approach is its tendency towards parochialism and bias, and this explains why care relationships may work better on a small group scale – religious organisations may thus be criticised on this front. But the chapter ended by arguing that in religious terms, care and justice were two sides of the same coin – religious people helped those in need not just because they deserved to be helped but because it was part of their religious duty and identity to do so.

Chapter 7 looked at the realm of poverty reduction in the work and discourse of religious organisations in the UK. It explored three dimensions of the meaning of poverty: material, spiritual and civic. Thus, the chapter highlighted that religious welfare organisations are also concerned with issues of economic justice, although it is the churches that have taken a lead position in this regard. Like its counterpart churches in Europe, the Church of England and other smaller church groups have regularly authored reports commenting on the cause of poverty and the shortcoming of government policy in combating poverty and inequality, especially in poor urban areas. Church groups have argued, for instance, that all people should have good work and that all work should be seen as vocational, with no one being branded lazy, and no such category as unemployment. Equally, the issue of globalisation and unequal terms of global trade have been raised by the church. The Jubilee Debt Campaign was pioneered by the churches and is a direct attempt at combating international poverty and injustice. The chapter ended with a review of the types of services offered by religious welfare organisations classed into four: in-cash assistance, such as charity and credit unions; in-kind assistance, such as food and clothing banks; employment and training services, which are part of government contracts and see religious organisations operating very much as secular organisations; and international poverty relief, which sees religious organisations diverting their attention to poverty and disaster relief outside of the UK. In some ways, this chapter raised more questions or pointed the direction towards new areas of research as the topic is poorly researched in the UK. It has highlighted that in spite of the good will and readiness for public outcry against inequality and poverty that religious groups demonstrate, they have much less power in actively being able to change things on the ground.

In Chapter 8, the focus was the contribution that religious organisations make to housing processes and urban regeneration more broadly. The chapter explored a variety of case illustrations in the areas of faith-based housing association, homeless services to the poor and political mobilisation by the community-organising network Citizens UK to show the variety of ways in which religious organisations contribute to civic renewal and political engagement. Although the Church of England and other Christian denominations have tended to dominate the arena of urban regeneration due to their stronger political and economic leverage, the landscape is fast changing as the UK's religious minorities are organising more effectively. Engagement in urban regeneration policy brings a variety of opportunities and challenges for the faith-based organisations, but a key issue this chapter discussed was that of good neighbourliness. Some faith communities may segregate themselves as they seek to live within their own congregations and perhaps protect themselves from discrimination, but religious organisations are socially active and extend services to their wider neighbourhood.

To conclude, this book explored the role of religion in social welfare and human wellbeing in contemporary Britain. The analytical journey on which it has taken us culminates in two central questions: first, are the services provided by religious welfare organisations simply 'scratch[ing] the surface' of social deprivation and inequality, as Taylor (2001, p 124) puts it, or are they pushing forward a structural endeavour that is truly able to change society and change lives? Or is it both? Second, how much of what religious welfare organisations do is about religion and how much of it is about social welfare? Or are the two connected in some inexorable way? The idea that human nature may involve more than the pursuit of individual happiness, preferences and utility and that issues of justice or duty matter just as fundamentally for religious welfare providers is the basis on which these questions may be answered.

Clearly there is a major research agenda here, but for now, it is possible to conclude the following: religion is more than just a part of the mixed economy of welfare. Political figures within British history and the church more generally have helped forge important social legislation, been guided by Christian morality in public matters and integrated church functions into the workings of government. The growth of minority faith groups is undoubtedly a reflection of the changing religious profile of the UK. Many are beginning to come of age as they seek to engage in local civic action that allows them to give back to society as UK citizens but also preserve the cultural heritage of their ethnic communities. Questions remain as to how far religious organisations are able to cater for members from outside of their communities, although they may take part in multi-faith consortiums; generally, where they are concerned with religious welfare activities, they help to enhance the capacities of their local communities and enable to engage better as local citizens.

In terms of achieving equality, justice and fulfilling needs, religious organisations first and foremost seek to respond to human need, and the chapters have shown that they do fulfil human need and they do work with some of those who are most in need. They can also empower communities by working closely with marginalised populations, quite literally those who would die without their help, as noted in Chapter 8. Religious organisations also care about economic justice, but this is where their achievements may fall short since much depends on the workings of the economy over which they have little control. It may be said that the church is close to the ruling elites and could do more to advance equality and justice. In any case, for religious groups, truth and justice are intimately linked: helping others in need is as much a personal outward act of faith which religious people believe they gain from personally as it is a valid response to the needs of others. Herein lies the crux of the argument about service and services that has animated much of the discussions in the book. How, then, can religious welfare organisations be accommodated in liberal societies?

Religious welfare in liberal democratic states

The extent to which liberal democracies can accommodate free religious expression in the public sphere has haunted Western European society for a long time, and undoubtedly, the question of religious welfare goes to the heart of this matter (Herbert, 2003). Concerns surround not only the eligibility of public funds going to organisations that have religious missions but also the risk that religious organisations are working undercover through the provision of social services.

This book has adopted what may be regarded as a conventional view of religion. This is because minority ethnic religions that are an important focus of this book would not necessarily sit well with individualist and humanistic definitions of spirituality. Likewise, Christian evangelical groups, which are at the forefront of social welfare action in Britain today, would want their ways of life to be directly integrated into their religious identity. As the research reported here and other contemporary research shows, adherence to scriptures or the laws of a particular religion as well as community-based rituals and practices are fundamentally connected to more individualist and amorphous notions of spirituality. Seeing religion as a way of life has conceptual implications for the concept of *ways of being* which is being proposed in this book, as discussed later.

Yet, such a stance poses important challenges for the place of religion in liberal society. It may be argued that religious welfare sits well with economic liberalism since it advocates community- or family-based provision of welfare that reinforces personal ties of charity and altruism. But this is not to say that religion is always a good bedfellow with capitalism. We have shown in this book that church and other religious groups have been at the forefront of the critique against the capitalist system. For Pacione (1990, p 201), the church has to coexist with the market and the state, and cannot negate their roles in society. So its main contribution would be to 'ameliorate the excesses of the capitalist system by using its various resources in ways that accord high priority to the disadvantaged'. This would require lobbying government at national level to review economic policy and accord more importance to issues of wealth redistribution and the common good. The church may also act as a conduit for the voices of the marginalised groups to be heard.

On the other hand, the more problematic equation is of how religion may be accommodated by politically and culturally diverse societies that depend on secular frameworks to ensure equality and freedom. Riordan (2011) sums up some of these key arguments below.

> What limits are there to the effectiveness of public agencies in working for people's wellbeing? What are the boundaries which public authorities should not overstep in caring for wellbeing? Reducing crime, maintaining public security and absence of anxiety merely establish the conditions for living a decent life. What a decent human life is to consist of and how it might be realised and shared cannot be the business of the public authorities. It is a matter for the freedom of each one and each group. But this is not to relegate the question to a supposedly private sphere. It is very definitely a matter of public concern, and what is required for its pursuit are public spaces in which the questions of the human good and the common good of our social cooperation may be aired and explored, without fear that somebody or group will be able to hijack the power of the state so as to impose its preferred answer on others. (Riordan, 2011, p 214)

These arguments echo those by White and Tronto (2004) in the discussion on social care in Chapter 6, that it is only true democratic processes that can allow open debate about social needs and social rights and how both the universal and the particular may be reconciled. Rawls himself, according to Bretherton (2010), did not support a view of Enlightenment that was against Christian values. Nelson (2010) also argues that liberalism may be viewed as a 'disguise' for modernist state power. The Enlightenment era did not produce independent rational principles on which to base rational discourse, and liberalism itself represents a particular worldview and a particular value system. The education system in Western societies like the UK is an important institution through which such values are transmitted. Seeing these overarching political philosophies in this way, as worldviews, may help illustrate the approach here in terms of how religion fits with social policy. What, then, are the opportunities and limits of this fit?

Opportunities and limits for dialogue between religion and social policy

At the most general level, it is possible to identify a common moral discourse of concern for welfare. This is argued by Deacon and Mann (1999) below:

> Welfare policy is either about enabling people to make responsible choices or it is a form of social engineering. If it is the former, then it must engage with behaviour and the moral decisions that people make. If it is the latter, then debate is about what sort of society it wants to engineer and which set of moral codes it wishes to impose. The tension between these options cannot be resolved; policy will either treat the poor as moral defectives or as moral agents. (Deacon and Mann, 1999, p 433)

Social policy, as Fitzpatrick (200) has argued, has tended to focus on the technical process of solving social problems as isolated objective units. But, as White (2006, p 29) argues in the context of health, there is a need to move beyond the Cartesian view of the human being as a machine whereby health is regarded as freedom from disease; perhaps it is also timely that we move beyond the notion of wellbeing as freedom from social problems to broader definitions that take into account issues of identity, moral value and the broader purposes of society.

The examples of religious welfare provision discussed here may thus be viewed in two ways: we may praise them as tailor-made services that respond to specific needs among specific people. It is difficult to escape the fact that members of the same religious faith will flock together – in the end, religion is about a system of shared beliefs. On the other hand, a senior and well-informed observer of this sector argues that this is a flawed argument. If communities are serving the needs of their members without discriminating against outsiders or instilling a sense of exclusiveness in their services, then this is a valid social welfare function. What is interesting is that for almost all religious organisations that took part in the research for this book there is no need to proselytise – faith can be spread by the example of good actions towards others.

Hence, religiously based social welfare provision has a great weakness and a great strength: it relies on a theological backdrop and is vulnerable to theological parochialism; this will potentially be entrenched by community-based discourse in the UK where a community living in a geographical vicinity is religiously homogeneous. In providing social welfare services, religious organisations have the potential to bridge a human gap and to develop a wider discourse of human wellbeing. But how easy is this in practice? History points in the other direction even though religious organisations may sit around a table to exchange views and experiences – in the end a Sikh, or Jewish or Zoroastrian elderly person may well prefer to go to a luncheon club of their own faith if they had to choose among various religious providers.

It is the need to balance or perhaps choose between mission and action that will provide the litmus test for religious welfare organisations in the UK. Can a service truly be 'distinctive' and 'universal' at the same time? This book certainly posits that religion is both mundane and distinctive – it is everywhere but it also has its own specific location. In the North American context, Wuthnow (2004) argues that the success of faith-based provision is based on its fluid boundaries. People move in and out of a free and open economy of religious organisations and worldviews, the pluralism of which is fostered by the lack of an established state religion. Might British social policy follow this model, seeing as the UK is a diversely religious society?

In the arena of social welfare and social action, perhaps, it is the outsider who needs to see that in enacting their own religiously inspired *ways of being*, religious groups are responding to specific human needs interpreted within a broader range of social relations and social purpose. How, then, does the concept of *ways of being* help us move forward in thinking about religious welfare and in rethinking social policy?

Ways of being and implications for social policy

The qualitative shift that religion makes in thinking about social welfare is that people are more than just individual citizens with rights and obligations towards a welfare state; they are conscious meaning-making purpose-seeking social agents. Wellbeing in this view is fundamentally related to human nature and morality, a point already made clear by some scholars of social policy (see, for example, Jordan, 2008; Spicker, 2011). This lays a premium on morality and duty as the main axes of social action, and not happiness as a transient form of pleasure (Kenny and Kenny, 2006).

This argument requires moving beyond utilitarian assumptions about the maximisation of individual pleasures and is more akin to Aristotle's notion of *eudaimonia* which points to deeper senses of meaning and personal fulfilment that amount to the literal translation of this term as 'a worthwhile life' (Kenny and Kenny, 2006, p 14). Aristotle defined happiness as an activity that follows the virtuous principles, meaning 'doing well what is worth doing and what we are good at' (Kenny and Kenny, 2006, p 15). It is the philosophical premise of utilitarian welfarism where wellbeing is depicted as a transient static outcome that this book has sought to challenge. This apparent tension between the religious (Christian) view of human nature and utilitarianism is a historical one (see, for example, Norman's [1987a] account of the Victorian Christian Socialists), as Layard (2005), an ardent advocate of Benthamite thinking, notes. But even a neo-utilitarian such as Layard has this to say about religion:

> The goal of self-realisation is not enough. No society can work unless its members feel responsibilities as well as rights.... Unfortunately, our current culture provides no clear answer. The decline of orthodox Christianity and then of social solidarity has left a moral vacuum.... Many of the ideas are as old as Buddhism and have recurred throughout the ages in all religious traditions that focus on inner life. In every case the techniques are offered for liberating the positive force in each of us, which religious people call divine. These techniques could well become the psychological basis of twenty-first-century culture. The secret is compassion towards oneself and others.... (Layard, 2005, pp 9, 93, 233)

The notion of compassion is central to the arguments of this book. In the world of religious welfare, it animates the core concept of *service*. Religious welfare caters for the needs of others not just because they are in need but because human life has a broader purpose. In many ways, religious welfare shares the idealism of 19th-century thinkers, as discussed in Offer (2006), who saw individual welfare as inseparable from social welfare. Themselves inspired by Christian morality, idealists such as Coleridge and Green sought to emphasise the spiritual and moral dimensions of human life: human flourishing could only exist within the ideal human society. So *ways of being* is a social concept: it is the personal welfare of the human being wrapped up in a way of life which is only such because it is shared by others. This reinforces the importance of cultural values and definitions in the design and delivery of social policy which have marked Clarke's (2003) thesis. Moreover, it stands in opposition to the utilitarian ideal that is willing to accept the happiness of the majority and the misery of the few. The only way this theory can be seen as flawed is if the fundamental principle is one of morality and not happiness. This is because morality is about social ethics and the social structure of society whereas happiness is about individual life.

Indeed, there is a long-standing debate about the meaning and nature of happiness and the centrality of its place as the supreme moral goal of human life (Kenny and Kenny, 2006, p 25). This debate has preoccupied philosophers of the ancient and modern world, and of both religious and secular leanings. For St Augustine and Thomas Aquinas, happiness was the ultimate goal of human life and intrinsically good. In utilitarian thinking, the same is true. Others thought differently, as found in the thinking of John Duns Scotus and Emmanuel Kant. Here, morality was bound up with duty (Kenny and Kenny, 2006, p 25). In this view, virtue is more important than happiness, which emphasises the role of self-sacrifice, perhaps for the happiness of others (Kenny and Kenny, 2006). Theological virtues such as faith, hope and love were gifts of divine grace. In sum, religious welfare actors do what they do not just because it makes them and those they are helping feel good but also because they know that it is right.

We may thus invoke the Kantian thesis that the nature of knowledge and experience is bound by conditions that are not directly accessible to empirical inquiry. The import of religion to social policy is therefore that it helps re-open long-standing debates about the meaning and nature of social welfare and wellbeing. It is worth reminding readers here that the concept of *way(s) of being* is based on the notion of religion as a way of life, but ultimately, as the research reported in this book shows, the concept points to the importance of *service* not just as the transfer of an output but as a human relationship between the person helping and the person being helped, whereby the self-identity of both is further realised. The welfare of the one is intricately bound up to the welfare of the many. That is why we have social policy.

References

Ahmed, M., Cantle, T. and Husain, D. (2009) 'Faith, multiculturalism and community cohesion: a policy conversation', in *Faith in the public realm: Controversies, policies and practices*, Bristol: The Policy Press, pp 83-104.

Alcock, P. (2008) *Social policy in Britain*, Basingstocke: Palgrave Macmillan.

Alcock, P., May, M. and Wright, S. (2012) (eds) *The student's companion to social policy*, London: Wiley Blackwell.

Alcock, P., May, M. and Rowlingson, K. (2008) (eds) *The student's companion to social policy*, London: Wiley Blackwell.

Alinsky, S.D. (1973) *Rules for radicals*, New York: Random House.

Anderson, C. (2008) 'The delivery of health care in faith-based organisations: parish nurses as promoters of health', *Health Communication*, vol 16(1), pp 117-28.

Armstrong, K. (2009) *The case for God*, New York: Knopf Doubleday.

Ashencaen Crabtree, S., Husain, F. and Spalek, B. (2008) *Islam and social work: Debating values, transforming practice*, Bristol: The Policy Press.

Aspinall, P. (2000) 'Should a question on "religion" be asked in the 2001 British Census? A public policy case in favour', *Social Policy & Administration*, vol 34, no 5, pp 584-600.

Atherton, J. (2011) 'Developing an overview as context and future', in J. Atherton, E. Graham and I. Steedman (eds), *The practices of happiness*, Oxford: Routledge, pp 1-20.

Bäckström, A., Davie, G., Edgardh, N. and Pettersson, P. (eds) (2010) *Welfare and religion in 21st century Europe, vol 1*, Aldershot: Ashgate.

Bäckström, A., Davie, G., Edgardh, N. and Pettersson, P. (eds) (2011) *Welfare and religion in 21st century Europe, vol 2*, Aldershot: Ashgate.

Baker, C. (2009) 'Blurred encounters: religious literacy, spiritual capital and language' in A. Dinham, R. Furbey and V. Lowndes (eds), *Faith in the public realm: Controversies, policies and practices*, Bristol: The Policy Press, pp 105-22.

Baldock, J. (2011) 'Social policy, social welfare, and the welfare state' in Baldock, J., Manning, N., Vickerstaff, S. and Mitton, L. (eds) *Social policy*, Oxford: Oxford University Press, pp 6-30.

Baldock, J., Manning, N., Vickerstaff, S. and Mitton, L. (eds) (2011) *Social policy*, Oxford: Oxford University Press.

Banks, S. (2003) *Ethics, accountability and the social professions*, London: Palgrave Macmillan.

Bayley, M. (1989) *Welfare – a moral issue? A Christian perspective*, Sheffield: Diocese of Sheffield Social Responsibility Committee.

Beaumont, J. (2008) 'Faith action on urban social issues', *Urban Studies*, vol 45, no 10, pp 2019-34.

Beaumont, J. and Baker, C. (eds) (2011) *Postsecular cities: Space, theory and practice*, London: Continuum.

Beckford, J.A. (2001) 'The tension between established church and equal opportunities in religion: the case of prison chaplaincy', in P.D. Nesbitt (ed) *Religion and social policy*, Walnut Creek, CA: AltaMira Press, pp 39-53.

Beckford, J.A. (2005) 'Muslims in the prisons of Britain and France', *Journal of Contemporary European Studies*, vol 13, no 3, pp 287-97.

Beckford, J.A. and Demerath, N.J. III (2007) 'Introduction', in J.A. Beckford and N.J. Demerath III (eds) *The Sage handbook of the sociology of religion*, London: Sage Publications, pp 1-16.

Beckford, J., Gale, R., Owne, D., Peach C. and Weller, P. (2006) *Review of the evidence base on faith communities*, Report for the Office of the Deputy Prime Minister, Coventry: University of Warwick.

Berger, P.L. (1999) 'The desecularization of the world: a global overview', in P.L. Berger (ed) *The desecularization of the world*, Washington, DC: Ethics and Public Policy Centre, pp 1-18.

Bevan, P. (2007) 'Researching wellbeing across the disciplines: some key intellectual problems and ways forward', in Gough, I. and McGregor, J.A. (eds) *Wellbeing in developing countries: From theory to research*, Cambridge: Cambridge University Press, pp 283-315.

Beveridge, W. (1948) *Voluntary action*, London: Allen & Unwin.

Booth, C. (1892) *Life and labour of the people in London*, London: Macmillan & Co.

Booth, W., General (1890) *In darkest England and the way out*, London: Charles Knight and Co Ltd.

Borell, K. and Gerdner, A. (2011) 'Hidden voluntary work: a nationally representative survey of Muslim congregations in Sweden', *British Journal of Social Work*, vol 41, no 5, pp 1-12.

Bowpitt, G. (1998) 'Evangelical Christianity, secular humanism, and the genesis of British social work', *British Journal of Social Work*, vol 28, pp 675-93.

Bowpitt, G. (2000) 'Working with creative creatures: towards a Christian paradigm for social work theory, with some practical implications', *British Journal of Social Work*, vol 30, no 3, pp 349-64.

Bradley, K. (2009) *Poverty, philanthropy and the state: Charities and the working classes in London, 1918–79*, Manchester: Manchester University Press.

Brahm Levey, G. (2009) 'Secularism and religion in a multicultural age', in G. Brahm Levey and R. Modood (eds) *Secularism, religion and multicultural citizenship*, Cambridge: Cambridge University Press, pp 1-24.

Brent, R. (1987) *Liberal Anglican politics: Whiggery, religion and reform 1830–1841*, Oxford: Clarendon Press.

Bretherton, L. (2010) *Christianity and contemporary politics*, Oxford: Wiley-Blackwell.

Bruce, S. (2003) *God is dead: Secularisation in the West*, London, Wiley Blackwell.

Burleigh, M. (2005) *Earthly powers: Religion and politics in Europe from the Enlightenment to the Great War*, London: Harper Perennial.

Bullis, R. (1996) *Spirituality in social work practice*, Washington, DC: Taylor & Francis.

Bursey, E. (2010) 'Introduction', in S. Sorajjakool, M.F. Carr and J.J. Nam (eds) *World religions for health care professionals*, London and New York: Routledge, pp 1-13.

CAF (Charity Aid Foundation) (2004) *Charity Trends 2004*, www. charitytrends.org/.

CAF (Charity Aid Foundation) and NCVO (National Council for Voluntary Organisations) (2005) *UK Giving 2004/2005: Results of the 2004/05 survey of individual charitable giving in the UK*, London: CAF and NCVO.

Campbell, D. (2009) 'Reconsidering the implementation strategy on faith-based policy initiatives', *Nonprofit and Voluntary Sector Quarterly*, vol 40, no 1, pp 130-48.

Casanova, J. (1994) *Public religions in the modern world*, Chicago, IL and London: University of Chicago Press.

Casanova, J. (2008) 'Public religions revisited', in H. de Vries (ed) *Religion: Beyond a concept*, New York: Fordham University Press, pp 101-19.

Castles, F.G. (ed) (1993) *Families of nations: Patterns of public policy in Western democracies*, Dartmouth: Aldershot.

Castles, F.G. (2010) 'The English-speaking countries', in F.G. Castles, S. Leibfried, J. Lewis, H. Obinger and C. Pierson (eds) *The Oxford handbook of the welfare state*, Oxford: Oxford University Press, pp 630-42.

Chambers, P. (2004) 'Religion, identity and change in contemporary Wales', in S. Coleman and P. Collins (eds) *Religion, identity and change: Perspectives on global transformations*, Aldershot: Ashgate, pp 69-83.

Chapman, R. (2009) 'Citizens of faith in local governance: opportunities, rationales and challenges', in C. Durose, S. Greasley and L. Richardson (eds) *Changing local governance, changing citizens*, Bristol: The Policy Press, pp 135-51.

CLG (Department for Communities and Local Government) (2010) *Ensuring a level playing field: Funding faith-based organisations to provide publicly funded services*, London: The Stationery Office.

Clarke, J. and Fink, J. (2008) 'Unsettled attachments: national identity, citizenship and welfare', in Van Oorschot, W., Opielka, M. and Pfau-Effinger, B. (eds) *Culture and the welfare state: Values and social policy in comparative perspective*, Cheltenham: Edward Elgar, pp 224-46.

Cloke, P., May, J. and Johnsen, S. (2010) *Swept up lives? Re-envisioning the homeless city*, Chichester : Wiley-Blackwell.

Cnaan, R. (2004) *The invisible caring hand: American congregations and the provision of welfare*, New York: New York University Press.

Coleman, P.G. (2011) 'Ageing and belief', in P.G. Coleman, *Belief and ageing: Spiritual pathways in later life*, Bristol: The Policy Press, pp 1-12.

Coleman, P.G. (2011) 'The changing social context of belief in alter life', in P.G. Coleman (ed) *Belief and ageing: Spiritual pathways in later life*, Bristol: The Policy Press, pp 13-34.

Coleman, P.G., McKiernan, F., Maills, M. and Speck, P. (2002) 'Spiritual belief and quality of life: the experience of older bereaved spouses', *Quality in Ageing: Policy, practice and research*, vol 3, no 1, pp 20-6, March.

Coleman-Brueckheimer, K., Spitzer, J. and Koffman, J. (2009) 'Involvement of Rabbinic and communal authorities in decision-making by Haredi Jews in the UK with breast cancer: an interpretive phenomenological analysis', *Social Science & Medicine*, vol 68, pp 323-33.

Commission on Urban Life and Faith (2006) *Faithful cities*, London: Church House.

Commission on Urban Priority Areas (1985) *Faith in the city*, London: Church House.

Conradson, D. (2008) 'Expressions of charity and action towards justice: faith-based welfare provision in urban New Zealand', *Urban Studies*, vol 45, no 10, pp 2117-41.

Cosedine, J. (2002) 'Spirituality and social justice', in M. Nash and B. Stewart (eds) *Spirituality and social care: Contributing to personal and community wellbeing*, London: Jessica Kingsley Publishers, pp 31-48.

Coyte, M.E., Gilbert, P. and Nicholls, V. (2007) *Spirituality, values and mental health: Jewels for the journey*, London: Jessica Kingsley Publishers.

CTBI (Churches Together in Britain and Ireland) (2005) *Prosperity with a purpose: Christians and the ethics of affluence*, London, Church House.

CTBI (2006) *Strong and prosperous communities: The Local Government White Paper*, London: DCLG.

CTBI (2008) *Face-to-face and side-by-side: A framework for partnership in our multi-faith society*, London: DCLG.

Cunningham, H. (1998) 'Introduction', in H. Cunningham and J. Innes (eds) *Charity, philanthropy and reform*, London: Macmillan Press Ltd.

Daly, M. and Lewis, J. (2000) 'The concept of social care and the analysis of contemporary welfare states', *British Journal of Sociology*, vol 51, no 2, pp 281-98.

Davie, G. (1994) *Religion in Britain since 1945*, Malden, Oxford and Victoria: Blackwell Publishing.

Davie, G. (1999) 'Europe: the exception that proves the rule?' in P.L. Berger (ed) *The desecularisation of the world*, Washington DC: Ethics and Public Policy Centre, pp 65-85.

Davie, G. (2006) 'Is Europe an exceptional case?', *International Review of Mission*, vol 95, nos 378/379, pp 247-58.

Davis, F. (2011) 'Spiritual progression in a time of economic recession', Talk given at Centre for Faiths and Public Policy, University of Chester, 17 March.

Davis, F., Paulhaus, E. and Bradstock, A. (2008) *Moral, but no compass: Church, government and the future of welfare*, Chelmsford: Matthew James Publishing.

Deacon, A. and Mann, K. (1999) 'Agency, modernity and social policy', *Journal of Social Policy*, vol 28, no 3, pp 413-35.

Demerath, N.J. (2003) *Crossing the gods: World religions and worldly politics*, New Jersey: Rutgers University Press.

Deneulin, S. and Rakodi, C. (2011) 'Revisiting religion: development studies thirty years on', *World Development*, vol 39, no 1, pp 45-54.

Dewsbury, J.D. and Cloke, P. (2009) 'Spiritual landscapes: existence, performance and immanence', *Social and Cultural Geography*, vol 10, no 6, pp 695-711.

Dinham, A. (2007) *Priceless, unmeasurable? Faith and community development in the 21st century England*, London: Faith-based Regeneration Network.

Dinham, A. and Lowndes, V. (2008) 'Religion, resources and representation: three narratives of faith engagement in urban governance', *Urban Affairs Review*, vol 43, no 6, pp 817-45.

Dinham, A. and Lowndes, V. (2009) 'Faith and the public realm', in A. Dinham, R. Furbey and V. Lowndes (eds) *Faith in the public realm: Controversies, policies and practices*, Bristol: The Policy Press, pp 1-20.

Dinham, A. and Shaw, M.a (2012) 'Measurement as reflection in faith-based social action' in *Community Development Journal*, vol 47, no 1, pp 126-41.

Dinham, A., Furbey, R. and Lowndes, V. (eds) *Faith in the public realm: Controversies, policies and practices*, Bristol: The Policy Press

Dobkin Hall, P. (1990) 'Religion and the social space for voluntary institutions' in R. Wuthnow, V. Hodgkison and Associates (eds) *Faith and philanthropy in America*, San Francisco, London: Jossey-Bass Publishers, pp 38-62.

Drake, R.F. (2001) *The principles of social policy*, London: Palgrave.

Durkheim, E. (1915) *The elementary forms of religious life*, London: Allen & Unwin Ltd.

Dwyer, P. (2007) *Understanding social citizenship*, Bristol: The Policy Press.

East of England Development Agency (2003) *Faith in action*, accessed on 10 May 2012 at www.faithneteast.org.uk/pdf/Faith_in_Action.pdf.

Easterlin, R. (1974) 'Does economic growth improve the human lot? Some empirical evidence', in I.P.A David and M.W. Reder (eds) *Nations and households in economic growth: Essays in honour of Moses Abramovitz*, New York: Academic Process.

Easterlin, R. (2001) 'Income and happiness: towards a unified theory', *The Economic Journal*, vol 111, no 473, pp 465-84.

Ebaugh, H.R., Pipes, P.F., Saltzman, J. and Chafetz, M.D. (2003) 'Where's the religion? Distinguishing faith-based from secular social service agencies', *Journal for the Scientific Study of Religion*, vol 42, no 3, pp 411–26.

Edwards, S. (2009) 'Three versions of an ethics of care', *Nursing Philosophy*, vol 10, pp 231-40.

Edwards, S. and Gilbert, P. (2007) 'Spiritual assessment – narratives and responses', in M.E. Coyte, P. Gilbert and V. Nicholls (eds) *Spirituality, values and mental health: Jewels for the journey*, London: Jessica Kingsley Publishers, pp 144-59.

Escott, P. and Logan, P. (2006) *Faith in LSPs? The experience of faith community representatives on local strategic partnerships. A report from the Churches Regional Network*, London: Churches Together in England.

Esping-Andersen, G. (1990) *The three worlds of welfare capitalism*, Princeton, NJ: Princeton University Press.

Faith-based Regeneration Network and Dinham, A. (2008) *Report for communities and local government in connection with the CLG Framework for Interfaith Dialogue and Local Action*, accessed on 10 May 2012 at www.fbrn.info/files/FbRN-report_0.pdf.

Farias, M. and Hense, E. (2009) 'Concepts and misconceptions in the scientific study of spirituality' in B. Spalek and A. Imtoual (eds), *Religion, spirituality and the social sciences: Challenging marginalisation*, Bristol: The Policy Press, pp 163-76.

Farnell, R., Furbey, R., Shams Al-Haqq Hills, S., Macey, M. and Smith, G. (2003) *Faith in urban regeneration? Engaging faith communities in urban regeneration*, York and Bristol: Joseph Rowntree Foundation and The Policy Press.

Farnsley, A.E. II (2007) 'Faith-based initiatives', in J.A. Beckford (ed) *The Sage handbook of the sociology of religion*, London: Sage Publications, pp 345-56.

Field, F. (1990) 'How well have Britain's poor fared?', in the Rt Hon Michael Alison MP and D.L. Edwards (eds) *Christianity and conservatism: Are Christianity and conservatism compatible?*, London: Hodder & Stoughton, pp 242-62.

Field, F. (2002) 'Making welfare work: the politics of reform', *Scottish Journal of Political Economy*, vol 49, no 1, pp 91-103.

Fischer, C. (2001) 'Work and its discontents: two cases of contemporary religious responses to unemployment', in P. Nesbitt (ed) *Religion and social policy*, Walnut Creek, CA, and Oxford: AltaMira Press.

Fitzgerald, S.T. (2009) 'Cooperative collective action: framing faith-based community development', *Mobilization: An International Journal*, vol 14, no 2, pp181-98.

Fitzpatrick, T. (2001) *Welfare theory*, Bristol: The Policy Press.

Fitzpatrick, T. (2008) *Applied ethics and social problems*, Bristol: The Policy Press.

Flint, J. (2009) 'Cultures, ghettos and camps: sites of exception and antagonism in the city', *Housing Studies*, vol 24, no 4, pp 417-31.

Flint, J. (2010) 'Faith and housing in England: promoting community cohesion or contributing to urban segregation?', *Journal of Ethnic and Migration Studies*, vol 36, no 2, pp 257-74.

Flora, P. and Heidenheimer, A.J. (eds) (1981) *The development of welfare states in Europe and America*, New Brunswick: Transaction Books.

Francis, L. (2008) 'Self-assigned religious affiliation: a study among adolescents in England and Wales' in B. Spalek and A. Imtoual (eds), *Religion, spirituality and the social sciences: Challenging marginalisation*, Bristol: The Policy Press, pp 149-61.

Fraser, D. (2009) *The evolution of the British welfare state*, London: Palgrave Macmillan.

Fraser, N. (1997) *Justice interruptus: Critical reflections on the 'postsocialist' condition*, New York and London: Routledge.

Furbey, R., Dinham, A. and Farnell, R. (2006) *Faith as social capital: Connecting or dividing?*, Bristol: The Policy Press [illustrated edition].

Furman, L.D., Benson, P.W., Canda, E.R. and Grimwood, C. (2005) 'A comparative international analysis of religion and spirituality in social work: a survey of UK and US social workers' in *Social Work Education*, vol 24, no 8, pp 813-39.

Furness, S. and Gilligan, P. (2010) *Religion, belief and social work*, Bristol: The Policy Press.

Gilbert, P. (2011) 'Seeking inspiration: the rediscovery of the spiritual dimension in health and social care in England', *Mental Health, Religion and Culture*, vol 13, no 6, pp 533-46.

Gilliat-Ray, S. (2003) 'Nursing, professionalism and spirituality', *Journal of Contemporary Religion*, vol 18, no 3, pp 335-49.

Gilliat-Ray, S. (2008) 'From "visiting minister" to "Muslim chaplain": the growth of Muslim chaplaincy in Britain, 1970–2007', in E. Barker (ed) *The centrality of religion to social life: Essays in honour of James Beckford*, Aldershot: Ashgate, pp 145-60.

Gilligan, C. (1982) *In a different voice*, Cambridge, MA: Harvard University Press.

Gilligan, P. (2010) 'Faith-based approaches', in M. Gray and S. Webb (eds) *Ethics and value perspectives in social work*, London: Palgrave Macmillan.

Glasby, J. (2007) *Understanding health and social care*, Bristol: The Policy Press.

Gorski, P.S. (2005) 'The return of the repressed: religion and the political unconscious of historical sociology', in J. Adams, E.S. Clements and A.S. Orloff (eds) *Remaking modernity: Politics, history and sociology*, Durham, NC and London: Duke University Press, pp 161-89.

Gough, I., McGregor, A. and Camfield, L. (2007) 'Theorising wellbeing in international development' in Gough, I. and McGregor, J.A. (eds) *Wellbeing in developing countries: From theory to research,* Cambridge: Cambridge University Press, pp 3-43.

Grønberj, K.A. and Never, B. (2004) 'The role of religious networks and other factors in types of volunteer work', *Nonprofit Management and Leadership*, vol 14, no 3, pp 263-89.

Grunwald, K. and Thiersch, H. (2009) 'The concept of the lifeworld orientation for social work and social care', *Journal of Social Work Practice*, vol 23, no 2, pp 131-46.

Habermas, J. (2006) 'Religion in the public sphere', *European Journal of Philosophy*, vol 14, no 1, pp 1-25.

Harlow, R. (2010) 'Developing a spirituality strategy – why, how, and so what?', *Mental Health, Religion & Culture*, vol 13, no 6, pp 615-24.

Harris, J. (2011) 'Voluntarism, the state and public–private partnerships in Beveridge's social thought', in M. Oppenheimer and N. Deakin (eds) *Beveridge and voluntary action in Britain and the wider British world*, Manchester: Manchester University Press, pp 9-20.

Harris, M., Halfpenny, P. and Rochester, C. (2003) 'A social policy role for faith-based organisations? Lessons from the UK Jewish voluntary sector', *Journal of Social Policy*, vol 32, no 1, pp 93-112.

Hay, D. (2006) *Something there: The biology of the human spirit*, Philadelphia, PA: Templeton Foundation Press.

Haynes, J. (2009) 'Introduction' in *Routledge handbook of religion and politics*, London: Routledge, pp 1-8.

Heclo, H. (1981) 'Toward a new welfare state?', in P. Flora and A.J. Heidenheimer (eds) *The development of welfare states in Europe and America*, New Brunswick, NJ: Transaction Books, pp 383-406.

Heelas, P. and Woodhead, L. (2004) *The spiritual revolution: Why religion is giving way to spirituality*, London: Wiley-Blackwell.

Heidenheimer, A.J. (1983) 'Secularization patterns and the westward spread of the welfare state, 1883-1983: two dialogues about how and why Britain, the Netherlands and the United States have differed', *Comparative Social Research*, vol 6, pp 3-65.

Hepworth, C. and Stitt, S. (2007) 'Social capital and faith-based organisations' in *The Heythrop Journal*, vol 48, no 6, pp 895-910.

Herbert, D. (2003) *Religion and civil society: Rethinking public religion in the contemporary world*, Aldershot: Ashgate.

Hewitt, M. (2000) *Welfare and human nature: The human subject in twentieth-century social politics*, Houndsmill and London: Macmillan Press Ltd.

Himmelfarb, G. (1995) *The de-moralisation of society: From Victorian virtues to modern values*, New York: Random House.

Hodgkinson, V.A. (1990) 'The future of individual giving and volunteering: the inseparable link between religious community and individual generosity', in R. Wuthnow and V.A. Hodgkinson (eds) *Faith and philanthropy in America*, San Francisco, CA and London: Jossey-Bass Publishers, pp 284-312.

Hollinger, F., Haller, M. and Valle-Hollinger, A. (2007) 'Christian religion, society and the state in the modern world', *Innovation*, vol 20, no 2, pp 133-57.

Holloway, M. and Moss, B. (2010) *Spirituality and social work*, London: Palgrave Macmillan.

Holman, C. and Holman, N. (2002) *Torah, worship and acts of loving kindness: Baseline indicators for the Charedi community in Stamford Hill*, Stamford Hill and London: Interlink.

Home Office (2001) *Community cohesion: A report of the Independent Review Team chaired by Ted Cantle*, London: Home Office.

Home Office (2004) *2003 Citizenship Survey*, London: Home Office.

Home Office Faith Communities Unit (2004) *Working together: Co-operation between government and faith communities*, London: Home Office.

Hornsby-Smith, M. (1999) 'The Catholic Church and social policy in Europe', in P. Chamberlayne, A. Cooper, R. Freeman and M. Rustin (eds) *Welfare and culture in Europe*, London: Jessica Kingsley Publishers, pp 172-89.

Housing Corporation (2007) *Housing Corporation assessment*, London: North London Muslim Housing Association, Housing Corporation.

Hudson, M. (1993) *The lost tradition of biblical debt cancellations*, Research paper, accessed on 25 February 2011 at http://michael-hudson.com/wp-content/uploads/2010/03/HudsonLostTradition.pdf .

Huntington, S. (1996) *The clash of civilisations and the remaking of the world order*, New York: Simon & Schuster.

Ilchman, W., Katz, S.N. and Queen, E.L. II (eds) (1998) *Philanthropy in the world's traditions*, Bloomington, IN: Indiana University Press.

Innes, J. (1998) 'State, church and voluntarism in European welfare, 1690–1850', in H. Cunningham and J. Innes (eds) *Charity, philanthropy and reform*, London: Macmillan Press Ltd.

Introvigne, M. (2004) 'The future of new religions', *Futures*, vol 36, pp 979-90.

Jawad, R. (2009) *Social welfare and religion in the Middle East: A Lebanese perspective*, Bristol: The Policy Press.

Jewell, A. (2004) 'Nourishing the inner being', in A. Jewell (ed) *Ageing, spirituality and wellbeing*, London: Jessica Kingsley Publishers, pp 11-26.

Jolley, D. and Moreland, N. (2011) 'Dementia care: spiritual and faith perspectives', *Nursing and Residential Care*, vol 13, no 8, pp 388-91.

Jordan, B. (2008) *Welfare and well-being*, Bristol: The Policy Press.

Judge, H. (2001) 'Faith-based schools and state funding: a parallel argument', *Oxford Review of Education*, vol 27, no 2, pp 463-74.

Kahl, S. (2005) 'The religious roots of modern poverty policy: Catholic, Lutheran, and reformed Protestant traditions compared', *European Journal of Sociology*, vol 46, pp 91-126.

Kahl, S. (2009) 'Religious doctrines and poor relief: A different causal pathway' in P. Manow and K. van Kersbergen (eds) *Religion, class coalitions and welfare states*, Cambridge: Cambridge University Press, pp 267-97.

Kellehear, A. (2002) 'Spiritual care in palliative care: whose job is it?', in B. Rumbold (ed) *Spirituality and palliative care: Social and pastoral perspectives*, Oxford: Oxford University Press, pp 166–77.

Kenny, A. and Kenny, C. (2006) *Life, liberty and the pursuit of utility*, Exeter: Imprint Academic.

Kohn, D. (2010) 'Judaism' in *World religions for health care professionals*, London and New York: Routledge, pp 113–129

Kosmin, B. (2005) 'Social housing and faith communities: A Jewish perspective', Speech delivered at the Housing Corporation Policy Forum, London, 15 April, www.jpr.org.uk/lectures/ social_housing_kosmin.htm.

Kwan Chan, C. and Bowpitt, G. (2005) *Human dignity and welfare systems*, Bristol: The Policy Press.

Layard, R. (2005) *Happiness: Lessons from a new science*, London: Penguin.

Le Grand, J. (1997) 'Knights, knaves or pawns? Human behaviour and social policy', *Journal of Social Policy*, vol 26, no 2, pp 149–69.

Lewis, J. (1999) 'Voluntary and informal welfare', in R.M. Page and R. Silburn (eds) *British social welfare in the twentieth century*, Basingstoke: Macmillan, pp 249–70.

Lindsay, D.M. and Wuthnow, R. (2010) 'Financing faith: religion and strategic philanthropy', *Journal for the Scientific Study of Religion*, vol 49, no 1, pp 87–111.

Lowndes, V. and Chapman, R. (2007) 'Faith, hope and clarity: faith groups and civil renewal', in T. Branman, P. John and G. Stoker (eds) *Re-energizing citizenship: Strategies for civil renewal*, Basingstoke: Palgrave Macmillan, pp 163–84.

Luckmann, T. (1967) *The invisible religion: the problem of religion in modern society*, London: Collier-Macmillan.

Lukka, P. and Locke, M. (2000) 'Faith, voluntary action and social policy: a review of the research', *Voluntary Action*, vol 3, no 1, pp 25–41.

Lupton, M. and Perry, J. (2004) *The future of BME housing associations*, Coventry: Chartered Institute of Housing.

Lynch, G. (2008) 'Dreams of the autonomous and reflexive self: the religious significance of contemporary lifestyle media' in B. Spalek, and A. Imtoual (eds) *Religion, spirituality and the social sciences*, Bristol: The Policy Press, pp 63–76.

MacKinlay, E. (2004) 'The spiritual dimension of ageing' in Jewell, A. (ed) Ageing, spirituality and wellbeing, London, Jessica Kingsley Publishers, pp 72–85.

Madeley, J.T.S. (2003) 'European liberal democracy and the principle of state religious neutrality', in J.T.S. Madeley and Z. Enyedi (eds) *Church and state in contemporary Europe: The chimera of neutrality*, London: Frank Cass Publishing, pp 1-22.

Mandair, A. (2010) 'Sikhism', in S. Sorajjakool, M.F. Carr and J.J. Nam (eds) *World religions for health care professionals*, London and New York: Routledge, pp 77-94.

Manow, P. (2004) *The good, the bad and the ugly: Esping-Andersen's regime typology and the religious roots of the Western welfare state*, Working Paper 04/3, Cologne, Germany: Max Planck Institute for the Study of Societies.

Manow, P. and van Kersbergen, K. (2009) 'Religion and the Western welfare state: the theoretical context', in P. Manow and K. van Kersbergen (eds) *Religion, class coalitions and welfare states*, Cambridge: Cambridge University Press, pp 1-38.

Martin, D. (1967) *A sociology of English religion*, London: SCM Press.

Martin, D. (1978) *A general theory of secularization*, Oxford: Blackwell.

Martin, D. (1999) 'The Evangelical Protestant upsurge and its political implications', in P.L. Berger (ed) *The desecularization of the world: Resurgent religion and world politics*, Washington, DC: Ethics and Public Policy Center, pp 37-50.

Mathews, I. (2009) *Social work and spirituality*, Exeter: Learning Matters.

Mavani, H. (2010) 'Islam', in S. Sorajjakool, M.F. Carr and J.J. Nam (eds) *World religions for health care professionals*, London and New York: Routledge, pp 95-112.

McAndrew, S. (2010) 'Religious faith and contemporary attitudes', in A. Park, J. Curtice, K. Thomson, M. Philips, E. Carey and S. Butt (eds) *British Social Attitudes 2009-2010, The 26th report*, London: Sage Publications, pp 65-86.

McGregor, J.A. (2007) 'conclusion: researching human wellbeing: from concepts to methodology' in Gough, I. and McGregor, J.A. (eds), *Wellbeing in developing countries: From theory to research*, Cambridge: Cambridge University Press, pp 316-50.

Melville, R. and McDonald, C. (2006) 'Faith-based organisations and contemporary welfare', *Australian Journal of Social Issues*, vol 41, no 1, pp 69-85.

Midwinter, E. (1994) *The development of social welfare in Britain*, Buckingham: Open University Press.

Milmo, C. (2002) 'Britain's first "eruv" enclave for Jews divides local opinion', *The Independent*, 3 August.

Milward, A. (1992) *The European rescue of the nation state*, London: Routledge.

Minkenberg, M. (2003) 'The policy impact of church–state relations: family policy and abortion in Britain, France and Germany', in J.T.S. Madeley and Z. Enyedi (eds) *Church and state in contemporary Europe: The chimera of neutrality*, London: Frank Cass Publishing, pp 194-215.

Mir, G. and Sheikh, A. (2010) '"Fasting and prayer don't concern the doctors … they don't even know what it is": communication, decision-making and perceived social relations of Pakistani Muslim patients with long-term illnesses', *Ethnicity and Health*, vol 15, no 4, pp 327-42.

Modood, R. (2009) 'Muslims, religious equality and secularism', in G. Brahm Levey and R. Modood (eds) *Secularism, religion and multicultural citizenship*, Cambridge: Cambridge University Press, pp 164-85.

Montagné-Villette, S., Hardill, I. and Lebeau, B. (2011) 'Faith-based voluntary action: a case study of a French charity', *Social Policy and Society*, vol 10, no 3, pp 405-16.

Morgan, K. (2009) 'The religious foundations of work–family policies in Western Europe', in P. Manow and K. van Kersbergen (eds) *Religion, class coalitions and welfare states*, Cambridge: Cambridge University Press, pp 56-90.

Morgan, P. and Lawton, C.A. (2007) *Ethical issues in six religious traditions*, Edinburgh: Edinburgh University Press.

Moss, B. (2005) 'Thinking outside the box: religion and spirituality in social work education and practice', *Implicit Religion*, vol 8, no 1, pp 40-52.

Multi-Faith Centre at the University of Derby (2007) *Religions in the UK* (ed P. Weller), Derby: University of Derby.

Musick, M.A., Wilson, J. and Bynum, W.B. (2000) 'Race and formal volunteering: the differential effects of class and religion' in *Social Forces*, vol 78, no 4, pp 1539-71.

Nash, M. and Stewart, B. (2002) *Spirituality and social care: Contributing to personal and community well-being*, Jessica Kingsley Publishers, London

NCVO (National Council for Voluntary Organisations) (2007) *Faith and voluntary action*, London: NCVO.

Nelson, J. (2010) 'Religious segregation and teacher education in Northern Ireland' in *Research Papers in Education*, vol 25, no 1, pp 1–20.

Nesbitt, P.D. (2001a) 'Introduction to religion and social policy: fresh concepts and historical patterns', in P.D. Nesbitt (ed) *Religion and social policy*, Walnut Creek, CA and Oxford: AltaMira Press, pp ix-xiii.

Nesbitt, P.D. (2001b) 'The future of religious pluralism and social policy: reflections from Lambeth and beyond', in P.D. Nesbitt (ed) *Religion and social policy*, Walnut Creek, CA and Oxford: AltaMira Press, pp 244-62.

NHS Scotland (2008) *Spiritual care and chaplaincy in NHS Scotland*, Scottish Executive: Edinburgh.

Norman, E. (1987a) *The Victorian Christian socialists*, Cambridge: Cambridge University Press.

Norman, E. (1987b) 'Stewart Headlam and the Christian socialists', *History Today*, April.

Norman, E. (1990) 'Do British parties need philosophies?', in the Rt Hon Michael Alison MP and D.L. Edwards (eds) *Christianity and conservatism: Are Christianity and conservatism compatible?*, London: Hodder & Stoughton, pp 164-78.

Norris, P. and Inglehart, R. (2004) *Sacred and secular: Religion and politics worldwide*, Cambridge: Cambridge University Press.

NWDA (Northwest Development Agency) (2003) *Faith in England's Northwest: The contribution made by faith communities to civil society in the region*, Warrington: NWDA.

NWDA (2005) *Faith in England's North West: Economic impact assessment*, Warrington: NWDA.

Obadia, L. (2010) 'Globalisation and the sociology of religion' in Turner, B.S (ed) The new Blackwell companion to the sociology of religion, Chichester: Blackwell Publishing, pp 483-95.

Offer, J. (2006) *An intellectual history of British social policy: Idealism versus non-idealism*, Bristol: The Policy Press.

Office of National Statistics (2004) *2001 Census*, accessed on 10 May 2011 at www.statistics.gov.uk/cci/nuggetasp?id=979.

Opielka, M. (2008) 'Christian foundations of the welfare state: strong cultural values in comparative perspective', in W. van Oorschot, M. Opielka and B. Pfau-Effinger (eds) *Culture and the welfare state: Values and social policy in comparative perspective*, Cheltenham: Edward Elgar, pp 89-116.

Oppenheimer, M. and Deakin, N. (2011) 'Beveridge and voluntary action', in M. Oppenheimer and N. Deakin (eds) *Beveridge and voluntary action in Britain and the wider British world*, Manchester: Manchester University Press, pp 1-8.

Orloff, A.S. (2005) 'Social provision and regulation: theories of states, social policies and modernity', in J. Adams, E.S. Clements and A.S. Orloff (eds) *Remaking modernity: Politics, history and sociology*, Durham, NC and London: Duke University Press, pp 190-224.

Ouseley, H. (2001) *Community pride not prejudice: Making diversity work in Bradford*, Bradford: Bradford Vision.

Pacione, M. (1990) 'The ecclesiastical community of interest as a response to urban poverty and deprivation', *Transactions of the Institute of British Geographers*, New Series, vol 15, no 2, pp 193-204.

Pacione, M. (2005) 'The geography of religious affiliation in Scotland', *The Professional Geographer*, vol 57, no 2, pp 235-55.

Page, R.M. and Silburn, R. (eds) (1999) *British social welfare in the twentieth century*, Basingstoke: Macmillan.

Pargament, K.I. (1997) *The psychology of religion and coping: Theory, research and practice*, London and New York: Guilford Press.

Park, K.-H. (2010) 'Chinese religions', in S. Sorajjakool, M.F. Carr and J.J. Nam (eds) *World religions for health care professionals*, London and New York: Routledge, pp 62-76.

Parker-Jenkins, M., Hartas, D. and Irving, B.A. (2005) *In good faith: Schools, religion and public funding*, Aldershot and Burlington: Ashgate.

Parry, J.P. (1986) *Democracy and religion: Gladstone and the Liberal Party 1867-1875*, Cambridge: Cambridge University Press.

Pattison, S. (2001) 'Dumbing down the spirit', in H. Orchard (ed) *Spirituality in health care contexts*, London: Jessica Kingsley, pp 33–46.

Pelling, H. (1965) *Origins of the Labour Party*, Oxford: Clarendon Press.

Pettersson, P. (2010) 'Majority churches as agents of European welfare: a sociological approach', in A. Bäckström, G. Davie, N. Edgardh and P. Pettersson (eds) *Welfare and religion in 21st century Europe, vol 2*, Aldershot: Ashgate, pp 15-60.

Pfau-Effinger, B. (2004) 'Culture and welfare state policies: reflections on a complex interrelation', *Journal of Social Policy*, vol 34, no 1, pp 3-20.

Phillips, D. (2006) 'Parallel lives? Challenging discourses of British Muslims self-segregation' in *Environment and Planning D: Society and Space*, vol 24, no 1, pp 24-40.

Pierson, C. and Leimgruber, M. (2010) 'Intellectual roots', in F.G. Castles, S. Leibfried, J. Lewis, H. Obinger and C. Pierson (eds) *The Oxford handbook of the welfare state*, Oxford: Oxford University Press, pp 32-45.

Plant, R., Lesser, H. and Taylor-Gooby, P. (1980) *Political philosophy and social welfare*, London: Routledge & Kegan Paul.

Polt, R. (1999) *Heidegger: An introduction*, London: UCL Press.

Powell, F. (2007b) *The politics of civil society: Neo-liberalism or social left?*, Bristol: The Policy Press.

Powell, M.A. (ed) (2007a) *Understanding the mixed economy of welfare*, Bristol: The Policy Press.

Prochaska, F. (1988) *The voluntary impulse: Philanthropy in modern Britain*, London: Faber and Faber.

Prochaska, F. (2006) *Christianity and social service in modern Britain*, Oxford: Oxford University Press.

Prochaska, F. (2011) 'The war and charity', in M. Oppenheimer and N. Deakin (eds) *Beveridge and voluntary action in Britain and the wider British world*, Manchester: Manchester University Press, pp 21-35.

Purdam, K., Afkhami, R., Crockett, A. and Olse, W. (2007) 'Religion in the UK: an overview of equality statistics and evidence gaps', *Journal of Contemporary Religion*, vol 22, no 2, pp 147-68.

Putnam, R. (2000) *Bowling alone: The collapse and revival of American community*, New York: Simon & Schuster.

Putnam, R. and Campbell, D.E. (2010) *American grace: How religion divides and unites us*, New York: Simon and Schuster.

Putnam, R., Light, I., de Souza Briggs, X., Rohe, W.M., Vidal, A.C., Hutchinson, J., Gress, J. and Woolcock, M. (2004) 'Using social capital to help integrate planning theory, research, and practice: preface', *Journal of the American Planning Association*, vol 70, no 2, pp 142-92.

Quadango, J. and Rohlinger, D. (2009) 'The religious factor in US welfare state politics', in P. Manow and K. van Kersbergen (eds) *Religion, class coalitions and welfare states*, Cambridge: Cambridge University Press, pp 236-65.

Rahnema, M. (1997) 'Poverty', in W. Sachs (ed), The development dictionary, London and New Jersey, NJ: Zed Books.

Rimor, M. and Tobin, G.A. (1990) 'Jewish giving patterns to Jewish and non-Jewish philanthropy', in R. Wuthnow and V. Hodgkinson (eds) *Faith and philanthropy in America*, San Francisco, CA and London: Jossey-Bass Publishers, pp 3-21.

Riordan, P. (2011) 'Human happiness as a common good: Clarifying the issues', in J. Atherton, in J. Atherton, E. Graham and I. Steedman (eds), *The practices of happiness*, Oxford: Routledge, pp 207-16.

Rodger, J.J. (2000) *From a welfare state to a welfare society: The changing context of social policy in a postmodern era*, London: Macmillan.

Romain, J.A. (1991) *Faith and practice: A guide to reform Judaism today*, London: RSGB (Reform Synagogues of Great Britain).

Rowlingson, K. and Connor, S. (2011) 'The deserving rich? Inequality, morality and social policy', *Journal of Social Policy*, vol 40, no 3, pp 437-613.

Rumbold, B. (ed) (2002) *Spirituality and palliative care: Social and pastoral perspectives*, OUP Australia & New Zealand.

Scervish, P.G. and Whitaker, K. (2010) *Wealth and the will of God*, Bloomington and Indianapolis, IN: Indiana University Press.

Sellick, P. (2004) *Muslim housing experiences*, London: Housing Corporation.

Shah, M. and Sorajjakool, S. (2010) 'Hinduism', in S. Sorajjakool, M.F. Carr and J.J. Nam (eds) *World religions for health care professionals*, London and New York: Routledge, pp 32-47.

Sheldrake, P. (2006) *A brief history of spirituality*, Oxford: Blackwell Publishing.

Sherr, M. and Straughan, H. (2005) 'Volunteerism, social work, and the church: A historic overview and look into the future', *Journal of the North American Association of Christians in Social Work*, vol 32, no 2, pp 97-115.

Sider, R. and Unruh, H. (2004) 'Typology of religious characteristics of social service and education organisations and programs', *Non-profit and Voluntary Sector Quarterly*, vol 33, no 1, pp 109-34.

SJPG (Social Justice Policy Group) (2007) *Breakthrough Britain: Ending the costs of social breakdown, Volume 6: Third sector*, London: Centre for Social Justice.

Skocpol, T. (2000) 'Religion, civil society and social provision in the US', in M.J. Bane, B. Coffin and R. Thiemann (eds) *Who will provide? The changing role of religion in American social welfare*, Boulder, CO: Westview Press, pp 21-50.

Smith, C. (1996) 'Correcting a curious neglect, or bringing religion back in', in C. Smith (ed) *Disruptive religion: The force of faith in social-movement activism*, New York and London: Routledge, pp 1-25.

Smith, G. (2004a) 'Faith in community and communities of faith? Government rhetoric and religious identity in urban Britain', *Journal of Contemporary Religion*, vol 19, no 2, pp 185-204.

Smith, G. (2004b) 'Implicit religion and faith-based urban regeneration', *Implicit Religion*, vol 7, no 2, pp 152-82.

Smith, S.R. and Sosin, M.R. (2001) 'The varieties of faith-related agencies', *Public Administrative Review*, vol 61, pp 651-69.

Sorajjakool, S. and Naewbood, S. (2010) 'Buddhism', in S. Sorajjakool, M.F. Carr and J.J. Nam (eds) *World religions for health care professionals*, London and New York: Routledge, pp 48-61.

Spalek, B. and Imtoual, A. (2008) *Religion, spirituality and the social sciences*, Bristol: The Policy Press.

Spargo, J. (1909) *The spiritual significance of modern socialism*, London: Arthur F. Bird.

Spicker, P. (2000) *The welfare state: A general theory*, London: Sage Publications.

Spicker, P. (2007) *The idea of poverty*, Bristol: The Policy Press.

Spicker, P. (2011) 'Generalisation and phronesis: rethinking the methodology of social policy', *Journal of Social Policy*, vol 40, no 1, pp 1-20.

Spreadbury, J.H. and Coleman, P.G. (2011) 'Religious responses in coping with spousal bereavement', in P.G. Coleman (ed) *Belief and ageing: Spiritual pathways in later life*, Bristol: The Policy Press, pp 79-96.

Stewart, B. (2002) 'Spirituality and culture: challenges for competent practice in social care', in M. Nash and B. Stewart (eds) *Spirituality and social care: Contributing to personal and community wellbeing*, London: Jessica Kingsley Publishers, pp 49-70.

Stoter, D. (1995) *Spiritual aspects of health care*, London: Mosby, Time Mirror International Publishers Limited.

Sutton, P. and Vertigans, S. (2005) *Resurgent Islam: A sociological approach*, Cambridge: Polity Press.

Swinton, J. (2001) *Spirituality and mental health care*, London and Philadelphia, PA: Jessica Kingsley Publishers.

Tangenberg, K. (2004) 'Spirituality and faith-based social services: exploring provider values, beliefs and practices', *Journal of Religion and Spirituality in Social Work*, vol 23, no 3, pp 3-23.

Taniguchi, H. and Thomas, L. (2011) 'The influences of religious attitudes on volunteering', *Voluntas*, no 22, pp 335-55.

Tawney, R.H. (1920) *The sickness of an acquisitive society*, London: Fabian Society.

Taylor, J. (2003) 'After secularism: British government and the inner cities', in G. Davie, P. Heelas and L. Woodhead (eds) *Predicting religion: Christian, secular and alternative futures*, Aldershot: Ashgate, pp 120-34.

Taylor, R. (1998) 'The ethic of care versus the ethic of justice: an economic analysis', *Journal of Socio-Economics*, vol 27, no 4, pp 479-93.

Taylor-Gooby, P. and Stoker, G. (2011) '*The Coalition programme*: a new vision for Britain or politics as usual?', *The Political Quarterly*, vol 82, no 1, January-March, pp 4-15.

Temple, W. (1942) *Christianity and social order*, Harmondsworth: Penguin.

Thane, P. (2011) 'Voluntary action in Britain since Beveridge', in M. Oppenheimer and N. Deakin (eds) *Beveridge and voluntary action in Britain and the wider British world*, Manchester: Manchester University Press, pp 121-34.

Thatcher, M. (1990) 'Preface', in the Rt Hon Michael Alison MP and D.L. Edwards (eds) *Christianity and conservatism: Are Christianity and conservatism compatible?*, London: Hodder & Stoughton.

Therborn, G. (1993) 'The politics of childhood' in F. Castles (ed) *Families of nations: Patterns of public policy in western democracies*, Dartmouth: Aldershot. Tinder, G. (1987) 'Christianity and the welfare state', *The Review of Politics*, vol 49, no 4, pp 549-69.

Tiggle, N. (2012) 'Overhaul in approach to elderly care needed', BBC news, 29 February (www.bbc.co.uk/news/health-17195679).

Tinker, C. (2006) 'Islamophobia, social cohesion and autonomy: challenging the arguments against state-funded Muslim schools in Britain', *Muslim Education Quarterly*, vol 23, no 1, pp 4-19.

Titmuss, R. (1970) *The gift gelationship: From human blood to social policy*, George Allen & Unwin, London.

Titmuss, R. (1976) *Commitment to welfare*, London: George Allen & Unwin.

Trigg, R. (2007) *Religion in public life: Must faith be privatized?*, Oxford: Oxford University Press.

Troeltsch, E. (1932) *The social teaching of the Christian churches*, Boston, MD: Beacon Press.

Tronto, J.C. (1958) *Protestantism and progress*, Boston, MD: Beacon Press.

Tronto, J.C. (1995) 'Care as a basis for radical political judgement', *Hypatia*, vol 10, no 2, pp 141-9.

van Kersbergen, K. (1995) *Social capitalism: A study of Christian democracy and the welfare state*, London and New York: Routledge.

van Kersbergen, K. and Manow, P. (2010) 'Religion', in F.G. Castles, S. Leibfried, J. Lewis, H. Obinger and C. Pierson (eds) *The Oxford handbook of the welfare state*, Oxford: Oxford University Press, pp 265-91.

van Oorschot, W., Opielka, M. and Pfau-Effinger, B. (2008) 'The culture of the welfare state: historical and theoretical arguments', in W. van Oorschot, M. Opielka and B. Pfau-Effinger (eds) *Culture and the welfare state: Values and social policy in comparative perspective*, Cheltenham: Edward Elgar.

Voas, D. and Ling, R. (2010) 'Religion in Britain and the United States', in A. Park, J. Curtice, K. Thomson, M. Philips, E. Carey and S. Butt (eds) *British Social Attitudes 2009–2010, The 26th report*, London: Sage Publications, pp 65-86.

Wallis, J. (2002) *Faith works: Lessons on spirituality and social action*, London: SPCK.

Warren, M. (2009) 'Community organizing in Britain: the political engagement of faith-based social capital', *City & Community*, vol 8, no 2, pp 99-127.

Weber, M. (1930) *The protestant work ethic and the spirit of capitalism*, London and New York: Routledge.

Weber, M. (1993) *The sociology of religion*, trs E. Fischoff, Boston, MA: Beacon Press.

Weller, P. (2009) 'How participation changes things: "inter-faith", "multi-faith" and a new public imaginary', in A. Dinham, R. Furbey and V. Lowndes (eds) *Faith in the public realm: Controversies, policies and practices*, Bristol: The Policy Press, pp 63-82.

West, H. (2006) 'Introduction' in H.R. West (ed) *The Blackwell guide to Mill's 'Utilitarianism'*, Oxford: Blackwell Publishing, pp 1-8.

Whelan, R. (1996) *The corrosion of charity*, London: The IEA Health and Welfare Unit.

White, G. (2006) *Talking about spirituality in healthcare practice*, London: Jessica Kingsley Publishers.

White, S. (2010) 'Ethics', in F.G. Castles, S. Leibfried, J. Lewis, H. Obinger and C. Pierson (eds) *The Oxford handbook of the welfare state*, Oxford: Oxford University Press.

White, J.A. and Tronto, J.C. (2004) 'Political practices of care: needs and rights', *Ratio Juris* vol. 17, no 4, pp 425–53.

Whiting, R. (2008) 'No room for religion or spirituality or cooking tips: exploring practical atheism as an unspoken consensus in the development of social work values in England', *Ethics and Social Welfare*, vol 2, no 1, pp 68–83.

Wilber, C.K. and Jameson, K.P. (1980) 'Religious values and social limits to development', *World Development*, vol 8, no 7/8, pp 467–80.

Wilensky, H.L. (1981) 'Leftism, Catholicism and democratic corporatism: the role of political parties in recent welfare state development', in P. Flora and A.J. Heidenheimer (eds) *The development of welfare states in Europe and America*, New Brunswick, NJ: Transaction Books, pp 345–82.

Wilkinson, R. and Pickett, K. (2010) *The spirit level: Why equality is better for everyone,* London: Penguin.

Williams, R. (2011) 'Leader: The government needs to know how afraid people are', *The New Statesman*, 9 June, at www.newstatesman.com/uk-politics/2011/06/long-term-government-democracy.

Williamson, S.A. and Hodges, V.G. (2006) 'It kind of made me feel important: client reflections on faith-based social services', *Journal of Religion and Spirituality in Social Work*, vol 25, no 2, pp 43–57.

Wineburg, R.J. (2001) *A limited partnership: The politics of religion, welfare, and social service*, New York: Columbia University Press.

Wolffe, J. (2007) 'Religion and "secularization" in 20th century Britain', in F. Carnevali and J.-M. Strange (eds) *Economic, cultural and social change*, Harlow: Pearson Education Limited.

Wuthnow, R. (1988) *The restructuring of American religion: Society and faith since World War II*, Princeton, NJ: Princeton University Press.

Wuthnow, R. (2004) *Saving America? Faith-based services and the future of civil society*, Princeton, NJ: Princeton University Press.

Zahl, M.-A. Furman, L.D., Benson, P.W. and Canda, E.R. (2007) 'Religion and spirituality in social work practice and education in a cross-cultural context: findings from a Norwegian and UK study', *European Journal of Social Work*, vol 10, no 3, pp 295–317.

Index

Page references for notes are followed by n